THIRD EDITION

Military Leadership

In Pursuit of Excellence

EDITED BY

Robert L. Taylor
University of Louisville

AND

William E. Rosenbach
Gettysburg College

WITH A FOREWORD BY

Walter F. Ulmer, Jr.

WestviewPress
A Division of HarperCollinsPublishers

Cover photo: Gen. Douglas MacArthur wades ashore during initial landings at Leyte, the Philippines, October 1944 (National Archives, photo no. 1207).

Copyright © 1984, 1992, 1996 by Westview Press, A Division of HarperCollins Publishers, Inc.

Published in 1996 in the United States of America by Westview Press, 5500 Central Avenue, Boulder, Colorado 80301-2877, and in the United Kingdom by Westview Press, 12 Hid's Copse Road, Cumnor Hill, Oxford OX2 9JJ

Library of Congress Cataloging-in-Publication Data
Military leadership : in pursuit of excellence / edited by Robert L.
  Taylor and William E. Rosenbach; with a foreword by Walter F.
  Ulmer.—3rd ed.
    p. cm.
  ISBN 0-8133-3025-4.—ISBN 0-8133-3024-6 (pbk.)
  1. Leadership.   I. Taylor, Robert L. (Robert Lewis), 1939–   .
II. Rosenbach, William E.
UB210.M55 1996
355.3′3041—dc20   96-25533
                                                                                      CIP

The paper used in this publication meets the requirements of the American National Standard for Permanence of Paper for Printed Library Materials Z39.48-1984.

10   9   8   7   6   5   4   3   2   1

Military
Leadership

Dedicated to the men and women of the Armed Services
who must cope with the expectations of
a peacetime military and serve a global mission of
peacekeeping in new, multicultural forces

Contents

Foreword

As the twentieth century comes to a close, some scholars have presaged a *Revolution in Military Affairs (RMA)*. This "revolution" would be driven by the continuous advances of technology, the central piece being the microprocessor. Combined with new generation sensors and communications linkages, these awesome "chips" would provide commanders with "real time" details of the battle arena. Military operations could then gain an order of magnitude enhancement of speed and precision. Smaller forces would seemingly be able to cope with challenges that just decades ago required formations of significantly greater size.

Most discussions of military "revolutions"—of "downsizing" and "streamlining" to meet economic and geopolitical realities—are remarkably focused on technology and structure. Yet not only the past thousand years of history but also American excursions since Vietnam have highlighted and magnified the role of people as the predominant factors determining military outcomes. Grenada, Panama, the Gulf War of 1990–1991; the deployments to Somalia, Haiti, and Bosnia; the unobtrusive but often violent drug interdictions; and the less warlike but demanding chores of healing the ravages of flood and forest fire at home were facilitated by technological creativity. Still, they were orchestrated and executed by dedicated, motivated individuals. In all these situations, courage and commitment were of larger importance than were modems and lasers.

Recall the young Army Specialist Four in the Persian Gulf who explained that he had "a duty" to pull his companions out of a burning vehicle and give them aid while keeping the enemy at bay—biting through cardboard to arm pyrotechnics when his bloody hands could no longer handle that chore. He may have been born with nerves of steel and the right stuff in the brain. But it wasn't genealogy that created his sense of "duty." That was learned. His invaluable outlook surely was nourished in his early years by family or teachers, then wonderfully reinforced by leaders working their magic years and miles away from cameras that brought the Gulf War and subsequent military deployments into our living rooms.

The years immediately prior to the publication of this book have seen unprecedented change in the global political, military, and economic landscapes. The magnitude and startling pace of these changes have grown through the boundaries of our mind-set. The inherent inefficiencies of totalitarian government, a natural thirst for the freedom to carve one's own destiny, a resurgence of ethnic and religious conflicts, and the awesome power of television have led to upheavals that continue to reshape the lives of a large segment of the world's people. Although technological developments and human intolerance of bondage have been the primary forces for change over the past 400 years, the form and direction of these changes have been determined largely by the somewhat mysterious process we call "leadership."

The selections in this volume tap into a very special domain of historical and behavioral studies about military leaders and leading. Warfare and the institutions dedicated to preparation for war have given us the richest lode to mine in our quest for understanding. Leadership in the worlds of science, education, politics, and the arts is of ultimate consequence to society's progress. Yet these environments—thankfully—provide fewer opportunities than does the military for routinely exposing the bedrock of character that underlies leader behavior.

Competitive world markets, the deluge and diversity of ideas roaming cyberspace, and localized brutal wars have pumped new energy into the search for answers to questions about leadership—a pursuit that had already been stimulated by America's earlier lag in the productivity race. Over 300 colleges and universities in the United States now offer undergraduate or mentored opportunities for those who wish to gain experience in leadership. American industry spends billions of dollars on in-house and contracted developmental training, partially aimed at enhancing leader effectiveness. (This seems appropriate because recent surveys still portray American managers as a key source of worker anxiety and disaffection!)

I agree with the editors' view that effective leaders in the military are more alike than different from leaders in other sectors of our society. In fact, executive functions grow more similar across the range of organizational types as we move into higher echelons. The totality of insights and anecdotes in this collection of thoughtful articles covers the broadest range of behavior. A review of leadership in any of its costumes would miss the mark if it avoided encompassing a wide expanse of human activity in disparate situations and degrees of effectiveness.

We have learned a lot about both military and civilian leaders. Yet there remains much to be learned. Leadership theory remains fragmented, without coherent models that recognize and integrate concepts for followership, for organization-building, for individual growth and development, for dealing sensitively with a heterogeneous workforce, for differentiating among leader tasks by organizational level, for enhancing self-awareness, for measuring leadership outcomes, or for providing a set of clear definitions. Further complicating our travels through the maze of leadership theory is the basic criterion problem: What is "good" leadership and how do we measure it? In a society where immediate results are highly prized, where spectacular outcomes frequently draw more praise than does the "cathedral mentality" that sacrifices some short-term gains to contribute to a longer-term enrichment of the institution, it is not surprising that high-quality, transformational leadership can play second fiddle to manipulative expediency. (A companion volume by the editors, *Contemporary Issues in Leadership* [third edition], provides an insightful analysis of many of these issues.)

These conceptual questions seem to fade into triviality as we watch Norman Schwarzkopf exemplify competence and commitment. Or we read of great captains of the ages, writings by or about the Spaatzes, Halseys, Lees, and Pattons that inspire us greatly. But they inform us incompletely. We need to add to essential history and biography the analyses of the Gardners and Cronins and Sorleys that are provided in this compilation. Perhaps the American military is more enamored of leaders than of leadership. By that I mean that we may concentrate—particularly in dissecting activity at the more senior levels—more on *what* happened than *how* or *why*. Understandably, we are more fascinated by the critical, single bold stroke than by the tedious crafting of the sword. Success in the Gulf War derived from years of individual and team development by thousands of leaders at squad and unit levels. In June 1991, when a frustrated Red Adair called for Schwarzkopf to lead the attack in extinguishing the Kuwaiti oil fires, Schwarzkopf would have been the first to tell Red that a sudden injection of top leadership cannot repair systemic derelictions or create instant values. In winter 1995–1996 some army engineers bridged the swollen Saba River and endured both awful weather and merciless television scrutiny to permit heavy armor to enter Bosnia. Again, these soldiers demonstrated more than the technical expertise of passive "followership." They reflected the results of collective leadership that over time had spawned unit commitment and, as Stokesbury mentions, "a cause that transcended themselves."

Leadership seems either disarmingly simple or awesomely complex. Yet mysterious as leadership remains, somehow the American military has sustained momentum for systematic leadership development throughout the ranks that has been equaled by few institutions in history. It is indeed remarkable that our armed forces are seen as representing models of opportunity for individual growth and simultaneously respected for rugged efficiency in mission performance. Lee Smith's "New Ideas from the Army (Really)" should assuage lingering concerns of some of the public about the capacity of military leaders to acknowledge a changing world, even if those leaders have not yet constructed a behavioral and organizational model that routinely bridges the gap between essential discipline and essential creativity.

David Campbell of the Center for Creative Leadership has collected extensive data wherein different groupings of leaders in our society are described in specific terms by their peers and followers—which happens to be the only true measure of the essence of individual leadership. Among thirty sample groups whose leadership competencies were measured from the peer and subordinate perspective, military officers in senior service colleges ranked, as a group, in the top three. That is good news. It is also good news that expectations regarding the behavior of military leaders are remarkably high, although not always met. Pockets of dissatisfaction among followers still dot the landscape. The articles on followership that the editors have chosen are particularly timely. Warren Bennis's "effective backtalk" is a neat phrase of enormous significance. It again highlights in its implementation the abiding role of courage on both ends of the leader-follower arrangement. We recognize that it is not leader activity but leader impact on subordinate productivity and stamina that is the measure of effectiveness. All kinds of data, along with common sense, tell us that the tools are on hand to improve leader behavior if we can marshal the necessary resolve.

The seminal work of S.L.A. Marshall, the wisdom of Matthew Ridgway, and the insights of James Stokesbury and Abraham Zaleznik provide both stimulation and guidance as we search for that elusive mix of characteristics, behaviors, and sensitivity in context that ensures effective leadership. Beneficially, the importance of self-awareness and the formula for continued growth among "successful" adults has been more prominently recognized in recent years. Kouzes and Posner's "conquer yourself" is a particularly appealing pronouncement.

The years just ahead pose special challenges to military leaders in our democratic society. Our experimentation with social engineering in and out of the military marches on. Some constraints on personnel utilizations continue to be imposed on the military establishment without mature consideration of their consequences on combat readiness. The most basic characteristics for warriors in battle have not changed greatly, yet the need to revalidate the criteria for military service is clear. We find ourselves in a fascinating period of questioning in our democracy as we continuously redefine the boundary between individual prerogatives and the public good.

Even as we reduce our forces, budgets evaporate more quickly than missions; needed upgrades of countable tanks, ships, and aircraft quietly divert funds from nourishment of spirit and toning of muscle; and silent deterioration of organizational climates can be discerned only by diligent professional watchfulness. These potential dangers to institutional effectiveness require countermeasures that only strong leaders can provide. What a noble challenge for leaders in our society. What a tribute their success will be to our predecessors. What a gift to future generations.

Lt. Gen. Walter F. Ulmer, Jr.
Former President and CEO
Center for Creative Leadership

Preface

Previous editions of this book were published in 1984 and 1992. Each focused on the various approaches that have been used over the years to study and understand military leadership. The collections proved to be timely and useful resources for those engaged in the development of their own leadership as well as those interested in learning more about the topic. We continue to get a great deal of helpful feedback on our ideas and the readings selected. Constantly engaging in searches for new material that is relevant to the contemporary scene, we find that current events produce two types of responses. One is a restating of previous work to fit the current environment. The other is a presentation of fresh insight that helps leaders and aspiring leaders to better understand the issues before them. Our quest is to assemble the best of the latter category into a concise, powerful framework for the reader.

Leadership remains an important topic, and much is written about the subject. Over the past fifteen years, we have reviewed more than 2,000 books and articles to try to identify the best in the military, politics, psychology, business, religion, sociology, education, and history that will be relevant to those in the military. Clearly, military publications address the topic with gusto. However, we find that in the general literature, little attention is given to the unique expectations and conditions of military leadership.

There is demand for one book or text that reduces leadership to a set of teachable techniques or—of greater importance—skills that can be learned. We continue to believe that no such book exists. Because leadership is a process of human interactions involving an infinite variety of individual personalities and situations, there is no one formula that will ensure leader effectiveness. There is no one right answer.

Today, shared leadership is the most common theme, and the sharing is between the leader and those expected to follow. As a result, this edition again addresses followership as an essential ingredient of effective leadership. We also remain certain that the most important elements of leadership development are self-knowledge and self-confidence.

New in our society is an ambivalence about the military and, consequently, rationalizations for reducing military expenditures; politicians who feel the pressure to downsize the military because of the end of the Cold War and industrial reorganizations; and increasing demands for military participation in peacekeeping operations throughout the world. Changing social attitudes also add to these contemporary challenges to military leadership.

In Part 1, we provide some thoughts about a perspective of leadership in this changing environment. By presenting several views, we identify the unique aspects of military leadership as well as the universal constructs associated with leadership in general. The comparisons and contrasts should be helpful.

New to this edition is Part 2, where we look at lessons from history relating to military leadership. With so much emphasis on the future and change, we believe it is important to reflect on the past to better understand how we created the present. We have many things to learn from the heroes of the past. The only frustration here was in identifying the right people to paint the broad picture—there are many from which to choose.

Followership is addressed in Part 3. We believe that effective leadership is possible only if one understands and appreciates effective followership. Equal time is necessary to develop both attributes. Our goal is to clearly outline what is necessary for developing good followers.

Because the leader is so closely associated with the organization or unit, we address climate, culture, and values in Part 4. Personal values in concert and in conflict with organizational values challenge followers and leaders. We address climate from the perspective of the leader as a role model and the follower as a participant. Individual and group responsibilities are affected by our awareness of who we are and the impact we have on others.

Finally, in Part 5 we select some current issues that are influencing the military today. Downsizing with increased mission expectations and social change are at the forefront of the challenges facing military leaders today. There are no quick solutions at this point, but a great deal of change—and, we hope, learning—is occurring. Through effective leadership, the challenges and opportunities of today will be the successes of tomorrow.

Our hope is that you will find intellectual and practical benefit in reviewing this collection. We are continually energized by the study of leadership. The diversity of perspectives and the views from multiple disciplines help to create a more comprehensive view of military leadership.

We are grateful to the men and women with whom we proudly served for giving us the commitment to learn more about leadership. We have tried to apply what we learned; for the results, we continue to look to those with whom we work.

Special thanks go to the people around us who make us look good. Doug Adams, a doctoral student at the University of Louisville, spent countless hours searching every available source for new articles on military leadership. Marda Numann, at the University of Louisville, was again the one person who could keep us organized and on track. Cindy McDonald and Jan Pollard provided incredible administrative support; without them, we could not have completed this project. Annette Rau of Westview Press helped us get feedback so that we are continuously improving the book. Finally, we are grateful to the people with whom we share our lives, Linda Shapiro and Colleen Rosenbach, for their patience and support.

Robert L. Taylor and William E. Rosenbach

PART ONE

Leadership in Perspective

Leadership is intangible, and therefore no weapon ever designed can replace it.
—General Omar Bradley
Command and General Staff College, May 16, 1967

Leadership is one of the most observed and studied concepts in the modern world. We recognize and appreciate good leadership; we abhor bad leadership. Beyond that, precise measurements and definitions of leadership elude us. Each individual develops an idea of leadership, and there are as many definitions and descriptions of the term as there are people who write and speak about it. However, most agree that leadership is an influence process dependent on the relationship between leaders and followers. Getting things done through others implies a process of people working together to achieve shared goals and aspirations.

Characteristics of Leadership

The first thing that differentiates leaders from others is that they have a *vision* for the future. Leaders have an ability to "see" and place matters in perspective. Such vision is not made up of daydreams but rather of goals for an organization and its people. The vision becomes the focus for the leader's commitment, drive, and energy. Followers often feel a sense of energy and excitement simply by being around their leader.

However, successful leadership entails more than just having a vision and being committed to it. The vision must be shared, and thus the leader must be skilled in *communicating*. This is a sensitive art, and the most effective leaders are able not only to communicate their own vision but to work with followers to co-create a vision. The result is that *all* share the vision as their own. Should something happen to the leader, the vision remains powerful in the hearts and minds of the followers; goals and objectives are pursued in a way that reflects that they are "ours."

Motivating people to work together to fulfill the vision is an exciting challenge. We hear a great deal today about teams and team building.

1

Teams are not driven by the leader. Effective leaders create an environment in which people motivate themselves. Leaders empower others, share authority, and provide the wherewithal for committed followers to accomplish the mission. The vision is translated into action because everyone wants to succeed. Motivation is a collective energy, allowing people to achieve personal and organizational goals.

Leaders must be prepared to take charge when needed; *timing* is everything. Too often people are placed in leadership roles without being prepared. The predictable result is failure. Failure also ensues when a leader prepares incessantly but does not recognize when it is time to act. The latter situation relates to the concept of *risk*; some are unwilling to take action that may result in success or failure. With self-knowledge and self-confidence, leaders can assess the situation and determine the time and place for action in the best interests of the organization and its people.

There is no effective leadership without *trust*. Leaders are dependent upon trust as a bond between them and their followers. This bond is a two-way process. Leaders must demonstrate their trust in followers through delegation and empowerment. The leader enables followers to be worthy of that trust by making sure that adequate training is provided and that goals are clearly communicated. At the same time, followers depend upon the leader to be trustworthy—honest, consistent, equitable, and humane. Of all the modern organizations, there is none so dependent on the bonds of trust as the military.

There are significant differences in military, business, political, religious, and social organizations. Each calculates a "bottom line" in a unique way. Nonetheless, there are commonalities in organizational leadership, and the military has provided models that have been adopted by other organizations. At this point in our history, the dynamic changes taking place in our technological, international, and psychosocial environments are having a profound effect on the military. Developments in communications and technology have created a world in which the boundaries are less clear than ever before, and it is increasingly important that the military share what it has learned about leadership.

Individuals who possess leadership qualities do not necessarily become effective leaders. Our understanding of leadership is incomplete because of ambiguity, inconsistency, and paradox. However, we do not believe that a definition is important at this point. Rather, we invite you to clear away your preconceptions and biases. Read this first section with an eye toward creating a framework in which you can understand the construct of leadership. Rather than searching for answers, examine your beliefs and values and resist adopting what others say or do. Think about who you are, what your situation is, and the needs of your organization. Leadership will come into focus, and it may or may not be what you originally thought.

The Concept of Leadership

Tom Cronin analyzes the issues associated with defining leadership in "Reflections on Leadership" (Chapter 1). He questions whether we can teach leadership, and he raises several important points. First, Cronin suggests that we cannot understand leadership without understanding followership; we agree with this tenet and explore it in depth. Second, he contends that leaders exist throughout society and we can identify them by searching in logical, practical ways. Finally, Cronin provides a set of leadership qualities, creating an interesting perspective to those who study leaders and leadership.

In a classic piece, the 1965 essay "The Antileadership Vaccine" (Chapter 2), John Gardner addresses the dispersion of power in society. He focuses on our failure to cope with the "big question." In his opinion, the antileadership vaccine is administered by our educational systems and by the structure of our society, causing people to lose confidence in their ability to assume a leadership role. In training people for leadership, we have neglected the broader moral view of shared values, thus inhibiting vision, creativity, and risk-taking. He argues that we appear to be approaching a point at which everyone will value the technical expert who advises the leader or the intellectual who stands off and criticizes the leader. Thus, no one will be concerned with the development of leadership itself.

Abraham Zaleznik rewrote his 1977 *Harvard Business Review* article, "The Leadership Gap" (Chapter 3), for the military. He suggests that during periods of stress and change, society feels an inherent tension between the need for leaders and the need for managers. Zaleznik shows how managerial goals are centered in the structure of the organization; leadership goals center on people. Leaders work to create change, are willing to take risks, and exhibit great self-confidence. Managers are less willing to take risks, tend toward careerism, and emphasize technical skills, such as planning, organizing, and controlling, at the expense of leadership. He emphasizes that we need both leaders and managers. However, we need to merge personal and organizational values in order to develop a stronger sense of true leadership. His message is important to both business and the military—the need for leaders is evident throughout society.

Majors Kevin Donohue and Leonard Hong present a more contemporary perspective in "Understanding and Applying Transformational Leadership" (Chapter 4). The authors cite resistance, compliance, identification, and internalization as the possible follower reactions to leadership. Leaders not only want to change behaviors, they want to change attitudes. Thus, Donohue and Hong differentiate transactional (changing behaviors) and transformational (changing attitudes) leadership. The latter is most effective during periods of crisis, change, and instability—the conditions characterizing today's military. Transformational leaders develop and communicate a vision, set high expectations for and put confidence in the followers, demonstrate individualized concern toward followers, and practice self-sacrifice. The authors contend that transformational leadership leads to higher levels of performance than transactional leadership. This performance is assessed by examining the followers' will to carry on—a trait essential to winning on the battlefield. Finally, the authors note that this is not a new concept. Rather, transformational leadership is a framework to study why and how effective leaders are successful.

We conclude this section with an article by Brig. Gen. Huba Wass de Czece, "A Comprehensive View of Leadership" (Chapter 5). He effectively summarizes leadership in four key functions. First is the providing and instilling of purpose. The effective leader must have a clear idea of how the unit or organization fits into the larger scheme. Second is effective direction. Through information gathering, analysis, decision making, giving orders, and monitoring outcomes, the effective leader establishes context for action. Third, the effective leader provides motivation; followers act at all levels with mutual trust and respect. Effectiveness depends upon the leader's values and ethics as well. Finally, the leader focuses on sustaining continued effectiveness. Long-term development of the unit or organization is essential; leaders should think of the group they lead as an organism, not a machine. The author then suggests that there are differences in levels of leadership with junior officers leading by example and the more senior officers influencing by the indirect leadership of shaping values and policies.

In "Leadership: Views from Readers," we conclude this section with reactions to the previous article. Gen. Wass de Czece's piece prompted a great deal of feedback—the mark of a provocative presentation. To assist you in understanding the breadth and depth of leadership perceptions, we selected representative letters that might assist in finalizing a concept of leadership that you might use for the rest of the book.

Remember that leaders aren't made leaders because they are college graduates. Leaders are invariably made leaders because they are caring and concerned about people.

—SP4 Mickey Howen

1

Reflections on Leadership

Thomas E. Cronin

Introduction

Leadership is one of the most widely talked about subjects and at the same time one of the most elusive and puzzling. Americans often yearn for great, transcending leadership for their communities, companies, the military, unions, universities, sports teams, and for the nation. However, we have an almost love-hate ambivalence about power wielders. And we especially dislike anyone who tries to boss us around. Yes, we admire the Washingtons and Churchills, but Hitler and Al Capone were leaders too—and that points up a fundamental problem. Leadership can be exercised in the service of noble, liberating, enriching ends, but it can also serve to manipulate, mislead and repress.

"One of the most universal cravings of our time," writes James MacGregor Burns, "is a hunger for compelling and creative leadership." But exactly what is creative leadership? A *Wall Street Journal* cartoon had two men talking about leadership. Finally, one turned to the other in exasperation and said: "Yes, we need leadership, but we also need someone to tell us what to do." That is to say, leadership for most people most of the time is a rather hazy, distant and even confusing abstraction. Hence, thinking about or defining leadership is a kind of intellectual leadership challenge in itself.

What follows are some thoughts about leadership and education for leadership. These thoughts and ideas are highly personal and hardly scientific. As I shall suggest below, almost anything that can be said about leadership can be contradicted with counter examples. Moreover, the whole subject is riddled with paradoxes. My ideas here are the product of my

Another version of this chapter appeared in *Presidential Studies Quarterly,* 14:1 (Winter 1984). Copyright © 1983 by Thomas E. Cronin. Reprinted by permission of the Center for the Study of the Presidency and of the author.

studies of political leadership and my own participation in politics from the town meeting level to the White House staff. Some of my ideas come from helping to advise universities and foundations and the Houston-based American Leadership Forum on how best to go about encouraging leadership development. Finally, my thoughts have also been influenced in a variety of ways by numerous conversations with five especially insightful writers on leadership—Warren Bennis, James MacGregor Burns, David Campbell, Harlan Cleveland and John W. Gardner.

Teaching Leadership

Can we teach people to become leaders? Can we teach leadership? People are divided on these questions. It was once widely held that "leaders are born and not made," but that view is less widely held today. We also used to hear about "natural leaders" but nowadays most leaders have learned their leadership ability rather than inherited it. Still there is much mystery to the whole matter. In any event, many people think colleges and universities should steer clear of the whole subject. What follows is a set of reasons why our institutions of higher learning generally are "bashful about teaching leadership." These reasons may overstate the case, but they are the objections that serious people often raise.

First, many people still believe that leaders are born and not made. Or that leadership is somehow almost accidental or at least that most leaders emerge from circumstances and normally do not create them. In any event, it is usually added, most people, most of the time, are not now and never will be leaders.

Second, American cultural values hold that leadership is an elitist and thus anti-American phenomenon. Plato and Machiavelli and other grand theorists might urge upon their contemporaries the need for selecting out and training a select few for top leadership roles. But this runs against the American grain. We like to think that anyone can become a top leader here. Hence, no special training should be given to some special select few.

Third is the complaint that leadership training would more than likely be preoccupied with skills, techniques, and the means of getting things done. But leadership for what? A focus on means divorced from ends makes people—especially intellectuals—ill at ease. They hardly want to be in the business of training future Joe McCarthys or Hitlers or Idi Amins.

Fourth, leadership study strikes many as an explicitly vocational topic. It's a practical and applied matter—better learned in summer jobs, in internships or on the playing fields. You learn it on the job. You learn it from gaining experience, from making mistakes and learning from these. And you should learn it from mentors.

Fifth, leadership often involves an element of manipulation or deviousness, if not outright ruthlessness. Some consider it as virtually the same as learning about jungle-fighting or acquiring "the killer instinct." It's just not "clean" enough a subject matter for many people to embrace. Plus, "leaders" like Stalin and Hitler gave "leadership" a bad name. If they were leaders, then spare us of their clones or imitators.

Sixth, leadership in the most robust sense of the term is such an ecumenical and intellectually all-encompassing subject that it frightens not only the timid but even the most well educated of persons. To teach leadership is an act of arrogance. That is, it is to suggest one understands far more than even a well-educated person can understand—history, ethics, philosophy, classics, politics, biography, psychology, management, sociology, law, etc. . . . and [is] steeped deeply as well in the "real world."

Seventh, colleges and universities are increasingly organized in highly specialized divisions and departments all geared to train specialists. While the mission of the college may be to educate "the educated person" and society's future leaders, in fact the incentive system is geared to training specialists. Society today rewards the expert or the super specialist—the data processors, the pilots, the financial whiz, the heart surgeon, the special team punt returners, and so on. Leaders, however, have to learn to become generalists and usually have to do so well after they have left our colleges, graduate schools and professional schools.

Eighth, leadership strikes many people (and with some justification) as an elusive, hazy and almost mysterious commodity. Now you see it, now you don't. So much of leadership is intangible, you can't possibly define all the parts. A person may be an outstanding leader here, but fail there. Trait theory has been thoroughly debunked. In fact, leadership is highly situational and contextual. A special chemistry develops between leaders and followers and it is usually context specific. Followers often do more to determine the leadership they will get than can any teacher. Hence, why not teach people to be substantively bright and well-read and let things just take their natural course.

Ninth, virtually anything that can be said about leadership can be denied or disproven. Leadership studies, to the extent they exist, are unscientific. Countless paradoxes and contradictions litter every manuscript on leadership. Thus, we yearn for leadership, but yearn equally to be free and left alone. We admire risk-taking, entrepreneurial leadership, but we roundly criticize excessive risk-taking as bullheadedness or plain stupid. We want leaders who are highly self-confident and who are perhaps incurably optimistic—yet we also dislike hubris and often yearn for at least a little self-doubt (e.g., Creon in *Antigone*). Leaders have to be almost singleminded in their drive and commitment but too much of that makes a person rigid, driven and unacceptable. We want leaders to be good listeners and represent their constituents, yet in the words of Walter Lippmann, effective leadership often consists of giving the people not what they want but what they will learn to want. How in the world, then, can you be rigorous and precise in teaching leadership?

Tenth, leadership at its best comes close to creativity. And how do you teach creativity? We are increasingly made aware of the fact that much of creative thinking calls upon unconscious thinking, dreaming and even fantasy. Some fascinating work is being done on intuition and the nonrational—but it is hardly a topic with which traditional disciplines in traditional colleges are comfortable.

Relationships

A few other initial observations need to be made about leadership. Chief among these is that the study of leadership needs inevitably to be linked or merged with the study of followership. We cannot really study leaders in isolation from followers, constituents or group members. The leader is very much a product of the group, and very much shaped by its aspirations, values and human resources. The more we learn about leadership, the more the leader-follower linkage is understood and reaffirmed. A leader has to resonate with followers. Part of being an effective leader is having excellent ideas, or a clear sense of direction, a sense of mission. But such ideas or vision are useless unless the would-be leader can communicate them and get them accepted by followers. A two-way engagement or two-way interaction is constantly going on. When it ceases, leaders become lost, out of touch, imperial or worse.

The question of leaders linked with followers raises the question of the transferability of leadership. Can an effective leader in one situation transfer this capacity, this skill, this style—to another setting? The record is mixed indeed. Certain persons have been effective in diverse settings. George Washington and Dwight Eisenhower come to mind. Jack Kemp and Bill Bradley, two well-known and respected members of Congress, were previously successful professional athletes. Scores of business leaders have been effective in the public sector and vice versa. Scores of military leaders have become effective in business or politics. Some in both. However, there are countless examples of those who have not met with success when they have tried to transfer their leadership abilities from one setting to a distinctively different setting. Sometimes this failure arises because the new group's goals or needs are so different from the previous organization. Sometimes it is because the leadership needs are different. Thus, the leadership needs of a military officer leading a platoon up a hill in battle may well be very different from the leadership requirements of someone asked to change sexist attitudes and practices in a large corporation or racist and ethnic hatred in an inner city. The leadership required of a candidate for office is often markedly different from that required of a campaign manager. Leadership required in founding a company may be exceedingly different from that required in the company's second generation.

Another confusing aspect about leadership is that leadership and management are often talked about as if they were the same. While it is true that an effective manager is often an effective leader and leadership requires, among other things, many of the skills of an effective manager, there are differences. Leaders are the people who infuse vision into an organization or a society. At their best, they are preoccupied with values and the longer range needs and aspirations of their followers. Managers are concerned with doing things *the right way*. Leaders are more concerned with identifying and then getting themselves and their organizations focused on *doing the right thing*. John Quincy Adams, Herbert Hoover and Jimmy Carter were often good, sometimes excellent, managers. Before coming to the White House, they were all recognized for being effective achievers. As businessmen, diplomats, governors or cabinet members, they excelled. As presidential leaders, they were found wanting. None was invited back for a second term. While none was considered an outright failure, each seemed to fail in providing the vision needed for the times. They were unable to lift the public's spirit and get the nation moving in new, more desirable directions.

As this brief digression suggests, being a leader is not the same thing as being holder of a high office. An effective leader is someone concerned with far more than the mechanics of office. While a good manager is concerned, and justifiably so, with efficiency, with keeping things going, with the routines and standard operating procedures, and with reaffirming ongoing systems, the creative leader acts as an inventor, risk taker and generalist entrepreneur ever asking or searching for what is right, where are we headed, and keenly sensing new directions, new possibilities and welcoming change. We need all the talented managers we can get, but we also need creative leaders. Ironically, too, an effective leader is not very effective for long unless he or she can recruit managers to help make things work over the long run.

Characteristics

One of the most important things to be said about leadership is that it is commonly very dispersed throughout a society. Our leadership needs vary enormously. Many of the great breakthroughs occur because of people well in advance of their time who are willing to agitate for change and suggest fresh new approaches that are, as yet, unacceptable to majority opinion. Many of the leadership needs of a nation are met by persons who do not hold high office and who often don't look or even act as leaders. Which brings us to the question of defining leadership. Agreement on a definition is difficult to achieve. But for the purposes at hand, leaders are people who perceive what is needed and what is right and know how to mobilize people and resources to accomplish mutual goals.

Leaders are individuals who can help create options and opportunities— who can help clarify problems and choices, who can build morale and coalitions, who can inspire others and provide a vision of the possibilities and promise of a better organization, or a better community. Leaders have those indispensable qualities of contagious self-confidence, unwarranted optimism and incurable idealism that allow them to attract and mobilize others to undertake demanding tasks these people never dreamed they could undertake. In short, leaders empower and help liberate others. They enhance the possibilities for freedom—both for people and organizations. They engage with followers in such a way so that many of the followers become leaders in their own right.

As implied above, many of the significant breakthroughs in both the public and private sectors of this nation have been made by people who saw all the complexities ahead of them, but so believed in themselves and their purposes that they refused to be overwhelmed and paralyzed by doubts. They were willing to invent new rules and gamble on the future.

Good leaders, almost always, have been get-it-all-together, broken-field runners. They have been generalists. Tomorrow's leaders will very likely have begun life as trained specialists. Our society particularly rewards the specialist. John W. Gardner puts it well:

> All too often, on the long road up, young leaders become "servants of what is rather than shapers of what might be." In the long process of learning how the system works, they are rewarded for playing within the intricate structure of existing rules. By the time they reach the top, they are very likely to be trained prisoners of the structure. This is not all bad; every vital system reaffirms itself. But no system can stay vital for long unless some of its leaders remain sufficiently independent to help it to change and grow.

Only as creative generalists can these would-be leaders cope with the multiple highly organized groups—each fighting for special treatment, each armed with its own narrow definition of the public interest, often to the point of paralyzing *any* significant action.

Overcoming fears, especially fears of stepping beyond the boundaries of one's tribe, is a special need for the leader. A leader's task, as a renewer of organizational goals and aspirations, is to illuminate goals, to help reperceive one's own and one's organization's resources and strengths, to speak to people on what's only dimly in their minds. The effective creative leader is one who can give voice and form so that people say, "Ah, yes—that's what I too have been feeling."

Note too, however, that leaders are always aware of and at least partly shaped by the higher wants and aspirations and common purposes of their followers and constituents. Leaders consult and listen just as they educate and attempt to renew the goals of an organization. They know how "to squint with their ears." Civic leaders often emerge as we are able to agree upon goals. One analyst has suggested that it is no good for us to just go looking for leaders. We must first rediscover our own goals and values. If we are to have the leaders we need, we will first have to agree upon priorities. In one sense, if we wish to have leaders to follow, we will often have to show them the way.

In looking for leadership and in organizational affiliations—people are looking for *significance, competence, affirmation, and fairness.* To join an organization, an individual has to give up some aspect of his or her uniqueness, some part of his or her soul. Thus, there is a price in affiliating and in following. The leader serves as a strength and an attraction in the organization—but psychologically there is also a *repulsion* to the leader—in part because the dependence on the leader. John Steinbeck said of American presidents that the people believe that "they were ours and we exercise the right to destroy them." Effective leaders must know how to absorb these hostilities, however latent they may be.

The leader also must be ever sensitive to the distinction between *power* and *authority.* Power is the strength or raw force to exercise control or coerce someone to do something, while authority is power that is accepted as legitimate by subordinates. The whole question of leadership raises countless issues about participation and the acceptance of power in superior-subordinate relationships. How much participation or involvement is needed, is desirable? What is the impact of participation on effectiveness? How best for the leader to earn moral and social acceptance for his or her authority? America generally prizes participation in all kinds of organizations, especially civic and political life. Yet, we must realize too that a part of us yearns for charismatic leadership. Ironically, savior figures and charismatic leaders often, indeed almost always, create distance and not participation.

One of the most difficult tasks for those who would measure and evaluate leadership is the task of trying to look at the elements that make up leadership. One way to look at these elements is to suggest that a leader has various *skills,* also has or exercises a distinctive *style* and, still more elusive, has various *qualities* that may be pronounced. By skill, I mean the capacity to do something well. Something that is learnable and can be improved, such as speaking or negotiating or planning. Most leaders need to have *technical skills* (such as writing well); *human relations skills,* the capacity to supervise, inspire, build coalitions and so on; and also what might be called *conceptual skills*—the capacity to play with ideas, shrewdly seek advice and forge grand strategy. Skills can be examined. Skills can be taught. And skills plainly make up an important part of leadership capability. Skills alone, however, cannot guarantee leadership success.

A person's leadership style may also be critical to effectiveness. Style refers to how a person relates to people, to tasks and to challenges. A person's style is usually a very personal and distinctive feature of his or her personality and character. A style may be democratic or autocratic, centralized or decentralized, empathetic or detached, extroverted or introverted, assertive or passive, engaged or remote. This hardly exhausts the diverse possibilities—but is meant to be suggestive. Different styles may work equally well in different situations. However, there is often a proper fit between the needs of an organization and the needed leadership style. A fair amount of research has been done in this area—but much more remains to be learned.

A person's *behavioral style* refers to one's way of relating to other people—to peers, subordinates, rivals, bosses, advisers, the press. A person's *psychological style* refers to one's way of handling stress, tensions, challenges to the ego, internal conflicts. Considerable work needs to be done in these areas—particularly if we are to learn how best to prepare people for shaping their leadership styles to diverse leadership situations and needs. But it is a challenge worth accepting.

James MacGregor Burns, in his book *Leadership*, offers us yet one additional distinction worth thinking about. Ultimately, Burns says, there are two overriding kinds of social and political leadership: *transactional* and *transformational leadership*. The transactional leader engages in an exchange, usually for self-interest and with short-term interests in mind. It is, in essence, a bargain situation: "I'll vote for your bill if you vote for mine." Or "You do me a favor and I will shortly return it." Most pragmatic officeholders practice transactional leadership most of the time. It is commonly a practical necessity. It is the general way people do business and get their jobs done—and stay in office. The transforming or transcending leader is the person who, as briefly noted earlier, so engages with followers as to bring them to a heightened political and social consciousness and activity, and in the process converts many of those followers into leaders in their own right. The transforming leader, with a focus on the higher aspirations and longer range, is also a teacher, mentor and educator—pointing out the possibilities and the hopes and the often only dimly understood dreams of a people—and getting them to undertake the preparation and the job needed to attain these goals.

Of course, not everyone can be a leader. And rarely can any one leader provide an organization's entire range of leadership needs. Upon closer inspection, most firms and most societies have all kinds of leaders and these diverse leaders, in turn, are usually highly dependent for their success on the leadership performed by other leaders. Some leaders are excellent at creating or inventing new structures. Others are great task leaders—helping to energize groups at problem solving. Others are excellent social (or affective) leaders, helping to build morale and renew the spirit of an organization or a people. These leaders are often indispensable in providing what might be called the human glue that holds groups together.

Further, the most lasting and pervasive leadership of all is often intangible and noninstitutional. It is the leadership fostered by ideas embodied in social, political or artistic movements, in books, in documents, in speeches, and in the memory of great lives greatly lived. Intellectual or idea leadership at its best is provided by those—often not in high political or corporate office—who can clarify values and the implications of such values for policy. The point here is that leadership is not only dispersed and diverse, but interdependent. Leaders need leaders as much as followers need leaders. This may sound confusing but it is part of the truth about the leadership puzzle.

Leadership Qualities

In the second half of this essay, I will raise, in a more general way, some of the qualities I believe are central to leadership. Everyone has his or her own list of leadership qualities. I will not be able to discuss all of mine, but permit me to offer my list and then describe a few of the more important ones in a bit more detail.

Leadership Qualities—A Tentative List
- Self-knowledge/self-confidence
- Vision, ability to infuse important, transcending values into an enterprise
- Intelligence, wisdom, judgment
- Learning/renewal
- Worldmindedness/a sense of history and breadth
- Coalition building/social architecture
- Morale building/motivation
- Stamina, energy, tenacity, courage, enthusiasm
- Character, integrity/intellectual honesty
- Risk-taking/entrepreneurship
- An ability to communicate, persuade/listen
- Understanding the nature of power and authority
- An ability to concentrate on achieving goals and results
- A sense of humor, perspective, flexibility

Leadership consists of a spiral upwards, a spiral of self-improvement, self-knowledge and seizing and creating opportunities so that a person can make things happen that would not otherwise have occurred. Just as there can be a spiral upwards, there can be a spiral downwards—characterized by failure, depression, self-defeat, self-doubt, and paralyzing fatalism.

If asked to point to key qualities of successful leadership, I would suggest [the following].

Leaders Are People Who Know Who They Are and Know Where They Are Going

"What a man thinks about himself," Thoreau wrote, "that is what determines, or rather indicates, his fate." One of the most paralyzing of mental illnesses is wrong perception of self. This leads to poor choosing and poor choosing leads to a fouled-up life. In one sense, the trouble with many people is not what they don't know, it is what they do know, but it is misinformed or misinformation.

Leaders must be self-reliant individuals with great tenacity and stamina. The world is moved by people who are enthusiastic. Optimism and high motivations count for a lot. They can lift organizations. Most people are forever waiting around for somebody to light a fire under them. They are people who have not learned the valuable lesson that ultimately you are the one who is responsible for you. You don't blame others. You don't blame circumstances. You simply take charge and help move the enterprise forward.

I am sure many of you have been puzzled, as I have been, about why so many talented friends of ours have leveled off earlier than needs to be the case. What is it that prevents people from becoming the best they could be? Often it is a lack of education, a physical handicap or a disease such as alcoholism. Very often, however, it is because people have not been able to gain control over their lives. Various things nibble away at their capacity for self-realization or what Abraham Maslow called self-actualization. Family problems, inadequate financial planning, and poor health or mental health problems are key factors that damage self-esteem. Plainly, it is difficult to handle life, not to mention leadership responsibilities, if people feel they do not control their own lives. This emotional feeling of helplessness inevitably leads people to believe they aren't capable, they can't do the job. It also inhibits risk-taking and just about all the qualities associated with creativity and leadership.

Picture a scale from, at one end, an attitude of "I don't control anything and I feel like the bird in a badminton game"—to the other end of the scale where there is an attitude of "I'm in charge." Either extreme may be pathological, but plainly the higher up, relatively, toward the "I'm in charge" end of the scale, the more one is able to handle the challenges of transforming or creative leadership.

Thus, the single biggest factor is motivating or liberating would-be leaders in their attitude toward themselves and toward their responsibilities to others.

Leaders also have to understand the situations they find themselves in. As observed in *Alice in Wonderland*, before we decide where we are going, we first have to decide where we are right now. After this comes commitment to something larger and longer term than just our own egos. People can achieve meaning in their lives only when they can give as well as take from their society. Failure to set priorities and develop significant personal purposes undermines nearly any capacity for leadership. "When a man does not know what harbor he is making for, no wind is the right wind."

Leaders Set Priorities and Mobilize Energies

Too many people become overwhelmed with trivia, with constant close encounters of a third rate. Leaders have always to focus on the major problems of the day, and on the higher aspirations and needs of their followers. Leadership divorced from important transcending purpose becomes manipulation, deception and, in the extreme, is not leadership at all, but repression and tyranny.

The effective modern leader has to be able to live in an age of uncertainty. Priorities have to be set and decisions have to be made even though all the information is not in—this will surely be even more true in the future than it has been in the past. The information revolution has tremendously enlarged both the opportunities and the frustrations for leaders. Knowing what you don't know becomes as important as knowing what you do know. A willingness to experiment and explore possible strategies even in the face of uncertainty may become a more pronounced characteristic of the creative leader.

The creative priority setter learns both to encourage and to question his or her intuitive tendencies. Oliver Wendell Holmes, Jr., said that "to have doubted one's own first principles is the mark of a civilized man" and so it continues to be. The ability to look at things differently, and reach out for more and better advice, is crucial. The ability to admit error and learn from mistakes is also vitally important.

Leaders need to have considerable self-confidence, but they also must have a dose of self-doubt. Leaders must learn how to communicate the need for advice and help, how to become creative listeners, how to empathize, and understand. In Sophocles' compelling play, *Antigone*, the tragic hero, King Creon, hears his son's advice but imprudently rejects it or perhaps does not even hear it. But it, Haemon's, is advice any leader should take into account:

Let not your first thought be your only thought. Think if there cannot be some other way. Surely, to think your own the only wisdom, and yours the only word, the only will, betrays a shallow spirit, an empty heart. It is no weakness for the wisest man to learn when he is wrong, know what to yield. . . .

So, father, pause and put aside your anger. I think, for what my young opinion's worth, that good as it is to have infallible wisdom, since this is rarely found, the next best thing is to be willing to listen to wise advice.

Leaders need to be able to discover their own strengths and the strengths of those with whom they work. They have to learn how to share and to delegate. They have to be able to make people believe they are important, that they are or can be winners. People yearn to think that what they are doing is something useful, something important. The transforming or creative leader knows how to nourish conviction and morale within an organization.

Good leaders know how to serve as morale-builders and renewers of purpose, able to get people to rededicate themselves to long-cherished but sometimes dimly understood values. Motivation is sometimes as much as 40 to 50 percent of the leadership enterprise. You can do very little alone with just faith and determination, yet you can do next to nothing without them. Organizations of all kinds need constantly to rediscover or renew their faith, direction, and sense of purpose.

Leaders Have to Provide the Risk-Taking, Entrepreneurial Imagination for Their Organizations and Communities

Leaders are able to see things in a different and fresh context. Warren Bennis suggests that creative leadership requires the capacity to recontextualize a situation. Willis Harmon suggests a leader is one who reperceives situations and challenges and comes up with new approaches, insights and solutions.

A third-grade class begins and the teacher says: "Class, take out your pencils and paper and draw a picture of anything you can think of." Students begin to draw balls, trees, automobiles, and so forth. Teacher asks Sally, in the second row: "What are you drawing?" Sally says, "I'm drawing a picture of God." Teacher says: "But no one has ever seen God; we don't know what he looks like." An undaunted Sally responds: "Well, they sure will when I get through!"

This little story illustrates the sometimes irrational self-confidence and "failure is impossible" factor that motivates the galvanizing leader. The founding revolutionaries in America, Susan Anthony, Martin Luther King, Jr., Saul Alinsky and countless others had the vision of a better and newer society and they, in effect, said, "They'll know a better or more just society when we get through."

Mark Twain once said, "a man is viewed as a crackpot until his idea succeeds." We need a hospitable environment for the dissenter and the creative individual. We need to avoid killing the spark of individuality that allows creativity to flourish. We kill it with rules, red tape, procedures, standard operating restrictions and countless admonitions "not to rock the boat."

Creativity is the ability to recombine things. To see a radio here and a clock there and put them together. Hence, the clockradio. Open-mindedness is crucial. Too many organizations are organized with structures to solve problems that no longer exist. Vested interest grows up in every human institution. People all too often become prisoners of their procedures.

Psychologist David Campbell points out that history records a long list of innovations that come from outside the "expert" organization. (See also John Jewkes, *The Sources of Invention.*) The automobile was not invented by the transportation experts of that era, the railroaders. The airplane was not invented by automobile experts. Polaroid film was not invented by Kodak. Handheld pocket calculators were not invented by IBM, digital watches were not invented by watchmakers. Apple computers and herbal tea are yet two more examples. The list is endless and the moral is vivid.

Leaders get organizations interested in what they are going to become, not what they have been. Creative leadership requires also not being afraid to fail. An essential aspect of creative leadership is curiosity. The best way to have inventive ideas is to have lots of ideas, and to have an organization that welcomes fresh ideas—whatever their merit. As any scientist knows, the art of research requires countless experimentation and failure before you get the results you want, or sometimes the unexpected result that constitutes the true breakthrough.

Leaders recognize the utility of dreaming, fantasy and unconscious thinking. One advocate of creative thinking writes,

> Production of dramatically new ideas by a process of purely conscious calculation rarely seems to occur. Unconscious thinking, thinking which you are unaware of, is a major contribution to the production of new ideas....

Leaders Need to Have a Sense of Humor and a Sense of Proportion

Leaders take their work seriously, but do not take themselves too seriously. Humor relieves strain and enables people to relax and see things in a slightly different or fresh light. Effective leaders usually can tell a joke, take a joke, and tell a good story. They also usually know the art of telling parables. Lincoln, FDR and JFK come quickly to mind, while Hoover, Nixon and Carter were humorless men. Adlai Stevenson put it this way: "If I couldn't laugh, I couldn't live—especially in politics."

In this same light, leaders need to be able to share the credit. Leadership sometimes consists of emphasizing the dignity of others and of keeping one's own sense of importance from becoming inflated. Dwight Eisenhower had a slogan he tried to live by which went as follows: "There's no telling how much one can accomplish so long as one doesn't need to get all the credit for it."

Thus, leaders need to have a sense of proportion and a sense of detachment. They must avoid being workaholics and recognize that they will have to be followers in most of the enterprises of life and leaders only a small fraction of the time. Emerson put it well when he tried to answer the question, "What is Success?"

> To laugh often and love much, to win the respect of intelligent persons and the affection of children; to appreciate beauty; to find the best in others; to give one's self; to leave the world a lot better whether by a healthy child, a garden patch, or a redeemed social condition; to have played and laughed with enthusiasm and sung with exaltation, to know even one life has breathed easier because you have lived—that is to have succeeded.

Humor, proportion and also *compassion*. A person able to understand emotions and passion and at least on occasion to express one's self with passion and conviction. Enthusiasm, hope, vitality and energy are crucial to radiating confidence.

Leaders Have to Be Skilled Mediators and Negotiators, But They Also Have to Be Able to Stir Things Up and Encourage Healthy and Desired Conflict

An old Peanuts cartoon has a dejected Charlie Brown coming off a softball field as the game concludes. In exasperation he whines, "How can we lose when we are so sincere?" Sincerity and purity of heart are not enough to succeed in challenging leadership jobs.

The strength of leaders often lies in their tenacity, in knowing how to deal with competing factions, knowing when to compromise, when to amplify conflict, and when to move an organization or a community away from paralyzing divisiveness and toward a vision of the common good.

Most citizens avoid conflict and find conflicts of any kind painful. The truly effective leader welcomes several kinds of conflict and views conflict as an opportunity for change or revitalization.

Stirring things up is often a prerequisite for social and economic breakthrough. Women's rights, black rights, consumer protection, tax reform movements and even our election campaigns are occasions for division and conflict. They are a reality the leader has to learn to accept, understand and turn to his advantage. Harry Truman said:

A President who's any damn good at all makes enemies, makes a lot of enemies. I even made a few myself when I was in the White House, and I wouldn't be without them.

George Bernard Shaw and others have put it only slightly differently. Reasonable people, they observe, adjust themselves to reality and cope with what they find. Unreasonable people dream dreams of a different, a better, world and try to adapt the world to themselves. This discontent or unreasonableness is often the first step in the progress of a person as well as for a community or nation.

But be aware that "stirrer uppers" and conflict-amplifiers are often threatening in any organization or society. In the kingdom of the blind, the one-eyed man is king. This may well be, as the proverb has it. But in the kingdom of the one-eyed person, the two-eyed person is looked upon with considerable suspicion and may even be considered downright dangerous.

Thus, it takes courage and guts as well as imagination and stamina to be the two-eyed person in a one-eyed world. Harlan Cleveland points out that just about every leader has had the experience of being in an office surrounded by experts. The sum of the meeting will be, "Let's do nothing cautiously." The leader is the one who has to say, "Let's take the first step." He or she is the functional equivalent of the first bird off the telephone wire, or what Texans call the "bell cow." The experts always have an excuse. They are like the losing tennis player whose motto is: "It's not whether you win or lose, it's how you place the blame."

An Effective Leader Must Have Integrity

This has been suggested earlier in several implicit ways, but it is perhaps the most central of leadership qualities. A leader must be able to see people in all of their relationships, in the wholeness of their lives and not just as a means to getting a job done, as a means for enhanced productivity.

Some may call it character, others would call it authenticity, compassion or empathy. Whatever we call it, character and integrity are much easier kept than recovered. People can see through a phony. People can readily tell whether a person has respect for others. Respect and responsibility generally migrate to those who are fair, compassionate and care about values, beliefs and feelings of others. People who cannot rise above their prejudices usually fail. People who permit a shell to be built up around their heart will not long be able to exercise creative leadership. Michael Maccoby captures this concern.

The exercise of the heart is that of experiencing, thinking critically, willing, and acting, so as to overcome egocentrism and to share passion with other people . . . and to respond to their needs with the help one can give. . . . It requires discipline, learning to concentrate, to think critically, and to communicate. The goal, a developed heart, implies integrity, a spiritual center, a sense of "I" not motivated by greed or fear, but by love of life, adventure and fellow feelings.

A leader's integrity requires also that he or she not be captured by peer pressures, protocol, mindless traditions or conventional rules. The truly effective leader is able to see above and beyond normal constraints and discern proper and desirable ends. The leader also possesses a sense of history and a concern for posterity. This ability, an exceptional capacity to disregard external pressures, is the ability that separates leaders from followers.

The Leader Has to Have Brains and Breadth

In the future, even more so than in the past, only the really bright individuals will be leaders.

Harlan Cleveland highlights this quality well when he writes:

> It used to be that a leader was a two-fisted businessman who chopped up the jobs that needed to be done, then left everyone alone and roared at them if they didn't work right. . . .
>   Loud commands worked if one person knew all things, but because of the way we [now] make decisions, through committees, a person charging around with a loud voice is just in the way.

Today's leaders must widen their perspectives and lengthen the focal point of their thinking. Leaders today have to learn how to thread or weave together disparate parts and move beyond analytical to integrative thinking. This will require well-read, well-traveled persons who can rise above their specialties and their professions. It will require as well persons who are not afraid of politics, but who rather view the art of politics as the art of bringing about the difficult and the desirable.

American Leadership

The creative political leader must work in a tension-filled world between unity and dissent, majority rule and minority rights and countless other contradictions. Tocqueville said of us, "These Americans yearn for leadership, but they also want to be left alone and free." The political leader is always trying to reconcile this and other paradoxes—but the important point is to be able to live with the paradoxes and dilemmas. And beyond this, the political leader must also be able to create, and preserve, a sense of community and shared heritage, the civic bond that ties us—disparate and feisty, rugged individualists—together.

Effective leaders of today and tomorrow also know how to vary their styles of leadership depending on the maturity of their subordinates. They involve their peers and their subordinates in their responsibility networks. They must be good educators and good communicators. They also have to have that spark of emotion or passion that can excite others to join them in the enterprise.

Most effective leaders will also be effective communicators: good writers, good speakers and good conversationalists. A few noted scientists may get by with mumbling, but they are the exception. For so much of leadership consists nowadays in persuading and informing that someone who cannot communicate well, cannot succeed. To paraphrase George Orwell, "If people cannot communicate well, they cannot think well, and if they cannot think well, others will do their thinking for them."

America is especially good at training experts, specialists and managers. We have plenty of these specialist leaders, but they are almost always one-segment leaders. We are in special need of educating multi-segment leaders.Persons who have a global perspective and understand that the once tidy lines between domestic and international, and public and private, are irretrievably blurred. Indispensable to a leader is a sense of breadth, the intellectual capacity to handle complex mental tasks, to see relationships between apparently unrelated objects, to see patterns in incomplete information, to draw accurate conclusions from inchoate data.

Vision is the ability to see all sides of an issue and to eliminate biases. Vision and breadth of knowledge put one in a strategic position—preventing the leader from falling into the traps that short-sightedness, mindless parochialism often set for people.

None of these qualities can guarantee creative leadership, but they can, when encouraged, provide a greater likelihood of it. We need all the leadership we can get—in and out of government. The vitality of nongovernmental America lies in our ability to educate and nourish more citizen leaders. Those of us who expect to reap the blessings of freedom and liberty must undergo the fatigues of supporting them and provide the leadership to sustain them.

Learning About Leadership

Permit me to return again to the question of whether leadership can be learned, and possibly taught. My own belief is that students cannot usually be taught to be leaders. But students, and anyone else for that matter, can profitably be exposed to leadership, discussions of leadership skills and styles, and leadership strategies and theories. Individuals can learn in their own minds the strengths as well as limitations of leadership. People can learn about the paradoxes and contradictions and ironies of leadership, which, however puzzling, are central to appreciating the diversity and the dilemmas of problem-solving and getting organizations and nations to function.

Learning about leadership means recognizing bad leadership as well as good. Learning about leadership means understanding the critical linkage of ends and means. Learning about leadership also involves the study of the special chemistry that develops between leaders and followers, not only the chemistry that existed between Americans and Lincoln, but also between Mao and the Chinese peasants, between Lenin and the Bolsheviks, between Martin Luther King, Jr., and civil rights activists, between Jean Monnet and those who dreamed of a European Economic Community.

Students can learn to discern and define situations and contexts within which leadership has flourished. Students can learn about the fallibility of the trait theory. Students can learn about the contextual problems of leadership, of why and when leadership is sometimes transferable, and sometimes not. Students can learn about the crucial role that advisors and supporters play in the leadership equation. Students can also learn about countless problem-solving strategies and theories, and participate in role playing exercises that sharpen their own skills in such undertakings.

Students of leadership can learn widely from reading biographies about both the best and the worst leaders. Plutarch's *Lives* would be a good place to start. Much can be learned from mentors and from intern participant observing. Much can also be learned about leadership by getting away from one's own culture and examining how leaders in other circumstances go about the task of motivating and mobilizing others. Countless learning opportunities exist that can sharpen a student's skills as a speaker, debater, negotiator, problem clarifier and planner. Such skills should not be minimized. Nor should anyone underestimate the importance of history, economics, logic, and a series of related substantive fields that help provide the breadth and the perspective indispensable to societal leadership.

Above all, students of leadership can make an appointment with themselves and begin to appreciate their own strengths and deficiencies. Personal mastery is important. So too the ability to use one's intuition, and to enrich one's creative impulses. John Gardner suggests, "It's what you learn after you know it all that really counts." Would-be leaders learn to manage their time more wisely. Would-be leaders learn that self-pity and resentment are like toxic substances. Would-be leaders learn the old truth that most people are not for or against you but rather preoccupied with themselves. Would-be leaders learn to break out of their comfortable imprisonments; they learn to cast aside dull routines and habits that enslave most of us. Would-be leaders learn how to become truly sharing and caring people—in their families, in their professions and in their communities. And would-be leaders constantly learn too that they have more to give than they have ever given, no matter how much they have given.

Let me conclude by paraphrasing from John Adams:

We must study politics [and leadership] and war [and peace] that our sons [and daughters] have the liberty to study mathematics and philosophy, geography, natural history and naval architecture, navigation, commerce, and agriculture, in order to give their children the right to study painting, poetry, music, architecture, statuary, tapestry, and porcelain.

2

The Antileadership Vaccine

John W. Gardner

It is generally believed that we need enlightened and responsible leaders at every level and in every phase of our national life. Everyone says so. But the nature of leadership in our society is very imperfectly understood, and many of the public statements about it are utter nonsense.

This is unfortunate because there are serious issues of leadership facing this society, and we had better understand them.

The Dispersion of Power

The most fundamental thing to be said about leadership in the United States is also the most obvious. We have gone as far as any known society in creating a leadership system that is not based on caste or class, nor even on wealth. There is not yet equal access to leadership (witness the remaining barriers facing women and Negroes), but we have come a long, long way from the family- or class-based leadership group. Even with its present defects, ours is a relatively open system.

The next important thing to be said is that leadership is dispersed among a great many groups in our society. The President, of course, has a unique, and uniquely important, leadership role, but beneath him, fragmentation is the rule. This idea is directly at odds with the notion that the society is run by a coherent power group—the Power Elite, as C. Wright Mills called it, or the Establishment, as later writers have named it. It is hard not to believe that such a group exists. Foreigners find it particularly difficult to believe in the reality of the fluid, scattered, shifting leadership that is visible to the

The Antileadership Vaccine, by John W. Gardner, president's essay reprinted from the 1965 Carnegie Corporation of New York Annual Report.

naked eye. The real leadership, they imagine, must be behind the scenes. But at a national level this simply isn't so.

In many local communities and even in some states there is a coherent power group, sometimes behind the scenes, sometimes out in the open. In communities where such an "establishment," that is, a coherent ruling group, exists, the leading citizen can be thought of as having power in a generalized sense: he can bring about a change in zoning ordinances, influence the location of a new factory, and determine whether the local museum will buy contemporary paintings. But in the dispersed and fragmented power system that prevails in the nation as a whole one cannot say "So-and-so is powerful," without further elaboration. Those who know how our system works always want to know, "Powerful in what way? Powerful to accomplish what?" We have leaders in business and leaders in government, military leaders and educational leaders, leaders in labor and in agriculture, leaders in science, in the world of art, and in many other special fields. As a rule, leaders in any one of these fields do not recognize the authority of leaders from a neighboring field. Often they don't even know one another, nor do they particularly want to. Mutual suspicion is just about as common as mutual respect—and a lot more common than mutual cooperation in manipulating society's levers.

Most of the significant issues in our society are settled by a balancing of forces. A lot of people and groups are involved and the most powerful do not always win. Sometimes a coalition of the less powerful wins. Sometimes an individual of very limited power gets himself into the position of casting the deciding ballot.

Not only are there apt to be many groups involved in any critical issue, but their relative strength varies with each issue that comes up. A group that is powerful today may not be powerful next year. A group that can cast a decisive vote on question A may not even be listened to when question B comes up.

The Nature of Leadership

People who have never exercised power have all kinds of curious ideas about it. The popular notion of top leadership is a fantasy of capricious power: the top man presses a button and something remarkable happens; he gives an order as the whim strikes him, and it is obeyed.

Actually, the capricious use of power is relatively rare except in some large dictatorships and some small family firms. Most leaders are hedged around by constraints—tradition, constitutional limitations, the realities of the external situation, rights and privileges of followers, the requirements of teamwork, and most of all the inexorable demands of large-scale organization, which does not operate on capriciousness. In short, most power is wielded circumspectly.

There are many different ways of leading, many kinds of leaders. Consider, for example, the marked contrasts between the politician and the intellectual leader, the large-scale manager and the spiritual leader. One sees solemn descriptions of the qualities needed for leadership without any reference at all to the fact that the necessary attributes depend on the kind of leadership under discussion. Even in a single field there may be different kinds of leadership with different required attributes. Think of the difference between the military hero and the military manager.

If social action is to occur, certain functions must be performed. The problems facing the group or organization must be clarified, and ideas necessary to their solution formulated. Objectives must be defined. There must be widespread awareness of those objectives, and the will to achieve them. Often those on whom action depends must develop new attitudes and habits. Social machinery must be set in motion. The consequences of social effort must be evaluated and criticized, and new goals set.

A particular leader may contribute at only one point to this process. He may be gifted in analysis of the problem, but limited in his capacity to communicate. He may be superb in communicating, but incapable of managing. He may, in short, be an outstanding leader without being good at every aspect of leadership.

If anything significant is to be accomplished, leaders must understand the social institutions and processes through which action is carried out. And in a society as complex as ours, that is no mean achievement. A leader, whether corporation president, university dean, or labor official, knows his organization, understands what makes it move, comprehends its limitations. Every social system or institution has a logic and dynamic of its own that cannot be ignored.

We have all seen men with lots of bright ideas but no patience with the machinery by which ideas are translated into action. As a rule, the machinery defeats them. It is a pity, because the professional and academic man can play a useful role in practical affairs. But too often he is a dilettante. He dips in here or there; he gives bits of advice on a dozen fronts; he never gets his hands dirty working with one piece of the social machinery until he knows it well. He will not take the time to understand the social institutions and processes by which change is accomplished.

Although our decentralized system of leadership has served us well, we must not be so complacent as to imagine that it has no weaknesses, that it faces no new challenges, or that we have nothing to learn. There are grave questions to be answered concerning the leadership of our society. Are we living up to standards of leadership that we have achieved in our own past? Do the conditions of modern life introduce new complications into the task of leadership? Are we failing to prepare leaders for tomorrow?

Here are some of our salient difficulties.

Failure to Cope with the Big Questions

Nothing should be allowed to impair the effectiveness and independence of our specialized leadership groups. But such fragmented leadership does create certain problems. One of them is that it isn't anybody's business to think about the big questions that cut across specialties—the largest questions facing our society. Where are we headed? Where do we want to head? What are the major trends determining our future? Should we do anything about them? Our fragmented leadership fails to deal effectively with these transcendent questions.

Very few of our most prominent people take a really large view of the leadership assignment. Most of them are simply tending the machinery of that part of society to which they belong. The machinery may be a great corporation or a great government agency or a great law practice or a great university. These people may tend it very well indeed, but they are not pursuing a vision of what the total society needs. They have not developed a strategy as to how it can be achieved, and they are not moving to accomplish it.

One does not blame them, of course. They do not see themselves as leaders of the society at large, and they have plenty to do handling their own specialized role.

Yet it is doubtful that we can any longer afford such widespread inattention to the largest questions facing us. We achieved greatness in an era when changes came more slowly than now. The problems facing the society took shape at a stately pace. We could afford to be slow in recognizing them, slow in coping with them. Today, problems of enormous import hit us swiftly. Great social changes emerge with frightening speed. We can no longer afford to respond in a leisurely fashion.

Our inability to cope with the largest questions tends to weaken the private sector. Any question that cannot be dealt with by one of the special leadership groups—that is, any question that cuts across special fields—tends to end up being dealt with by government. Most Americans value the role played by nongovernmental leadership in this country and would wish it to continue. In my judgment it will not continue under the present conditions.

The cure is not to work against the fragmentation of leadership, which is a vital element in our pluralism, but to create better channels of communication among significant leadership groups, especially in connection with the great issues that transcend any particular group.

Failure of Confidence

Another of the maladies of leadership today is a failure of confidence. Anyone who accomplishes anything of significance has more confidence than the facts would justify. It is something that outstanding executives have in common with gifted military commanders, brilliant political leaders, and great artists. It is true of societies as well as of individuals. Every great civilization has been characterized by confidence in itself.

Lacking such confidence, too many leaders add ingenious new twists to the modern art which I call "How to reach a decision without really deciding." They require that the question be put through a series of clearances within the organization and let the clearance process settle it. Or take a public opinion poll and let the poll settle it. Or devise elaborate statistical systems, cost-accounting systems, information-processing systems, hoping that out of them will come unassailable support for one course of action rather than another.

This is not to say that leadership cannot profit enormously from good information. If the modern leader doesn't know the facts he is in grave trouble, but rarely do the facts provide unqualified guidance. After the facts are in, the leader must in some measure emulate the little girl who told the teacher she was going to draw a picture of God. The teacher said, "But, Mary, no one knows what God looks like"; and Mary said, "They will when I get through."

The confidence required of leaders poses a delicate problem for a free society. We don't want to be led by Men of Destiny who think they know all the answers. Neither do we wish to be led by Nervous Nellies. It is a matter of balance. We are no longer in much danger, in this society, from Men of Destiny. But we are in danger of falling under the leadership of men who lack the confidence to lead. And we are in danger of destroying the effectiveness of those who have a natural gift for leadership.

Of all our deficiencies with respect to leadership, one of the gravest is that we are not doing what we should to encourage potential leaders. In the late eighteenth century we produced out of a small population a truly extraordinary group of leaders—Washington, Adams, Jefferson, Franklin, Madison, Monroe, and others. Why is it so difficult today, out of a vastly greater population, to produce men of that caliber? It is a question that most reflective people ask themselves sooner or later. There is no reason to doubt that the human material is still there, but there is excellent reason to believe that we are failing to develop it—or that we are diverting it into nonleadership activities.

The Antileadership Vaccine

Indeed, it is my belief that we are immunizing a high proportion of our most gifted young people against any tendencies to leadership. It will be worth our time to examine how the antileadership vaccine is administered.

The process is initiated by the society itself. The conditions of life in a modern, complex society are not conducive to the emergence of leaders. The young person today is acutely aware of the fact that he is an anonymous member of a mass society, an individual lost among millions of others. The processes by which leadership is exercised are not visible to him, and he is bound to believe that they are exceedingly intricate. Very little in his experience encourages him to think that he might some day exercise a role of leadership.

This unfocused discouragement is of little consequence compared with the expert dissuasion the young person will encounter if he is sufficiently bright to attend a college or university. In those institutions today, the best students are carefully schooled to avoid leadership responsibilities.

Most of our intellectually gifted young people go from college directly into graduate school or into one of the older and more prestigious professional schools. There they are introduced to—or, more correctly, powerfully indoctrinated in—a set of attitudes appropriate to scholars, scientists, and professional men. This is all to the good. The students learn to identify themselves strongly with their calling and its ideals. They acquire a conception of what a good scholar, scientist, or professional man is like.

As things stand now, however, that conception leaves little room for leadership in the normal sense; the only kind of leadership encouraged is that which follows from the performing of purely professional tasks in a superior manner. Entry into what most of us would regard as the leadership roles in the society at large is discouraged.

In the early stages of a career, there is a good reason for this: becoming a first-class scholar, scientist, or professional requires single-minded dedication. Unfortunately, by the time the individual is sufficiently far along in his career to afford a broadening of interests, he often finds himself irrevocably set in a narrow mold.

The antileadership vaccine has other more subtle and powerful ingredients. The image of the corporation president, politician, or college president that is current among most intellectuals and professionals today has some decidedly unattractive features. It is said that such men compromise their convictions almost daily, if not hourly. It is said that they have tasted the corrupting experience of power. They must be status seekers, the argument goes, or they would not be where they are.

Needless to say, the student picks up such attitudes. It is not that professors propound these views and students learn them. Rather, they are in the air and students absorb them. The resulting unfavorable image contrasts dramatically with the image these young people are given of the professional who is almost by definition dedicated to his field, pure in his motives, and unencumbered by worldly ambition.

My own extensive acquaintance with scholars and professionals on the one hand and administrators and managers on the other does not confirm this contrast in character. In my experience, each category has its share of opportunists. Nevertheless, the negative attitudes persist.

As a result the academic world appears to be approaching a point at which everyone will want to educate the technical expert who advises the leader, or the intellectual who stands off and criticizes the leader, but no one will want to educate the leader himself.

Are Leaders Necessary?

For a good many academic and other professional people, negative attitudes toward leadership go deeper than skepticism concerning the leader's integrity. Many have real doubts, not always explicitly formulated, about the necessity for leadership.

The doubts are of two kinds. First, many scientific and professional people are accustomed to the kinds of problems that can be solved by expert technical advice or action. It is easy for them to imagine that any social enterprise could be managed in the same way. They envisage a world that does not need leaders, only experts. The notion is based, of course, upon a false conception of the leader's function. The supplying of technically correct solutions is the least of his responsibilities.

There is another kind of question that some academic or professional people raise concerning leadership: Is the very notion of leadership somehow at odds with the ideals of a free society? Is it a throwback to earlier notions of social organization?

These are not foolish questions. We have in fact outgrown or rejected several varieties of leadership that have loomed large in the history of mankind. We do not want autocratic leaders who treat us like inferior beings. We do not want leaders, no matter how wise or kind, who treat us like children.

But at the same time that we were rejecting those forms of leadership we were evolving forms more suitable to our values. As a result our best leaders today are not out of place in a free society—on the contrary, they strengthen our free society.

We can have the kinds of leaders we want, but we cannot choose to do without them. It is in the nature of social organization that we must have them at all levels of our national life, in and out of government—in business, labor, politics, education, science, the arts, and every other field. Since we must have them, it helps considerably if they are gifted in the performance of their appointed task. The sad truth is that a great many of our organizations are badly managed or badly led. And because of that, people within those organizations are frustrated when they need not be frustrated.

They are not helped when they could be helped. They are not given the opportunities to fulfill themselves that are clearly possible.

In the minds of some, leadership is associated with goals that are distasteful—power, profit, efficiency, and the like. But leadership, properly conceived, also serves the individual human goals that our society values so highly, and we shall not achieve those goals without it.

Leaders worthy of the name, whether they are university presidents or senators, corporation executives or newspaper editors, school superintendents or governors, contribute to the continuing definition and articulation of the most cherished values of our society. They offer, in short, moral leadership.

So much of our energy has been devoted to tending the machinery of our complex society that we have neglected this element in leadership. I am using the word "moral" to refer to the shared values that must undergird any functioning society. The thing that makes a number of individuals a society rather than a population or a crowd is the presence of shared attitudes, habits and values, a shared conception of the enterprise of which they are all a part, shared views of why it is worthwhile for the enterprise to continue and to flourish. Leaders can help in bringing that about. In fact, it is required that they do so. When leaders lose their credibility or their moral authority, then the society begins to disintegrate.

Leaders have a significant role in creating the state of mind that is the society. They can serve as symbols of the moral unity of the society. They can express the values that hold the society together. Most important, they can conceive and articulate goals that lift people out of their petty preoccupations, carry them above the conflicts that tear a society apart, and unite them in the pursuit of objectives worthy of their best efforts.

3

The Leadership Gap

Abraham Zaleznik

Five years ago in the *Harvard Business Review* (*HBR*),[1] I raised the question of whether managers and leaders have distinctly different types of personality. I said that American business had created a new breed called the manager, whose function is to ensure the "competence, control, and the balance-of-power relations among groups with the potential for rivalry." The managerial ethic has fostered a bureaucratic culture that minimizes imaginative capacity and the ability to visualize purposes and to generate values at work, all important attributes of leaders who interact with followers.

The manager was seen as a person with practical responsibilities, who sees that problems are resolved in such a way that people at different levels of responsibility will continue to contribute effectively to the organization. Managerial practice focuses on the decisionmaking process rather than ultimate events, and managers themselves are typically hard working, intelligent, analytical, and tolerant of others. Individuals who are usually thought of as leaders, on the other hand—more dramatic in style and unpredictable in behavior—seem to dominate the swirl of power and politics with an authority that stems from personal magnetism and commitment to their own undertakings and destinies.

During periods of stress and change, society feels an inherent tension between its need for both managers and leaders, for both stability and innovation, and shows symptoms of the deficiency it may have created by stimulating an adequate supply of one type at the expense of the other.

Reprinted from *The Washington Quarterly, A Review of Strategic and International Issues,* 6:1 (Winter 1983), pp. 32–39. Copyright © 1982 by the Center for Strategic and International Studies and reprinted by permission of the Massachusetts Institute of Technology Press Journals.

Managerial goals are deeply embedded in the structure of the organization, in contrast to entrepreneurial or individual leadership goals, which actively attempt to shape public ideas and tastes. Instead of boldly adopting technical innovation or taking risks with untested ideas, managers tend to survey constituents' needs and build their goals on a rational anticipation of the response. They tend to avoid direct confrontation or solutions that could stir up strong feelings of support or opposition. To reconcile differences among people they often seek ways to convert win-lose situations into win-win situations. They focus subordinates' attention on procedures rather than on the substance of decisions, communicate in signals rather than in clearly stated messages, and play for time to take the sting out of win-lose. These tactics frequently create a climate of bureaucratic intrigue and control, which may account for subordinates often viewing managers as inscrutable, detached, and manipulative.

A leader is more interested in what events and decisions mean to people than in his own role in getting things accomplished. The atmosphere leaders create is often one of ferment, which intensifies individual motivation and often results in unanticipated outcomes. Risk is involved in the uncertainty of whether this intensity produces innovation and high performance, or is just wasted energy.

A sense of belonging, of being part of a group or organization, is important to a manager. Perpetuating and strengthening existing institutions enhances his sense of self-worth: he is performing in a role that harmonizes with the ideals of duty and responsibility. Leaders tend to feel somewhat apart from their environment and other people; their relationship toward individuals in a group and their own approach to work are more important to them than group membership and work roles. It is this separate sense of self that makes leaders agents of change, whether technological, political, or ideological.

Even great talent will not guarantee that a potential leader can achieve his ambitions, or that what he achieves will benefit the world. Leaders, like artists, are inconsistent in their ability to function well, and some may give up the struggle.

Is the Distinction Valid?

Our recent concern over declining U.S. productivity, declining standards of quality, and the low state of our work ethos testifies to some missing element in the way we organize economic activity in our society. I think this is directly related to the failure of modern bureaucracies to make use of one kind of leadership talent. If managers and leaders are both needed—one to maintain order by controlling the processes of strategy and operations, the other to effect necessary change by raising standards and defining future goals—we now face the serious challenge of how to build alliances or coalitions not merely between people who work at different jobs but between different kinds of personality types. Leadership involves the personal effect of the leader as an instrument of change on the thinking and behavior of other people.

In my *HBR* article, I used the example of Alfred P. Sloan, whose genius for management was responsible for introducing such new concepts as marketing programs related to product line segmentation, a new kind of distribution organization, and a balanced program of centralization and decentralization that is still a classic model of formal organizational structure. I showed how he handled a conflict between the heads of the manufacturing companies in General Motors, who wanted to go ahead with production of a water-cooled engine that they could make easily and take to market, and Charles Kettering, who was the head of research and development (R&D) and wanted more time and resources to develop an air-cooled engine. Sloan needed a solution that would not alienate Kettering or his ally, Pierre S. du Pont. Instead of exercising his authority to make the practical decision in favor of the manufacturing heads, he threaded his way through the problem by creating a new structure, a mythical organization called the air-cooled engine company, with Kettering in charge. Sloan knew that Kettering was an inventor and not a manager and that the air-cooled engine would probably not materialize, but his maneuver was brilliant because it solved the problem so everyone concerned accepted the process rather than saw it as a win-lose situation.

Such manipulations are useful to managers when the only apparent alternative solutions would hurt the organization or interfere with its output. A leader might have plunged headlong into the conflict, relying on his own powers to steer things through to what he saw as a sound long-range solution, but he might only have aggravated the problem by holding the manufacturers at bay and blocking production in the waiting factories.

Most American managers would probably take umbrage at the notion their profession overlooks any important element. To understand why effective management is not enough, I would like to point out four management assumptions that seem to me mistaken.

One assumption is that the goals of the organization are inherently sound. Managers do not think of themselves as having responsibility for rapid changes in orientation and attitudes, but instead they perpetuate existing goals. One of the elements missing in management, as well as in our economic institutions, is a willingness to question the goals inherent in organizations.

A second assumption is that setting up structures and forms to solve problems involves no cost to the organization. There is in fact a cost that should be calculated for every structural innovation, and if we were able to calculate these, managers would less frequently manipulate structures and think more directly about the nature of the problem they are trying to solve.

A third assumption that may be wrong is that the motivations, beliefs, needs, and desires of human beings are constants and will automatically support the structures that managers try to implement. I think this assumption should be questioned very seriously. There is ample evidence that human motivations vary not only according to incentives and rewards, but also with the social setting and culture of the organization.

The fourth and weakest link in the whole foundation of ideas that supports the management ethos is the assumption that behavior is predictable. We do not yet know enough about behavior, and I do not think we ever will. If behavior could be predicted, organizations could be run with a great deal more assurance than is actually possible simply by calculating the likely effects of doing certain things.

Leadership involves more of the personal effect of the leader as an instrument of change in raising the aspirations and values of other people. Leaders center their assumptions on people—why they act as they do, what they think, what is important to them—rather than on structures.

Leaders assume they can and will be responsible for directing and bringing about any appropriate change. Their primary job is to work persuasively on the values, beliefs, and ideas of people who are going to be part of this change. James MacGregor Burns, in his impressive synthesis drawn from a broad range of disciplines that have tackled the subject of leadership, shows how this "transforming" process worked in the lives of dominant world figures who changed the course of events.[2] During periods of upheaval the leaders tapped the immediate needs and desires of constituencies and transformed them into a higher stage of aspiration and expectation that led to effective action. Burns distinguished this transforming from a transactional kind of leadership, which is kept within contractual boundaries and is based on exchange of one thing for another, such as services rendered in return for money or responsibility accepted in exchange for tenured rank. This corresponds more to the work of managers and their concern with the orderly processes and getting things done through contractual relationships in a structure with a minimum of emotional engagement.

In his book *Leadership*, Professor Burns points out that in the past there have been two approaches to the subject: leaders are viewed either as heroic and famous figures, which is essentially an elitist and exclusive point of view, or as agents from the perspective of followers. He proposes a more realistic concept for the twentieth century, uniting these two views, in which the processes and interplay of leadership are seen as part of the dynamics of conflict and power, with leadership as something more than power holding. In the more complex and potent form of transformational leadership, a leader's power is based on an inherent sensitivity to followers' latent ideas, and his ability to raise them toward higher goals. Interaction between leader and followers is mutually stimulating and elevating, and the change in motives and goals of both has a direct effect on social relations—and morale—ranging from the small and hardly noticed to the creative and historic.

Leadership also involves risk. In contrast to the manager's reliance on structure, the leader risks losing his authority or an erosion of his power base by putting his personal desires on the line. Nothing is as perishable as power if it is used unwisely, or held without being used. The conservatism of managers may well be based on the necessity of guarding the extent to which they risk erosion of their power base. But leaders assume, more often than not, that the impetus for action comes from within themselves rather than from an imposed structure, and accept this inner challenge.

Probably the most important characteristic of leaders is that they must understand themselves before they can work on others. Because they view themselves as instruments of action, Socrates' maxim "Know thyself" is fundamental to leadership. Whereas the burden of responsibility for managers is basically on the structural network of people contributing to output, the essential responsibility of a leader is to himself and to effective interaction with his constituents. Leadership is meaningless without values. An organization or hierarchy can set its values and hope to develop leaders who will articulate them, but values cannot be imposed. They must correspond to the values latent in leaders and followers that can mesh with those of the organization.

The only values that can be relied on are those that are deeply felt and have been absorbed from experience. The styles and standards that evolve from the experience of a functioning relationship between leader and followers will survive even though they may be diverse and occasionally conflicting. The healthy expression of a loyal opposition strengthens the development of durable policies in well-run governments and institutions. There is no reason why democratic institutions, including corporations, cannot thrive by accepting the positive value of different attitudes, expressions, styles, opinions, and personalities.

Is There a Leadership Gap?

The increasing imbalance in our society weighted toward management has created a shortage of leaders in American institutions. One prevalent symptom of this gap is the loss of confidence in authority. Without the bond of confidence between those in authority and those responsive to it, achieving unity of purpose or any common understanding of what a business enterprise, university, or government is trying to accomplish becomes difficult.

Simultaneous with a decline in confidence, a dangerous trend toward careerism has developed. More often than not, people think of their own advancement or personal goals in terms of salary and status rather than the long-range effects of their work on others or on larger organizational objectives. Nothing destroys mutual confidence between a person in authority and the subordinates more than an awareness that the supervisor, executive or officer is fundamentally looking out for his own self-interest. We must find ways to counteract careerism. I think it is a dangerous symptom—at least as destructive at middle and lower levels as at the top—reflecting deterioration in a culture that does not adequately recognize the importance of personal or human values. If we respect power and money above personality, intelligence, and ideas, we establish careerist incentives and rewards that blur the significance of personal accomplishment or of higher social goals.

Executives often reject my view that managers and leaders are different. Because complexity makes their jobs so extremely demanding, they feel that being a top manager takes more talent and ability than I appreciate. Others contend that real managers have to be leaders to cope with elaborate, accumulated layers of hierarchies, especially in the defense area where the structure has been described as "just there." Layers of management and review and the anonymity of upper echelon staffs make it difficult to run a sprawling enterprise encompassing a tremendous range of personnel, operations, equipment, and supplies and seem to require leadership in managers as well as managerial expertise in leaders. I certainly would not minimize the burdens of responsibility at these levels, or the need for talent. The anonymity so keenly felt even by top officials in the defense organization is, however, the product of a managerial culture that has restricted the development of networks of individual leaders as an integral force in the organization.

Does not the mobility of people in responsible positions—the general lack of anchors—again indicate that our institutions have encouraged management at the expense of leadership? We find an illustration of this in the army's attempt to encourage unit cohesion by introducing a cohort system to keep enlisted men committed to their units and to the goals of the military organization. A military sociologist's observation that the . . . system has prompted positive mentor relationships between unit leaders and soldiers demonstrates again that a leadership gap has had its demoralizing causal effects.

The application of systems analysis and econometric models to the All Volunteer force is, of course, another structural attempt at solving the problems of efficiency in a large multiunit organization. That it is a civilian-imposed change, a deviation from the long-time military tradition, makes it no less a characteristically managerial structural solution, stressing skills over rank but neglecting to incorporate subjective, qualitative factors like cohesion and commitment on the very mechanistic ground that such factors don't lend themselves to the quantitative analysis.

Looking closely at the issues of leadership in organizations, I come back to the concept that it is essential and possible to underline the necessity for a coherent structure of authority in which individuals view themselves as major agents of action without readily shifting responsibility on to structures over which they have no feeling of control or personal investment. We could enhance our work ethos and our quality of production if organizations emphatically adopted the point of view that to direct people and communicate policy you must believe what you say and say only what you believe. Production indicators might rise dramatically when supervisors are encouraged to probe problems, propose improvements, and stimulate those working under them to adopt new attitudes and practices. It could reasonably be expected that through more widespread use of individual example and engagement the transformational process would prove far more efficient than consultants' surveys or organizational directives.

We all know by now that the American automobile industry, for instance, cannot be turned around by cautious piecemeal solutions or structural adjustments. Not only will bold decisions have to be made, but many risks will have to be taken in adopting technical innovations. The kind of initiative needed may be outside the experience of U.S. managers, but it can be found in the personality pattern of leaders whose self-reliance and ties with their followers give them the power to steer through problems toward the decisions that must be made for long-range solutions.

The complaint is made that Americans will not become followers because they have lost a sense of values. It has even been proposed that we should organize followers first around a set of goals or programs before leaders step forward to attach themselves to the appropriate cause. But as I have said, these proposals fail to consider the overriding aspect of leadership: the leader's intuitive abilities and personal qualities are essential in eliciting a response from followers in order to extend their energies and attitudes toward larger goals and values. Organizational attempts to prefabricate scenarios or instill prescribed values are futile, because they dodge the issue of personal influence and engagement by leaders and draw one more veil of anonymity between people and programs.

Can We Educate for Leadership?

Historians note that leaders emerge in times of crisis, as if the crisis itself had brought them forth to satisfy a public yearning for one individual to symbolize people's hopes, desires, ambitions, and determination. Apart from the disadvantages of waiting for crises to produce leaders, we can in our own time wonder whether the apparent phenomenon of crisis leadership is as dependable as it seems to have been in the past. The opposing influence of man-made bureaucratic structures may have been too effective. Our institutions will have to reassess their needs and determine not only how they can encourage and develop leaders at many different levels, but where the particular gaps are that leaders could most effectively fill.

"How do we recognize leadership? And do we understand it?" managers ask. It is true that we cannot pinpoint potential leaders in advance, but we can give them opportunities. Mentors can test the willingness of younger people to shape and mediate conflict and to step forward with their own criticisms and proposals for work problems—especially where structural solutions have not worked.

In the early days of the American republic an astonishing number of great men were prominently active in public life. Before schools of law, medicine, science, and technology had been established, the political arena was virtually the only field held open to men of talent, so they concentrated there and shone brilliantly. The talent they represented is widely diffused today through many specialties in the arts, sciences, and professions, but it is far less conspicuous in the bureaucracies of those institutions that shape our social standards: business, education, government.

It is a mistake to assume that people have changed from one generation to another and can no longer respond to initiative. Our system of training and educating people has denied [those with] a certain kind of leadership talent enough significant participation in the life of the organization. Managers, teachers, and people in responsible positions in the society can recognize potential leaders more easily when they understand that freely developed personal relationships between supervisors and subordinates can benefit the culture of the group, that questions and challenges can yield results, and that encouraging experimentation can produce a more dynamic environment where talent can grow.

Is it an elitist concept to train selected individuals to become leaders because of talent, personality, and potential influence over followers? Americans have always felt a tension between the polarized ideals of looking up to a select group of leaders and participation in a democracy.

The fundamental tension in our society between elitist and populist viewpoints tends to focus on a version of leadership representing either extreme. As a result we do not think much about the many effective leaders who have not captured headlines or appeared in history books. I think it is time to separate the term "charisma" from the concept of leadership. Charisma leads but can also mislead followers. It is not a necessary ingredient of leadership and certainly inclines toward elitist and mystical conceptions, as well as singles out certain leaders and diminishes others whose influence on followers may have been as enduring and significant.

Above all, charismatic leadership as a concept diverts attention from the important educational function of leadership. The energy and time expended in trying to bring out a talent for management in leaders, or leadership traits in good managers, could be allocated more realistically to teaching managers and leaders to understand their different approaches to work relationships without becoming destructively competitive, and for each to see the need for the other. This would also focus more attention on how to overcome the many obstacles to early identification of leaders.

Manager and Leader Orientations—Both Have Value

Our management culture is based on the rational principle of contract, which binds individuals to terms covering an exchange of something for something else without further infringements on their freedom. Contractual relationships are the key to a democratic economy and the free enterprise system, although extending the principle of contract into all family or community relationships tends to leave people deprived of the benefits of important human relationships.

The leader-manager distinction has been viewed by the sociologist Charles Moskos as a contrast between commitment to the institution, whose purpose and values transcend self-interest, and to occupational categories, where responsibilities are purely contractual, exchanging work for cash. I think this may miss the important potential synergistic effects of leadership and management in improving the ways in which people approach work and the solution of problems. Although executives' personal goals, according to this proposed theory, are more explicitly linked to institutional goals, the relationship with followers that leaders can develop in the professional and occupational categories could be at least as significant to the character and quality of the organization.

A more useful analogy might compare the effects of leaders and managers to those of strategy and operations, with strategists staking out the direction, relative position, and objectives of the organization in its competitive setting, and operations managers dealing with current applications and implementation of specifications and programs. Strategy is the job of projecting into the future: surveying a company's situation and deciding between alternative courses of action with many possible consequences. Operations coordinates the work of implementing decisions that have been made and getting the job done. Strategy corresponds to leadership in making decisions and taking actions that affect others, while operations corresponds to the many interrelating responsibilities of management.

This analogy suggests how the synergistic relationship between strategy and operations would apply also in a fully functioning relationship of mutual respect between leaders and managers in large organizations. To view the distinction as one between ideals and commitment, on one hand, and occupations and material self-interest, on the other, seems to oversimplify and even distort the real difference.

The notion that managers deal with things and leaders deal with people is another oversimplification. Managers deal with a great many people and have to be aware of their needs. The difference I would stress is that managers deal with people in interacting groups, aiming at consensus agreement and on the whole minimizing the one-to-one relationship that is essential to a leader's makeup and development. Both managers and leaders can contribute to a society and its institutions. The art of business management has obscured the importance of personal initiative and leadership by its emphasis on structural arrangements, processes, and order, to the point where personal leadership needs to be retrieved and drawn out in individuals whose talents predispose them in that direction.

Experimenting with one-to-one relationships, such as apprenticing junior executives to senior mentors, could inject a healthy elixir into the managerial culture. Peer alliances, through which corporations attempt to differentiate responsibilities equally among persons of equal status, theoretically promote learning uninhibited by the restraints of authority or criticisms of superiors, but I believe such alliances consistently develop team players rather than the kind of individual who might become a leader. In a one-to-one relationship with a superior, a junior executive can learn first hand about power, performance, and integrity. These relationships could teach senior executives that a direct exchange of ideas, open challenges, and the competitive impulses of subordinates can be creative and stimulating without shattering their own authority. Furthermore, apprenticeships prepare individuals to move more rapidly into strategy-related positions where they can put their ideas to work.

To undergo the necessary transformation in this decade, management will have to accept the feasibility of working alliances with leaders who question old practices and propose new solutions, and to think of the link between them as essential as the link between strategy and operations. While guarding against the cult of elitism, managers must nevertheless lean toward a culture of individualism. Only when the values of an organization also can be expressed as the personal values of those within the organization can they have any real meaning.

Notes

1. Abraham Zaleznik, "Managers and Leaders: Are They Different?" *Harvard Business Review*, May-June 1977, pp. 67–68.

2. James MacGregor Burns, *Leadership* (New York: Harper & Row, 1978), chapters 1, 3, 6, 7, 9, 11.

4

Understanding and Applying Transformational Leadership

*Majs. Kevin S. Donohue
and Leonard Hong*

Transformational leadership—the notion that a leader can influence followers to transcend self-interests and commit themselves to excellence—has been receiving a lot of attention lately. An increasing number of our senior leaders are talking about "empowerment" and "vision," two concepts identified with transformational leadership. So what exactly is new about this approach to leading? Is it the leadership "secret" behind the success of our greatest leaders? Most important, the bottom line: can it still work for us after it has been "painted green"?

To better understand where the field of leadership theory is going, let us start by briefly reviewing where it has been. From the end of World War II until the 1980s, the focus of leadership theorists and researchers has been on "situational," "interactionist" or "contingency" approaches to leadership. These approaches were heavily influenced by the behaviorist movement in American psychology and organizational behavior, so they normally revolved around the notion of observing and changing behaviors. In such theories, leaders use different styles of leadership, depending on various situational characteristics which in turn cause the followers to work more efficiently and get the mission accomplished.

The general assumption of most of these earlier theories was that the leader gave pay support, recognition or some other type of reward or threat of punishment in exchange for follower compliance. Many of us in the profession of arms, understanding how important leadership is, wanted to believe there was something truly useful in these theories. We learned how to

Reprinted by permission from *Military Review,* 74:8 (August 1994), pp. 24–41.

become a "9,9" leader, or how a "low LPC" leader should interact in structuring a task, but these leadership theories somehow felt hollow and we usually left them in the classroom. They looked good on paper, but they really did not address the things that attracted soldiers to their profession, such as patriotism, selfless service or duty. We thought about the greatest leaders we have worked with and for, and there seemed to be more going on than these leadership theories could account for. These theories had missed the *heart* of leadership. In fact, these theories are sometimes collectively called "transactional" theories, because they suggest that leadership is essentially a transaction between the follower(s) and the leader.

Transformational theories of leadership (occasionally referred to as "theories of excellence") became increasingly popular in the 1980s. These newer theories went beyond the earlier, more simplistic approaches to leadership by focusing on the attitudes and values underlying any of these behaviors—the "heart" of leadership. The transformational leader gets followers to transcend their own self-interest for the sake of the leader, team, unit or organization. The transformational leader obtains more from his or her followers than superficial change in their attitudes or minor increments in their temporary level of motivation.

Transformational leadership theories offer tremendous promise, but they still have some rough spots. One of the issues that needs further development is how, and indeed if, a leader can become transformational. For instance, it is common, but not very informative, for transformational theorists to note that a transformational leader has "charisma." Charisma, a Greek word meaning "divine gift," has often been used to describe some unexplainable, even mystical leader trait. The whole point of transformational leadership, however, is that we can understand what causes followers to be magnetically attracted to a leader's cause. Therefore, our interpretation will present the leader behaviors that lead to charismatic appeal.[1]

Before the application of transformational leadership can be discussed, it is essential to consider the different ways in which followers react to the influence attempts of a leader. After discussing these differences, we will focus on what conditions are most favorable for the use of transformational leadership. Finally, this article will propose a set of behaviors that may serve as foundations for the application of transformational leadership in the Army. (See Figure 4.1)

Follower Reactions to Leadership

Organizational leadership is commonly defined as the process of influencing human behavior so as to accomplish the goals prescribed by the organizationally appointed leader. Of course, it is not as simple as that; follower

	Transactional	*Transformational*
Leader's source of		
Power	Rank, position	Character, competence
Follower reaction	Compliance	Commitment
Time frame	Short Term	Long Term
Rewards	Pay, promotion, etc.	Pride, self-esteem, etc.
Supervision	Important	Less important
Counseling focus	Evaluation	Development
Where change occurs	Follower behavior	Follower attitude, values
Where "leadership" found	Leader's behavior	Follower's heart

FIGURE 4.1   A Comparison of Transactional and Transformational Leadership

behavior is ordinarily based upon a complex set of needs and motivations. When a leader attempts to influence a follower, four possible outcomes may occur: resistance, compliance, identification and internalization.[2]

Resistance is the refusal or reluctance of a follower toward a leader's request. Resistance occurs when soldiers actively avoid complying with the attempted influence. This may take subtle forms such as refusing to enforce an organizational policy, bathroom graffiti or looking the other way. It might also reach tragic dimensions, such as the mutiny of the French and Russian Armies during World War I or the "fragging" of noncommissioned officers and officers in Vietnam. Needless to say, resistance is an unacceptable outcome for any leader.

Compliance is the acceptance of the leader's influence and a corresponding change in behavior, but not necessarily a change in attitude.

Compliance involves accepting the leader's influence in order to receive social and material rewards or to avoid social and material punishment. Since the source of influence retains control over the rewards and punishment, public acquiescence without private commitment to the influence may be demonstrated.

Unlike resistance, it is usually possible for a leader to accomplish a short-term mission with nothing more than follower compliance. Even this is not always the case. For instance, consider the dilemma of Generals Richard Montgomery and Benedict Arnold, commanding a small force of the Continental Army during the 1775 invasion of Canada. The American conscripts, ravaged by weather and starvation, eagerly awaited the expiration of their enlistment contracts in the new year. Montgomery, knowing that most of his men would return to their homes as soon as they had fulfilled their obligation, rushed into a desperate attack on the fortress of Quebec on the last day of the year. The American force, attacking in a snowstorm at night, was decisively defeated. The invasion of Canada had failed, at least in part because the soldiers were willing to comply with the terms of their contract, but no more.

Much of the leadership practiced in today's Army achieves compliance from followers. But is compliance enough? The Greek commander Xenophon (circa 430–355 B.C.) probably identified the key insight of transformational leadership theory when he concluded that "willing obedience always beats forced obedience." It is perhaps too obvious to state that if the followers are committed to the leader and the mission, the likelihood of success increases; yet, if we focus simply on observing follower behaviors, we might never know whether the followers are complying or are committed. More recently, General of the Army Dwight D. Eisenhower suggested, "I would rather try to persuade a man to go along, because once I have persuaded him, he will stick. If I scare him, he will stay just as long as he is scared, and then he is gone."

According to these theories, then, an effective leader wants to do more than change behaviors; the leader wants to change attitudes—the leader seeks commitment. There are two follower reactions to the leader's influence that can achieve this commitment: identification and internalization.

Identification is the acceptance of influence because the source is an attractive, likable source, worthy of emulation. An attitude change in the follower due to identification may essentially resemble imitation, because the follower may wish to be like the leader. When the leader is gone, however, the follower may revert back to the original attitude and behaviors, since a lasting change did not really occur. We do not hear soldiers using the term "identification" too much, but such words as trust, respect, loyalty, cohesion and admiration are all types of identification.

Internalization is the acceptance of influence and consequent attitude change due to the intrinsically rewarding nature of the influence attempt. Followers take on the ideas or values from a trusted, sound leader because the followers see the wisdom of the influence attempt. The new attitude is durable and deeply rooted because it becomes "owned" by the follower. Ideally, it becomes a value. While complex concepts such as "self-actualized" and "empowered" are frequently used to describe a committed follower, commitment is frequently evident in the pride and self-confidence that a person has in his or her work.

As noted earlier, identification and internalization are both forms of commitment. As an example of follower commitment, consider the love that the Confederate soldiers of the American Civil War had for their commander, General Robert E. Lee. The Confederate soldiers' attachment to their commander in chief was nowhere more evident than at the battle of Spotsylvania Court House, where a Union attack threatened to overwhelm the Confederate position. Lee, sensing the precarious situation, rode forward to personally lead a desperate counterattack. The distraught Confederate soldiers, fearing for their commander's safety, implored Lee to let them take his place, shouting "General Lee to the rear!" Lee relented, and the vicious and costly counterattack went forward without him.

Conditions Ripe for Transformational Leadership

Transformational leadership is often associated with certain contexts. Since the word means to transform or change, it should be little surprise that transformational leadership may be cultivated when followers perceive that conditions of crisis, change and instability exist.[3] During this time, traditional values and beliefs may be questioned. The old ways of doing things may not help the organization through the crisis. Thus, a transformational leader may appeal to the values of his followers or even ask them to transcend their own self-interest to get the organization through the turbulent times.

Transformational leadership is not only found during an acute crisis, but also when the values of a culture are being attacked during a particularly unstable time. It carries with it a challenge to the old order, a break with continuity, a risky adventure, ferment and change. For example, Franklin D. Roosevelt was able to transform the American people with his fireside chats, inspiring addresses and encouragement of intellectual solutions to national problems during the unstable periods of the Great Depression and World War II.

Likewise, the leader may detect the need to go above and beyond the current conditions of mediocrity. The job may be getting done, but there may be a general "malaise" present in the organization. The leader may observe the members of the organization merely going through the motions. In other words, is their "heart" in their work? In a situation where the followers do not see any need to change, some leaders have deemed it necessary to "whip up a crisis" in order to create conditions more favorable for transformational leadership.

Conditions may also be favorable for transformational leadership when there are high levels of *follower disenchantment*.[4] During a time when followers are disenchanted with current conditions, a transformational leader will provide the direction and vision needed to energize the organization. Disillusioned followers are particularly receptive to the emotional, inspirational influence attempts made by a transformational leader.

Misguided leaders have capitalized on the conditions favorable for transformational leadership to suit their own purposes. For example, many cult leaders gather a large following by attracting those who are frustrated or dissatisfied with present relationships. Jim Jones was able to use transformational leadership to convince hundreds of followers dissatisfied with relationships and conditions in the United States to move to Guyana and, later, to commit mass suicide. Jones is also an example, along with other infamous leaders such as Adolf Hitler and Charles Manson, of the "dark side" of transformational leadership.

Transformational Leader Behaviors

It should be apparent that true transformational leadership requires a change in how the followers perceive themselves, their mission, their unit and their leader. Several leader behaviors appear to promote such changes. There is no guarantee that leaders can be transformational simply by employing one of more of these behaviors. However, it appears that certain behaviors, used when situational conditions are most favorable for their employment, provide the greatest likelihood of eliciting increased follower internalization and identification.

A transformational leader develops and communicates a vision.[5] A leader may realize the need for a major revitalization of the organization and develop a vision based on the needed changes. The leader's vision serves as a source of self-esteem and common purpose for organizational members. The vision should convey an inspiring, appealing picture of what the organization can be in the future without discounting the past.[6] For example, two bricklayers were working side by side at a construction site. When the first was asked what he was doing, he replied that he was laying bricks. When the other was asked, he responded that he was creating a great cathedral. The first bricklayer was only following blueprints—the other had a vision.

The vision of a transformational leader is more than a goal or unit objective, or even the commander's intent for a particular operation. It is a value or collection of values that the soldiers of a unit can rally around. General George Washington considered it essential that leaders "impress upon the mind of every man, from the first to the lowest, the importance of the cause and what it is they are contending for." It represents what the unit is all about, how it does things and why it does those things. It is not simply words, but an accepted personal value. It may be expressed in a revered motto, such as "duty, honor, country" or "Rangers lead the way," or it may be a more abstract concept such as wanting our unit to be so proficient that none of us would hesitate to have our sons or daughters assigned to it. (See Figure 4.2.)

Transformational leaders dream and can translate these dreams so that others can share them. A historical example of a leader who possessed and communicated his vision was Martin Luther King Jr. In his "I Have A Dream" speech, King was not just interested in getting the freedom to eat at dimestore lunch counters or changing segregation laws. Instead, he com-

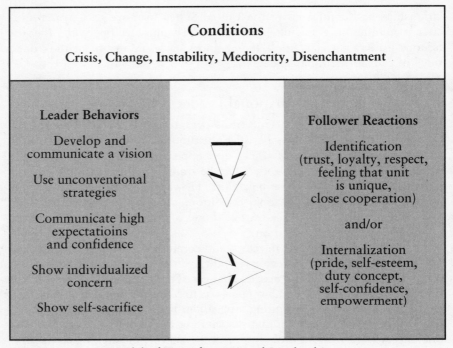

FIGURE 4.2 A Model of Transformational Leadership

municated the vision that the hearts of Americans would be changed to make these political developments possible. He framed his mission around those values found in the Constitution and the Declaration of Independence. Visions are often communicated through speeches, policies, behaviors or symbols.

The vision that provides a common purpose to the unit does not have to be communicated through a speech. Often, the leader's vision is communicated through the leader's use of unconventional strategies.[7] Since transformational visions normally seek to change the status quo, nonstandard ways of reinforcing the vision are likely to get more attention. Furthermore, innovative techniques add to the followers' attributions that the leader, the organization and the vision are extraordinary and unique.

An example of an unconventional strategy is a commander perpetuating a "think war" vision by directing that all unit physical training be conducted in flak vests. Another unconventional strategy that communicates a vision would be a newly arriving medical unit commander who goes through her unit's morning sick call without calling attention to who she is. She could later use her description of that experience to reinforce her vision that the unit's primary focus must always remain on caring for soldiers.

Transformational leaders go beyond the ordinary in expressing the vision. It should be noted that as these unconventional strategies become familiar to the followers, they diminish in their contribution to transformational leadership since they become routine, possibly even expected.

Along with communicating the vision to the followers the transformational leader also communicates high expectations and confidence in the followers.[8] Policies directed by the leader and behavior exhibited by the leader reflect a trust and faith in the competence and abilities of the followers. Indeed, the vision expressed by the leader and shared by the followers may be more alluring due to the conviction of the leader toward the unit. For instance, Brigadier General Anthony C. McAuliffe rallied the soldiers of the 101st Airborne Division, encircled in Bastogne, with his reply of "nuts!" to the German offer to accept a US surrender. While a brigade commander in World War I, Douglas MacArthur went forward to the battalion that was about to lead the way on an offensive. Upon finding the major in command, MacArthur encouraged this officer to lead the way bravely. MacArthur then removed the Distinguished Service Cross from his own tunic, explained that he knew the major would earn this award for his heroism in the battle to come, and pinned it upon him just as the barrage lifted and the attack was to commence. In doing so, MacArthur had communicated his complete confidence in this leader.

A transformational leader also shows individualized concern toward followers.[9] This is not simply "supportive behavior" or "taking care of the welfare of the troops" collectively. This may take the form of developmental orientations, such as delegation and mentoring, to an individualized orientation such as counseling and "leadership by walking around." One battalion commander at the National Training Center, Fort Irwin, California, described this aspect of transformational leadership as the ability to "know your soldiers by the backs of their heads." A leader who takes time to know more than impersonal numbers about his or her soldiers builds a bond between the leader and led. Once this bond is formed, an appeal to values in going beyond compliance is more easily accomplished. Although it is almost certainly an exaggerated claim, Julius Caesar could reportedly recognize every man in his legions by name. During inspections and speeches, Napoleon also showed the ability to single out campaign veterans by name, asking about their families and other personal details (although his recognition was aided by an adjutant's advance briefing).

A transformational leader shows self-sacrifice in achieving the vision.[10] This self-sacrifice may be evident in personal risk taking and incurring high costs to attain the vision the leader espouses. This self-sacrificing attitude adds to the trust the followers have in the leader, since they may have more faith in a leader who advocates a strategy that shows more concern for the soldiers and unit than for the leader's self-interest. Anyone can "talk the talk," but soldiers pay attention to the leader who "walks the talk." Self-sacrificing leaders also clearly communicate that they really believe in what they are doing.

It is virtually a requirement for any discussion of successful combat leadership to document heroic leadership in battle, but setting the example through selfless sacrifice can also be demonstrated away from the battlefield. While commanding a tank brigade in World War I, Colonel George S. Patton Jr. was observing 37mm gun practice. A round exploded in one gun's muzzle, wounding some soldiers. The next round fired from this gun exploded in the breech, killing the gunner. Fearing that the troops would lose confidence in their equipment, Patton went to the gun and personally fired the next three rounds without incident.

Transformational leadership begins with a vision. Once developed, this vision is communicated to followers through various conventional and unconventional strategies. Additionally, the leader expresses confidence in the followers in attaining the vision, demonstrates sincere individualized concern for the followers and shows the willingness for personal risk and sacrifice in fulfilling the vision.

The transformational leader goes beyond basic emotions such as fear, jealousy or greed to appeal to ideals and moral values such as justice, liberty, patriotism and equality. Such an appeal, if successful, inspires followers to transcend their own self-interest for the sake of the leader, team, unit or organization. Such a leader obtains more from his or her followers than superficial change in their attitudes or minor increments in their temporary level of motivation.

Transformational leadership leads to performance beyond the level elicited by transactional leadership. However, transactional and transformational leadership are not mutually exclusive, nor is transformational leadership a panacea for all of a leader's problems. There are clearly times when transformational leadership is less appropriate—the prospect of a three-day pass may motivate the post support detail to be more thorough in police call than exhorting them to pick up garbage for the leader's warfighting vision. Transactional leadership is generally easier to use, and for certain tasks or missions where a short-term behavior is all that is required, it may be enough.

Hence, it is possible for a leader to exhibit a complementary mix of both transactional and transformational leadership styles. How the leader mixes the two types of leadership is probably largely affected by a number of factors, including the organizational climate, unit mission and the leader's own experience and "comfort zone." Another factor that appears to have a major influence on the mix between transformational and transactional leadership is the level of the organization at which the leader is operating. Transformational leadership appears relatively more appropriate for senior leaders concerned with longer term horizons, but this does not imply that junior leaders have no use for it.

Perhaps the most significant implication of transformational leadership is the conditions under which it is best assessed—after the leader is gone, or at least when the leader is not supervising the unit's accomplishment of the mission. In the words of the American journalist Walter Lippman, "The final test of a leader is that he leaves behind him in other men the conviction and the will to carry on." In no other organization is this more true than in the profession of arms, and nowhere is this more vital than on the battlefield.

This interpretation of transformational leadership is an attempt to recast our Army's traditional perspectives on leadership in terms of the newest frameworks being explored by leadership theorists and researchers. We have tried to take some pretty abstract concepts and anchor them in the context of an Army. leader's daily life, in the hope that we can all gain a better grasp of transformational leadership theory. This is just a start. We hope that other Army leaders will take these concepts still further to foster a better understanding of how to use transformational leadership behaviors.

Can the principles of transformational leadership be applied in our Army? The question is moot—they already have been! Some of our best leaders have been the ones who understood how to frame their vision in order to wake other soldiers out of a sleepy routine, energize them and commit them to excellence. Transformational leadership theory is not some amazing new discovery; it simply provides a framework by which we can better understand their successes. The challenge that now lies before us is to capture the power of transformational leadership for ourselves.

Notes

1. For those who are interested in exploring transformational leadership at a more theoretical level, two of the "classic" works in the area are James M. Burns, *Leadership* (New York: Harper and Row, 1978) and Bernard M. Bass, *Leadership and Performance Beyond Expectations* (New York: Free Press, 1985). See also the more recent discussion in James G. Hunt, *Leadership: A New Synthesis* (Newbury Park, CA.: Sage Publications, 1991), 181–215.

2. H. C. Kelman, "Compliance, Identification, and Internalization: Three Processes of Attitude Change." *Journal of Conflict Resolution* (Vol. 2, 1958): 51–60. Resistance was suggested as an outcome of leader influence by Gary A. Yukl, *Leadership in Organizations* (Englewood Cliffs, NJ: Prentice Hall, 1989), 44. Jane Howell connects these processes to the charismatic leadership in "Two Faces of Charisma: Socialized and Personalized Leadership in Organizations" in *Charismatic Leadership*, eds. Jay A. Conger and Rabindra N. Kanungo (San Francisco: Jossey-Bass, 1968), 213–36.

3. Jay A. Conger and Rabindra N. Kanungo, "Conclusion: Patterns and Trends in Studying Transformational Leadership" in *Charsmatic Leadership*, 324–36.

4. Ibid., 333. See also Conger and Kanungo, "Toward a Behavioral Theory of Charismatic Leadership in Organizational Settings," *Academy of Management Review* (October, 1967), 637–47.

5. For a complete description of visionary leadership, see Marshall Sashkin, "The Visionary Leader" in *Charismatic Leadership*, 122–60, or F. R. Westley and H. Mintzberg, "Visionary Leadership and Strategic Management," *Strategic Management Journal* (Summer, 1989), 17–32.

6. For an excellent discussion of the components of an effective vision, see Tom Peters, *Thriving on Chaos: Handbook for a Management Revolution* (New York: Alfred A. Knopf, 1967) or Warren Bennis and Burt Nanus, *Leaders: The Strategies for Taking Charge* (New York: Harper and Row, 1985).

7. Conger and Kanungo, "Toward a Behavioral Theory."

8. For a complete description of expressing confidence in subordinates, see W. Burke, "Leadership as Empowering Others" in *Executive Power: How Executives Influence People and Organizations*, eds. S. Srivastva and Associates (San Francisco: Jossey-Bass, 1986).

9. Bass, 81–97. See also B. J. Avolo and Bernard M. Bass, "Transformational Leadership: Charisma and Beyond," in *Emerging Leadership Vistas*, eds. J. G. Hunt, B. R. Baliga, H. P. Dacher, and C. A. Schreisheim (Lexington, MA: Lexington Books, 1988), 29–50.

10. Conger and Kanungo, "Toward a Behavioral Theory."

5

A Comprehensive View
of Leadership

Brig. Gen. Huba Wass De Czece

Every Army leader, active or retired, should be considered knowledgeable on the subject of leadership. This is only natural since this has been the essence of the military profession. I have learned much from the views of others and have developed my own way of thinking about leadership and how to talk to younger leaders about it.

Before one can understand and write about what leaders ought to *be*, *know* and *do* (and that is a good way to talk about leadership), one ought to be clear about what leaders are for in a more fundamental sense. What are the critical leadership functions performed by Army officers as they lead small and large units within an Army preparing for, deterring and conducting war on behalf of a free society? How are these functions performed differently as one proceeds up the scale from sergeant to general? How do *being, knowing* and *doing* change at each level and how do we prepare our leaders to advance? The purpose of this article is to propose a systematic way to ask and answer those questions and to thus learn more about the science and art of leadership.

There is general agreement that leadership is the art of influencing others to take action toward a goal, and that military leadership is the art of influencing soldiers in units to accomplish unit missions. It is also generally understood that small-unit leaders rely on direct-influence processes while senior leaders rely more on indirect processes in proportion to their seniority. This is a slim framework for understanding the leadership function—why we *have* leaders.

Reprinted by permission from *Military Review,* 72:8 (August 1992), pp. 21–29.

What are the key leadership functions that must be performed to produce truly effective military organizations? Effective organizations have clearly defined purposes, respond to direction, are composed of people motivated to pursue organizational purposes along clearly identified paths and have programs that sustain their effectiveness over time. Organizations without these critical characteristics are not effective. Leaders provide purpose. They also establish direction, generate motivation and sustain effectiveness. They really do more, but they cannot do less. Thus effectiveness can be reduced to four leadership functions—providing purpose, establishing direction, generating motivation for unit actions and sustaining the effectiveness of the unit for future tasks (providing for continuity and constant improvement of the organization). All other functions are really subfunctions of these four; they facilitate the accomplishment of one or more of these four primary functions. For instance, setting the proper unit values may facilitate all four, but the reason for having the proper values is not that they are an end in and of themselves but they are a means to an ultimate end—a unit that can be led to accomplish its intended aims with greater effectiveness.

Four Primary Functions of Effective Military Leadership

Although the four primary functions of effective leadership are interdependent, we discuss purpose first because effective directing, motivating and sustaining require a focus or aim. We discuss directing next because it is composed of the actions the leader takes to guide the unit in the direction of purpose. Motivating follows this because it comprises the actions the leader takes to impel individuals within the unit to follow the directing guidance. We discuss sustaining effectiveness last because it is primarily an activity with long-range payoffs.

Provide and Instill Purpose. The effective leader must be an effective link in the chain of command. The leader must possess a broad vision to guide the organization drawing meaning or purpose from this vision for unit activity. The leader must have a clear idea of how the organization fits into a larger scheme—why they are doing what they are doing. The leader imparts a sense of purpose on subordinates and instills a sense of purpose in soldiers, aligning unit missions, goals and objectives within broader schemes and purposes.

To shape the vision, the effective leader may draw upon many sources:

- Beginning with the oath of office to defend and support the Constitution, or even higher moral and spiritual imperatives.
- Draw on institutional and national values, goals and aspirations to formulate the concept of purpose he articulates to subordinates.

A leader's commander and the next higher headquarters will transmit their articulation of purpose both directly and indirectly. In combat, this may be directly and clearly expressed (paragraphs 1b., 2 and 3 of the operations order he receives). A leader may have to read between the lines of their words or actions to clearly understand the commander's intent (or the vision from which they derive purpose). This is called "restating the mission" and "identifying the implied tasks." A leader must remain aware of events beyond those involving the unit. In reality, this may require filling gaps in the picture of purpose by deductive or inductive logic.

However arriving at the conception of purpose, the effective leader passes on a coherent picture of how the unit mission fits into the "big picture." Imparting a sense of importance of the tasks to be accomplished and how success or failure of the unit mission will affect the world beyond the unit. In combat, events will not unfold as planned, assumptions may prove to be wrong and assigned tasks may not be appropriate. Knowing the purpose of the unit mission helps subordinates judge what new tasks would be more appropriate. Understanding the purpose of unit missions (the "intent of higher commanders") aids them in coordinating their unit's actions with those of others and leads to overall harmony in execution and economy of effort toward common goals. It provides a frame of reference for independent thought and decision making by subordinates to solve unanticipated problems, which are best resolved and acted on rapidly.

As one proceeds from squad to the highest strategic levels, the leader must become more active in clarifying and transmitting purpose as it becomes more conceptual, longer range and ephemeral. At the highest levels, there may be a great deal of latitude in shaping, articulating and refining purpose. And higher values such as the oath of office and moral and spiritual imperatives, while important at all levels, play a more significant role because less specific guidance is provided. At squad level, it may be simply to know, pass on and imbue squad members with a simple idea such as "We must take out that bunker because it is holding up the platoon or company advance," or "We will train hard because we want to be the best squad in the company."

At all levels, it is the duty of leaders to clarify the purpose of their missions by asking appropriate questions, if time permits, and to inform subordinates appropriately. (It is also well known that there is a motivational side benefit of letting soldiers know the purpose of their sacrifices—the more important the purpose, the greater the motivational benefit.) The key benefit of providing and instilling purpose is to ensure that what is to be done is accomplished so as to fit into a higher scheme. This is the mechanism that aids synchronization in an environment where initiative is highly valued.

Providing Direction. Effective leaders provide unambiguous direction and guidance for action. They have a clear vision of what must be done, what is necessary to get the job done and how to proceed. They clearly articulate and assign objectives, missions and goals to subordinates. In addition to such direct guidance, they also provide indirect guidance. They promote values; set standards for accomplishment of tasks; enforce discipline; establish standard operating procedures; ensure the training of soldiers and units in appropriate doctrine, methods and techniques; and establish policies and regulations. At the highest levels, military leaders also may be responsible for development of doctrine, methods and techniques in some or all areas.

Providing direction effectively requires command and control skills, processes and functions—information gathering, analysis, decision making, issuing instructions or orders performing appropriate supervision and monitoring the effectiveness of the resulting actions. Effective leadership in combat is measured in terms of the speed and effectiveness of this cycle (often called the decision cycle) relative to that of the enemy.

As leadership advances from the squad to the highest levels, the function of providing direction becomes more complex. Setting and communicating standards, promoting values, enforcing discipline, establishing methods and procedures, and command and control processes become more dependent on systems and organizational functionaries than on direct interpersonal relations. Management, the control of things and the coordination and sequencing of events, while applicable at all levels, becomes an important tool in providing direction at senior levels of leadership. It is in this sense that it relates to leadership.

Effective senior leaders know that even the act of gathering information about the activities of subordinates may cause a reorientation of those activities. They take this into account in designing systems that will gather information purposefully. They ask for meaningful reports and develop unobtrusive ways to find out what they need to know without unintentionally reorienting the focus of subordinate activity.

Providing Motivation. Effective leaders provide motivation—they harness the willingness of subordinates to work toward common goals, missions, objectives and tasks. All combat is, in the end, a test of will, both of soldiers and leaders. In combat, leaders must motivate soldiers to do difficult things in trying circumstances. In peacetime, motivation to perform tasks well is important. In combat, it can be decisive. Marshal Maurice de Saxe, writing in the 18th century, pointed out that "a soldier's courage must be reborn daily," and Ardant du Picq, writing in the 19th, remarked that "you can reach into the well of courage only so many times before the well runs dry."

It is common knowledge that motivation promoted by rewards is more effective in generating commitment than motivation promoted by punishments. Providing positive motivation should be the aim of all leaders, but

negative sanctions are also important for delineating the limits of acceptable behavior. Effective leaders elicit willing compliance and devote a considerable effort to obtaining it.

Means and methods for motivating soldiers differ at various levels. At all
levels of authority, mutual trust and confidence are key, but styles may differ.

The moral force that impels subordinates to action at all levels is rooted
in mutual trust and respect. This in turn stems from a record of association
and a reputation for ethical behavior and sound decision making. Values,
or held beliefs, when appropriate and shared in the unit, are important motivators. "This unit can't be beat" and "This unit doesn't leave its dead on
the battlefield" are examples. Ethics are standards of behavior in relation to
values. Mutual trust and respect derive in part from perceptions of ethical
behavior and in part from a record of success. Mutual trust and respect
also derive from "taking care of the troops." When troops know that their
efforts will not be wasted on unnecessary tasks; that the leader recognizes
the value and quality of their labors and is doing the best to meet their
needs within the constraints imposed; is concerned about them as human
beings; listens to their grievances; and respects subordinates and builds
their self-esteem; they will give their full measure of support. All of these
factors combine to provide the leader the moral force he needs to motivate
in stressful situations in combat, or anytime.

American soldiers have always fought well when they feel they are in a
good outfit and trust their leaders. At the lowest levels, direct daily face-to-
face appeals to values, insistence on standards and a record of fairness, self-
discipline, competence, displays of example, courage and resourcefulness
are the most effective motivators. At times, especially in combat, resorting
to intimidation may be necessary, but intimidation never elicits a full measure of commitment. At the highest levels, personal displays of courageous
example, self-discipline, fairness, competence, and force of personality (in
both a positive and negative sense) are occasionally necessary and effective,
but a more complex system of authority, mutual trust, and confidence must
be established.

At the higher levels, soldiers learn to trust the collective leadership of
"higher headquarters" when that leadership is reliable and demonstrably
sound. A trusted and respected senior leader will have difficulty overcoming the deleterious efforts of a fumbling staff. Senior leaders ensure a positive command climate because they understand that they must influence
soldiers through layers of their subordinate leaders. They cultivate positive
leadership among their immediate subordinates and resort to face-to-face
persuasion to bolster will as the occasion warrants (but usually with subordinate commanders and staffs).

While discipline is primarily a direction-providing tool, in the sense that
a disciplined soldier or unit does what is expected even when the "boss" is

absent, maintaining discipline also plays a motivational role. A disciplined unit is responsive. One of its internalized values is "We always do what's right," and what is "right" is following the direction of the leader toward the purpose to be achieved.

Commanders at all levels establish or administer formal systems of rewards and punishments. Traditionally, on the positive side, this has been in the form of pay and benefits, promotions, decorations, skill badges, service ribbons, symbols of unit recognition, and time off. On the negative side have been judicial and nonjudicial punishments ranging from extra training to the gallows, as well as release from the service and so forth. They use the provisions of military regulations and the Uniform Code of Military Justice to administer punishments. In order to motivate effectively, these systems must be seen to be fair by those they seek to motivate.

Commanders at higher levels have a more powerful, more important, and perhaps more difficult role in establishing and maintaining a just system of formal rewards and punishments. They have a more powerful role in that they have more latitude and authority. The importance of their role stems from the impact they have in this powerful tool to motivate positively through an effective system, and the potential damage they can cause with an ineffective system. Their role is difficult because they have to work through many people who administer the system.

As mentioned earlier, soldiers who understand why an action is necessary and worthy of their sacrifices will fight more fiercely or work harder toward unit goals and missions. This function of informing and educating also becomes more complex with seniority of position. At more senior levels, it involves command information programs of great complexity and subtlety.

Sustaining Continued Effectiveness.   The final function of military leadership is different in that it orients to the future. Providing purpose, direction and motivation has immediate payoffs, but leaders must also ensure the continuity, health and further development of the organization. It is difficult to find one word to describe this function; the closest would be sustainment—sustaining the effectiveness of the organization over time. This implies continuity in a Darwinian rather than a static sense—the ability to remain a viable organism through adaptation as conditions change. It implies health in that all elements of an organism remain sound and function as intended. It implies further development in that leaders should never be satisfied with the current levels of proficiency and always seek to improve in areas which are weakest. Leaders should think of organizations they head as organisms and not as machines. Machines have no built-in recuperative powers, and they perform best when new. They wear out with use. This is not the case with organisms and organizations. Organisms can learn, adapt, grow, become more effective and stronger. They can also unlearn, maladapt, shrink, become less effective and weaker. And they can die. An organism cannot be stressed near maximum capacity for too long a time before it becomes less capable, but an organism can peak well above normal levels of effectiveness for short periods. Effective military leaders recognize these characteristics of military organizations and lead them accordingly.

Some have said that the most effective leaders provide for their succession. Others have said that they develop "high-performing" units. They do both and more. The good squad leader cross-trains the new man on the machinegun, teaches the machinegunner to be a team leader and coaches the team leaders. This squad leader trains the squad to be a cohesive and highly adaptive organism; looks for ways to take the pressure off when no expenditure of effort is required and ensures that squad members get needed rest when possible. When a tough chore is to be performed, the squad peaks for it.

Leaders at higher levels do essentially the same. The higher the level, the more systematic and institutionalized the process becomes. Senior leaders must prepare for attrition of key personnel, the introduction of more modern weapons and a myriad of environmental changes affecting the health and effectiveness of their command. In performing current tasks, they must consider future tasks. In combat, they may mortgage the future for a vital present mission or hold back to save strength and peak for a more vital task to come. They train their soldiers and leaders in peacetime and during lulls in battle. They build or rebuild morale or physical strength. They build teamwork between units of different branches and develop "high performing" staffs. The essential elements of this function are present at all levels, but at the most senior levels these efforts are formalized and highly organized. In the long term, tending to this function is as important as providing purpose, direction and motivation.

Effective military leadership requires that four key functions be performed well to influence soldiers and units to successfully accomplish tasks and missions over time. To be successful, military leaders must:

- Provide purpose and meaning for unit activity—fitting the specific mission into a broader framework of guidance derived from higher purpose, direction, motivation and sustaining sensings.
- Establish direction and guidance for the actions of subordinates leading to mission accomplishment.
- Generate or instill in his subordinates the will, or motivation, to perform assigned missions well.
- Sustain the effectiveness of his organization over time—provide for the continuity, improvement and future effectiveness of the organization.

The effectiveness of large military organizations depends on the performance of all of these functions up and down the chain of command. Although these functions are performed at every link in the chain, they are performed differently at each level. While there is room for variations in style (or the way functions are performed), there is little room for variations in values and ethical standards or in the understanding of doctrinal fundamentals. These and the purpose function at each level provide the glue that binds smaller organizations together to form larger ones—to make them one organism.

Differences in Levels of Leadership.   Intuition tells us that there may be distinct differences in the way the purpose, direction, motivation, and organizational sustainment functions are performed, and what leaders must be, know, and do to perform them at different levels. What follows is an intuitive sketch of some key distinctions by level based on 28 years of fallible experience and some historical reading over that time.

Junior noncommissioned officers (NCOs) who serve as squad leaders and team leaders and their equivalents practice "do as I do" leadership almost exclusively. For them, "showing" is as important as "telling." In combat, "do as I do" leaders are at or near the front of their organizations to direct and to motivate effectively. They derive purpose from company-level goals, missions, and values. They embody the warrior ethic of their branch and specialty and reflect the values inculcated in them by more senior NCOs. They provide direction by leading from the front, by establishing and enforcing squad standards and values, by demonstrating "how to do it." They enforce discipline directly and on the spot. They motivate by example and by the respect they have earned within the squad. They work to achieve a cohesive, "high-performing" squad. They care for and about their men. They provide for continuity by identifying talent among the younger soldiers and by providing for their own succession from among them. They cross-train soldiers to perform more than one task in the squad, and perform necessary individual training.

Senior NCOs (platoon sergeants, master sergeants, first sergeants, and sergeants major) also practice "do as I do" leadership, often not as directly, but they do more. They are primarily responsible for junior NCO development. They execute policies, supervise activities, and advise officers in the performance of all of their purpose, direction, motivation, and organizational sustainment functions. They are the repository of organizational values.

Company grade officers also practice "do as I do" leadership. They lead literally and directly, face-to-face. (Some headquarters company commanders with close to 300 men performing disparate functions over a wide area may not fit this mold; they face a challenge similar to the next higher level.) They act as important value setters, making short-term policies, setting short-term goals, and executing short-range tactical schemes. They make a given organization function. Their longer-range policies and goals are interpretations of higher-level ones, and their plans are very dependent upon plans and priorities set above their level. They are expected to display initiative and continuity in the short-term execution of tasks.

Junior field grade officers alternate between indirect and "do as I do" leadership. They are the first level of real value shapers. They are responsible for company grade officer development. They make longer-term policies and set longer-term goals. They execute short-range combined arms tactical schemes. They make a task force with nonorganic parts function.

Indirect leadership is characterized by some physical detachment due to time and space. These leaders must work harder to maintain intellectual and spiritual attachment. Every leader beyond the lowest levels must understand that time and space limits those in the organization whom the leader can touch personally. And this implies a decision as to whom within the organization, to how many and how far, he can spread his personal influence. The leader must choose carefully, for there are pitfalls to spreading too thin as well as to staying too near the headquarters. One can visualize this as a series of concentric circles. There is a pitfall in bypassing a circle or two and trying to reach all the way down to deal with the soldier in the ranks too often. This affects the mutual trust within a chain of command. It is best to reach out by degrees and occasionally "test the waters" beyond the three rings any leader can influence effectively. Some may be better at reaching out farther. Each leader should know this "range" and stay within it.

Senior field grade and junior general officers practice mostly indirect leadership. They are important value shapers and are responsible for junior field grade development. They shape command climates in the Army. They are long-term policy makers and goal setters. They execute complex combined arms tactical schemes. They create task forces, shape organizations, and make large, complex organizations function.

Senior general officers practice indirect leadership except on rare occasion and with a small segment of their subordinates. They lead other general officers and senior field grade officers in direct ways and work hard to shape consensus among their peers. They are the very long-range institutional value shapers. They are responsible for the development of field grade and junior general officers. They shape the command climate on Army posts, within major commands, and within the Army for long periods of time. They make policies and set goals that have impact many years beyond their tenure. They are responsible for the execution of complex operational and strategic schemes. They create organizations and set long-range trends. They shape institutions and make long-term important decisions frequently based on intuition because easily recognizable tradeoffs are not apparent.

There are differences other than those identified in this short sketch, and they should be identified and studied. Study may reveal that this intuitive grouping of ranks is not the best. Whatever grouping is used, a matrix can be developed. This could be useful for developing effective leaders because we could then identify what the *be, know,* and *do* requirements are for each level.

There is much written on the subject of leadership. U.S. Army Field Manual (FM) 22-100, *Military Leadership,* and FM 22-103, *Leadership and Command at Senior Levels,* are the best leadership manuals we have had. The historical record is full of useful material, as are more recent studies by behavioral scientists. But until we undertake an orderly and scientific study of the functions of leadership and understand more fully what leaders must be, know, and do at each level to effectively perform those functions in peace and war, we will only be partly informed.

6

Leadership: Views from Readers

Leadership: A Dependent's View

Green rows of mud-covered men silently marching past my front yard; sergeants and officers excitedly "talking shop" in my quarters' living room; and the solemn, respectful, changes of command that I have attended— each has given me the opportunity to see what leaders can and should be. As a dependent, I've seen the kind of commanders who watch their drenched, red-clayed soldiers slide up and down ravines while they sit in a dry, clean jeep. But growing up through countless Hails and Farewells, I've talked to leaders who stress participating in training, not just observing. These are the commanders for whom coldness and fatigue may threaten, yet cannot hinder, a mission from being accomplished. The leader who is known for thinking ahead, for inspirational actions, for always remaining flexible, and focusing on the important is the leader I can strive to become.

—Ms. Kerith Dana Dubik, Fort Leavenworth, Kansas

Thomas "Stonewall" Jackson

Leadership's concepts are epitomized in General "Stonewall" Jackson. He personifies FM 22-100's 11 attributes of good leadership. He sought self-improvement, was proficient at the art, responsible and soundly decisive; he led by example, cared for his troops, developed subordinates, ensured task completion, trained his team, and used his unit according to its capabilities. By using these sound principles long before they were set down formally, his units performed feats far in excess of what other commanders extracted from their men. His flanking maneuver at Chancellorsville is the historical forerunner of General H. Norman Schwarzkopf's "Hail Mary."

—Major Warner D. Farr, USA, Brooks AFB, Texas

Reprinted by permission from *Military Review,* 72:8 (August 1992), pp. 53–62.

The Ability to Articulate a Vision

Leadership does not seem to follow any type of template, each "Great Captain" achieving greatness on his own merits based on the challenges encountered. But the truly great leaders seem to have similar characteristics. All have a vision, and more important, the ability to articulate that vision to their soldiers. They have a sense of selflessness, always ensuring they maintained this perspective, no matter to how high an office they had ascended. Part of this selflessness involved taking the jobs that were not always the most popular, or the most "career enhancing." The great leaders were also unique in that they took the time to train and develop subordinates, usually in their own mold, and had a great love for our country, the plain old flag-waving type of patriotism.

—Major Eduardo Martinez Jr., USA, Fort Leavenworth, Kansas

R. E. Lee: Example of Personal Integrity

Robert E. Lee was a great captain. His brilliance and audacity on the battlefield inspired his men. Yet it was his personal integrity—his moral fortitude—that gave his soldiers unity, identity, purpose and loyalty. It enabled them to go beyond their physical limitations. General Lee became the center about which everything revolved within the Army of Northern Virginia, center of gravity for an army.

—Chaplain (CPT) Robert N. Neske, USA, Fort Leavenworth, Kansas

Furthermore:

To me leadership is the art of wisdom, intelligence and decisiveness to handle a crisis situation, turn it around, and get it under control or solve the problem that it represents. Examples of this would be General Matthew Ridgway in the Korean War and General Ulysses Grant in the American Civil War.

Jimmy Doolittle is my idea of a "great captain" because he served in both the Army and the Air Force. He also showed the proper balance of vision, intelligence and decisiveness in his handling of air power in the years of World War II.

—Charles Trudell, West Carrollton, Ohio

Words on Leadership

Realization: recognize the present.
Vision: know where organization ought to go.
Prescience: anticipate needs.

Involvement: participate,
- teach: train and educate,
- learn: commit to self-improvement,
- practice: "practice, practice, practice."

Incisiveness: dig for details and truth; mediocrity fails.

Linkage: inter-relationship of events; go beyond the obvious.

Responsibility: keep subordinates and superiors informed, on time, and out of trouble.

Thick skin: withstand trivial and professional denigration.

Dignity: exercise your vocabulary, but avoid "profane" and "vulgar" language.
- compliment people, say "thank you" and mean it,
- do not "touch" people—may be perceived as patronizing and presumptuous,
- treat people fairly, with respect and honor.

Reward: recognize good and bad, appropriately.

Courage: physical, moral and professional; "do the right thing."

—Major Eben H. Trevino Jr., USAF, MacDill AFB, Florida

Leadership: Sergeant's Business

The great captain I am going to talk about is my Command Sergeant Major, Johnnie Riley. Although Riley is not well known, he has the three qualities that make a great captain—he is a thinker, a motivator and most important a warrior. During the two years I have known him, I have consistently been in awe of his tactical acumen, his rapport with the soldiers and his overall knowledge of the Army. An example of his tactical brilliance was his input into the plan for our 80-mile air assault into Iraq. His recommendations were sound. In hearing that Riley was in a defensive position during a brigade field training exercise, the division's assistant division commander for operations said Riley was such a combat multiplier that it was like having another platoon in that position. Perhaps the essence of Riley's philosophy on being a soldier can best be described by this quote: "People say that war is hell, well if that's true it is our duty as soldiers to put out the fires and kill the devil."

—LTC Frank R. Hancock, USA, Fort Campbell, Kentucky

The Virtues of Followership

I believe that in order for one to be a successful leader, he must first understand and appreciate what it takes to be a good follower. The successful leader must experience what it is like to be on the receiving end of commands. He must gain this experience so that he can comprehend the strength that his own actions and words will one day have upon others.

This appreciation is essential because he understands what it takes to inspire and motivate just as he realizes what rewards they appreciate for a job well done.

—Cadet Allen T. Thiessen, US Military Academy

How to Be an Effective Leader

I was very proud the day my dad pinned my second lieutenant's bars on me; he was a colonel in the mature years of a distinguished career. His guidance on leadership summed up what he had practiced all his life:

"Keep your troops out of the sun and don't BS the old man."

Dad summed up a lot of books with those 13 pithy words, which have guided me ever since: take care of your soldiers and they will take care of you and your mission; tell it like it is, even when it hurts; uncompromising integrity in all you do.

—Colonel John B. Haseman, USA, US Embassy, Indonesia

Ike and the Limits of Intuition

Field Manual 22-103 states that leadership vision "can be an intuitive sensing." There is no question that Eisenhower "sensed" the right moment to launch Operation *Overlord*. Whether he sensed it intuitively is subject to question. He did, however, have all of his commanders present when he made his decision, including his meteorologist. Had any one commander been adamant or had even seriously taken exception, for whatever reason, the chances are that the invasion of Normandy would not have taken place on June 6th, and no amount of "intuition" on Eisenhower's part could have cajoled the members of the coalition into going along with him. Intuition has definite limitations in decision making. Eisenhower was aware of the limits and relied heavily upon his staff to help him with his decision.

—David Craig, New Orleans, Louisiana

Intangible Inspiration

Leadership is that intangible quality which inspires subordinates to follow with assurance and confidence when hardship and danger are present. Leadership is therefore of the utmost importance to soldiers at all levels since success depends wholly upon the leader's ability to control and direct. In fact, it may be said that the effectiveness of our Army depends more upon the quality of its leadership than any other factor. Inferior numbers and inferior material, coupled with superior leadership may always be counted upon to win against superior numbers, superior material and inferior leadership.

—Colonel Dennis P. Vasey, USA (Retired), Naples, Florida

Stuck in Transmit?

We lead people, we manage programs.

We all lead people sometimes, so are we good at it?

Can we change our leadership style, or were we cast in final form?

Should we adopt some clever leadership style, or should we be ourselves?

If we lead by fear, do we get the top effort?

If we lead with a firm human touch, do the hearts and minds follow?

Do we lead alone, or do we seek advice from all levels?

Do we learn each day how to be a better leader, or are we stuck in transmit?

—Colonel David K. Burke, USAF, Fort Leavenworth, Kansas

A Great Captain at Vera Cruz

Winfield Scott, bold but not brash, epitomizes the phrase "Great Captain." His Vera Cruz campaign shows these characteristics. Designing his own landing craft and doctrine, he led the Army's first large-scale amphibious invasion. Outnumbered, he boldly advanced on Mexico City without a supply line. With his small professional army, he outmaneuvered his adversary on three battlefields with minimal losses. After a march of 200 mountainous miles, he captured Mexico City, thus winning the war.

—LTC Timothy T. Tilson, USA, Wauwatosa, Wisconsin

The Techniques of Leadership

Leadership techniques are not concrete, nor guaranteed to be successful. Being able to adjust to changing situations and using the available resources are traits that a successful leader must exhibit. Successful leadership integrates consideration for subordinates and goal planning.

—Cadet Marshall Arthur McKay, US Military Academy

For the Troops

Leadership is an intangible concept, exercised in many ways, dependent on many factors. Some, including personal charisma, are beyond one's control. Others, such as use of troop leading procedures (TLP), are within one's control. In my opinion the key element in leadership is personal commitment to one's troops and involvement in their activities. The commander who is on the scene participating in training (or combat) will know his troops and their problems and sees in person what must be done. His presence motivates them and his presence at the site of critical action may in itself determine the outcome.

—Brigadier General Peter W. Clegg, USA, Fort Devens, Massachusetts

Bottom Line Orientation

In most organizations, there are few people at the top, a bunch in the middle, and a large number at the bottom. The bottom is where products are made, and where services are delivered. This work defines not just the worker's purpose, but the organization's purpose. The trenches is where the organization happens—the true "bottom line."

The real purpose of leadership is to reduce the uncertainty of those at the next echelon below, until, finally, when the decision making of the chain-of-command finally meets with the energy of the worker, there is, ideally, no uncertainty in the minds of either party.

Too often, the people in the trenches have unmet information needs, even at the moment when human energy is finally applied to the actual doing. This is not ignorance; it is uncertainty. Bottom-line uncertainties reflect failures on the part of leaders, at all levels, to provide workers with timely, accurate, coherent information.

The next time you see an organization chart, look at the trenches. You'll realize that the levels and the positions above the trenches, all the way up to and including the chief executive officer, are of no value whatsoever unless they somehow serve the information needs of people down there on . . . the bottom line.

—LTC Mike McGee, USA, Washington, D.C.

"I Propose to Fight on This Line . . ."

As general in chief of the Union armies, Grant conducted multiple campaigns over half a continent, commanding over 500,000 troops in 21 army corps. Grant spoke little and listened well. Self-reliant, he was calm amid excitement, patient, sure in judgment and foresight, and not depressed by reverses or unduly elated by success. He was tenacious and could discipline himself and others. Tireless in action he once personally wrote 42 important dispatches in one day. Fearless in battle, he had empathy for his soldiers. Setting an austere example in the field, he provided the steadfast command and control around which everything else turned. His magnanimity to Lee at Appomattox saved the country from prolonged guerrilla warfare. He was all the Union Army wanted, a leader.

—LTC Thomas D. Morgan, USA (Retired), Leavenworth, Kansas

The Leadership Paycheck

In my previous assignment as an ROTC instructor, we had a cadet in our battalion who thought that leadership was like a contest. Show up with the shiniest boots and win the prize. Become a fair-haired boy of a few superiors and rest on your hands.

Nothing could be further from the truth. Unfortunately, too many of us in leadership positions forget (in fact some never learn to begin with) that leadership of men and women is really a paycheck—it has to be earned every day. More important, the check is signed by our troops, not by our superiors. Our troops are the ones who grant us the privilege of leading them. They alone decide whether or not we've earned our "pay."

—Major Joseph W. T. Pugh, USA, Fort Bliss, Texas

Communicating Success

Before one can discover the essential qualities of a successful leader, he first has to communicate his definition of success to his audience. Although there are many ways to assess the success of a leader, the most resourceful is to measure the success of his unit in accomplishing given tasks. Regardless of whether the leader epitomizes one's concept of a great leader or not, a leader whose unit is successful is successful as well.

—Cadet Landy Donnell Dunham, US Military Academy

The Hallmark of a Leader

By definition, leadership is the art of influencing others to accomplish the mission. To paraphrase Napoleon, the great leader is not the one who can lead men. The great leader is the one the men will follow. This is truer today than it ever was, owing in large part to the intelligence of today's soldiers. Any officer or NCO can give orders, and the troops will have no choice but to obey. To be a leader, however, means understanding your soldiers and what makes them tick. A leader is one who can make the tough choices, who will roll up his sleeves and "get dirty" when he's short-handed.

—SFC Terence L. Johnson, USA, Fort Leavenworth, Kansas

Killer Angel

Joshua Lawrence Chamberlain is a great captain whose example few can match but all can follow. He voluntarily answered the call to serve; self-motivated himself to study the profession of arms; accepted mentoring by his commander; trained his soldiers for combat with available time; continually inspired his soldiers through his personal example, even when wounded; was tested at Fredericksburg; innovated at Gettysburg; took up his unit colors and moved forward at Petersburg; marched to the sound of the guns at Five Forks; respected his enemy's capabilities and honor; continued to serve his state and country after leaving the Army.

—Captain Edward S. Loomis, USA, Fort Polk, Louisiana

What Are the Essential Qualities of a Successful Leader?

There are those who fail, those who survive, and those who succeed. Any man charged with the leadership of others who is lacking integrity, morality, honesty, and concern is doomed to fail. Any leader possessing these qualities at a minimum has at least established a platform to succeed. Finally, there are those who seem to rise above the platform. That leader is the one who has the courage, foresight, and persistence to ask: Why? A successful leader will question the status quo. A response of "It has always been that way" will not satisfy a leader seeking improvement. That leader recognizes that nothing is perfect and everything needs improving. He views the old adage "If it ain't broke, don't fix it" as an excuse for complacency. The strive for excellence is, and will always be the determining factor between the successful and the survivor.

—Captain Phil Deaton, USA, White Sands Missile Range, New Mexico

The Basics of Leadership

I believe all successful leaders have one fundamental quality that stands out—the quality of human understanding. All soldiers need to know that they are more important than a weapon system. With all of our new technological advances and the downsizing of the Army, the soldier remains the key ingredient for success. Too often the needs of the soldier are subordinate to the needs of the Army. When a soldier knows that he has a chain of command that really cares and listens, his attitude and performance is magnified. "Leaders work with people and feelings."

—Captain Joseph C. Lopez, USA, APO AE 09630

Successful Leaders Develop Successful Subordinates

Successful leaders develop confidence and aggressive, independent action in their subordinates. They take a moment after a brutal after-action review to express continued confidence in a subordinate who has made a mistake while attempting to faithfully achieve the commander's intent. The successful leader does not sanction poor judgment; he reaffirms aggressive initiative on the part of junior leaders. In the darkest moments of an NTC rotation, a future leader's aggressive spirit can be formed or broken by a single word.

—CPT Frederick C. Hellwig, USA, Columbia, South Carolina

Improvisation

Successful leadership has many facets to it. A leader must know the fundamentals of leadership, but must also be able to improvise. Answers to most leadership puzzles will never be found in a book because the people involved will change constantly, causing new puzzles. A successful leader must be able to understand people and human nature. Leaders need to know the limits and capabilities of those they lead to maximize their potential. Being able to adapt to changing situations quickly and effectively has always been the hallmark of the more successful leaders.

—2LT Lawrence E. Collins Jr., USA, DeKalb, Illinois

For Want of a Nail

A former commander of mine used the metaphor of leadership as the process of making a good horseshoe. He began by noting that you need a skilled blacksmith, a hammer, a heated strip of metal and an anvil to make a good horseshoe.

The blacksmith in this case is any leader from general officer to section leader. The leader must be proficient and should have a vision of what goals the unit has set out to accomplish. The hammer is one of many tools available to us as leaders. It's equivalent to position, authority, knowledge or the ability to make things happen. The metal is the unit and soldiers. In almost every situation, soldiers want to do well. They're malleable metal ready to take shape under the direction of the leader. The anvil is the key item of equipment. Without it you can bang away at the metal and get the sparks and sound of a blacksmith, but the finished product will look nothing like the horseshoe. You need the firm evaluative base of an anvil to make things go right.

—Major Stephen P. Walsh, USA, Mt. Clemens, Michigan

Words of Wisdom

In his search to be a great leader, the young centurion sought out the Republic's veteran warrior. Looking up from his labor, the sage spoke:

"I know not what beats beneath your tunic, but what I saw in a leader from foot soldiers to proconsul is thus:

One who makes drill bloodless combat and combat bloody drill . . .

One who disciplines the offense and not the offenders . . .

One whose heart is with the Legion and whose loyalty is to the Republic...

One who seeks the companionship of the long march and not the privilege of position . . .

One whose commission is assigned from above and confirmed from below . . .

One who knows the self and, therefore, is true to all . . .

One who seeks to serve and not to be served . . .

This is the one who leads best of all."

—LTC Jeffrey L. Spara, USA, Syracuse, New York

Getting There

Leaders are first and foremost individuals of character. Although Army leadership doctrine does not neglect this attribute—and even places it first in the Be, Know, Do trinity—practice places Be far behind Know and, especially, Do. Army practice looks at leadership as an algorithm: in such-and-such a situation, do the following and you too will be a leader. It's all a question of technique. We have missed the leadership boat. We talk about history while encouraging our officers to spend their spare time earning business administration degrees. We publish lists of professional books but reward reading military fantasy novels. The first orients on Do; the second kills time. The Chief of Staff encourages us to grow leaders of character, and Harry Summers suggests future readiness will emerge from education. Without an institutional change, we won't get there from here.

—Major Steve G. Capps, Fort Leavenworth, Kansas

Leadership—Old Testament Style

Nehemiah was an Old Testament leader who was able to translate commander's intent into mission accomplishment and the Old Testament book bearing his name is perhaps the first written manual on effective leadership. He clearly epitomized the four values—courage, candor, commitment, and competence—that leaders should possess. As cup bearer to King Artaxerxes, Nehemiah showed considerable courage by asking for an extended TDY to rebuild Jerusalem's walls. He demonstrated candor by requesting specific assistance. Despite active opposition, Nehemiah remained unwavering in his commitment to the mission. Nehemiah's proficiency in communications, planning, reconnaissance, and decision making attest to his competence. His adherence to the four "Cs" resulted in the rebuilding of the walls in only 52 days.

—LTC Russell V. Olson Jr., USA, Fort Leavenworth, Kansas

From the Napoleonic Era

Marshall Louis Nicholas Davout, of Napoleon's Army, possessed three qualities that are the hallmark of a great leader—character, competence and caring. Marshall Davout believed in honesty, loyalty and courage. Even though men made fun of his devout Christian beliefs, no one ever doubted Davout's purity of character. Davout's competence on the battlefield saved Napoleon from defeat at Austerlitz. Davout's concern for his soldiers was evident to them. The soldiers, who didn't like their commander personally could look around and see that he kept them supplied better than any other unit in the French Army. Marshall Davout's reward for his leadership ability was the respect and obedience of his men.

—Cadet Veronica D. Robertson, US Military Academy

Leadership and Modern Technology

The complexity of the integrated battlefield and application of technology to complete mission objectives as demonstrated during Operation *Desert Storm* suggests that leaders should possess the ability to identify individuals, irrespective of rank, who possess relevant knowledge, skills, and attitudes and to effectively and efficiently utilize these individuals to complete assigned missions. This essential quality if possessed and applied by leaders will provide participating soldiers with enhanced self esteem and the pride of accomplishment. Consequently unit esprit de corps and combat readiness may he enhanced through the demonstrated recognition of and reliance on individual capabilities.

—1LT Doug Rokke, USA, Rantoll, Illinois

The Right Leader at the Right Place

Writing on Sir Garnet Joseph Wolsely, Archibald Forbes says, "The heaven-born soldier is he who achieves startling success with apparently inadequate means." Only good leadership turns defeat into victory. Good leaders set personal standards that harden individual and unit resolve and take risks because they trust subordinates to do the right thing at every level of command. Great Captains have the flexibility of mind to seize every initiative the enemy allows them and have the physical and mental toughness to stand firm on their decisions. Thus, leadership is the right mix at the right time of trust, flexibility, and firmness.

The "Great Captain" who epitomizes my definition of leadership was Field Marshall Sir William Slim, commander of Allied Land Forces in South East Asia, perhaps the toughest and least resourced World War II front. His commoner roots, his experience teaching the poor before he became a soldier and his service in the colonial army taught him to value the humanity of those he led regardless of race or class. From his World War II experience and his wounds at Gallipoli, Slim learned the importance of not wasting soldiers lives. A rare blend of improvisation and determination, he did not repeat the same mistakes. He was a leader who knew his trade, had great rapport with the men he led, and had the physical and mental resilience to turn a hopeless defeat in India into a remarkable victory over the Japanese in Burma.

—Colonel Joseph T. Cox, USA, US Military Academy

The Human Quality

The best leaders, in all walks of life, are honest and humane. As a noncom once remarked to me "You don't lead men into battle by telling them you're taking them to the Post Exchange." And as General Schwarzkopf observed: men don't die for abstract ideals like "Mom and apple pie" but for the buddies at their side. A leader's most important job is to inspire—by being trustworthy and protecting the lives of his men.

—Mrs. D. J. Collier, China Grove, North Carolina

Caring Is Key

The ability to care, guide, and teach are essential components for successful leadership. Weaving these components into a solid foundation, a leader makes subordinates better people. The first component, caring, creates a trusting relationship between leader and follower. Both parties show the other empathy, compassion, and understanding. This caring gives the leader the ability to guide subordinates to self-improvement by providing guidelines and perspectives. Teaching, the final component strengthens the caring and guiding foundation. Leaders teach subordinates through positive role models and examples. Working together, these three components make successful leaders by creating better subordinates.

—Cadet Heidi Strubbe, US Military Academy

Qualities of Leaders

The three most essential qualities of a successful leader are competence, courage, and wisdom. Competence is essential because a leader must know what he or she is doing. Without competence, the followers will not have confidence in him or her. Courage is essential because a leader must keep trying when the followers want to give up. Without courage, a leader cannot push his or her followers in tough times, which is when they most need a leader. Wisdom is essential because a leader must know how to react to circumstances. Without wisdom, a leader will make wrong decisions.

—Cadet Steven Park, US Military Academy

Leadership as Instinct

Leadership is not an art nor a technique, but an instinct occurring at a precise moment in time. A moment which might be critical on a smoke-filled battlefield or important to a boardroom problem-solving process. It exists just below the level of consciousness yet essential to its environment. Its absence creates a void which is often filled by a randomness of undefined and unguided efforts. The leader sees clearly at the critical moment and acts to focus available energies to seize that moment and turn it to its conclusion. The study of this instinct creates an art and the imitation of its characteristics defines the technique.

—Major John W. Lemza, USA, Fort Lee, Virginia

PART TWO

Lessons from History

Why and how are words so important that they cannot be used too often.
—Napoleon

We can learn a great deal from history. Once the major source in the study of leadership, history has provided chronicles of leaders and their successes and failures. In our fast-paced world of change, we often fail to review what has happened in the past, as if that is irrelevant. Our life experiences appear to have little in common with the days gone by. Yet, there are many lessons we can learn, for history often repeats itself.

In this section, we present some leadership lessons from history. You will immediately note similarities between the articles here and in the first section. We are not being repetitive. Rather, we are trying to show that much of what we discuss about leadership today is very much what students of leadership have been discussing for centuries. How leaders have succeeded may change, but the ways in which they influence do not. Leadership is still the relationship between the leader and his or her followers.

One shortcoming in our review of history is that very little has been written about women leaders. This is especially true of the military, where it is only in recent times that women have played important roles. One is tempted to cite Joan of Arc and her attributes, but beyond that, we can find little that might suggest commonalities and differences between men and women in effective leadership. Where history has important lessons is in the realization that different cultures and different generations have produced effective leaders with great similarities. We will assume that future historians will be able to say the same thing about gender.

The military is rich with the legends of great leaders. These heroes are called upon from time to time as a way of inspiring us in the present. You might take issue with those we chose to present in this section. There are many others, to be sure. However, those represented in the following chapters had common characters, values, and commitments that continue to influence effective leaders today.

Now that you have a framework for leadership, read about these leaders to test your construct. Reflect upon the times and the mission described. In many ways, the opportunities and challenges of the past are relevant to today and tomorrow. One is tempted to suggest that the individuals presented would not have been successful in today's world. That is speculation we will never have the opportunity to prove. Our belief is that the person, the character, and the qualities of leadership exemplified by these leaders would stand the test of time. Situation is important, but effective leaders adapt. You may agree or disagree. Our objective is to stimulate your thinking.

Historical Perspectives

In James Stokesbury's "Leadership as an Art" (Chapter 7), we focus on the leader as a person distinct from those who merely serve as heads of organizations. Interestingly, the author suggests that we are trapped by inadequacies of definitions for leadership and we often wind up with tautological definitions. Stokesbury deals with this dilemma by defining leadership as an art, and he further suggests that the best way to learn about leadership is to study the examples provided by history. Thus, this initial piece gives context to the study of history. Stokesbury chooses four leaders from history: the Marquis of Montrose, Alexander Suvorov, Robert E. Lee, and Henri Philippe Petain. All had little in common other than sharing attributes that the author believes define the art of leadership. He concludes by observing that the higher elements of leadership can be learned scientifically and can be manipulated by artifice. Stokesbury ironically observes that the better times are, the less artifice works and the more art is needed.

General S.L.A. Marshall writes in "Leaders and Leadership" (Chapter 8) that great military leaders of the past possessed a certain set of qualities. These were inner qualities rather than outward marks of greatness. Relatively few leaders were acclaimed for leadership in their early years. Marshall's thesis is that most successful leaders are molded by the influences around them and that they have the average person's faults and vices. Leaders have a common desire for substantial recognition (ego) and the will to earn it fairly. Too often, people with great inner strength hold in contempt those less well endowed by nature than themselves and, hence, fail as leaders. He cites courage, humor, presence, and integrity as the ingredients for successful military leadership.

In "Leadership" (Chapter 9), General Matthew Ridgway acknowledges that leadership is probably a combination of art and science. Like Stokesbury, he thinks there is far more art than science involved. He describes the chief ingredients of leadership as character, courage, and competence. His advice for developing leadership is to read history and biography, work hard, be humble, and be oneself. Ridgway's inability to specifically define activities or events that create success helps demonstrate why many keep returning to the concept of leadership as an art.

Lewis Sorley, in "The Art of Taking Charge" (Chapter 10), presents a series of vignettes about General Creighton Abrams's style and methods. Bringing the human element of leadership to real situations, Sorley provides a number of important elements of leadership. Gaining confidence, identifying and solving problems, setting the example, living one's values, listening, and developing followers are presented as ways in which one leader, Abrams, was exceptionally effective as a leader. The lessons relate to standards, morale, and self-worth—characteristics that defined the general and the organization long after he was its leader. Leadership in the broad context is described by Albert Hunt in "The Greatest Man Churchill and Truman Ever Met" (Chapter 11). Insights about General George C. Marshall highlight the importance of self-knowledge and self-confidence. Vision and integrity characterized General Marshall. At the same time, Hunt reflects on the miscalculations of this great person to suggest that the most effective leaders have, at one time or another, failed, but they have learned from their failures. Marshall was a politician but did not promote himself. Winner of the Nobel Peace Prize, Marshall served in key military and civilian roles; he was one of the very few people who were successful leaders in very different environments. The author muses about whether Marshall would be successful today. After all, timing is an element of effective leadership. Perhaps there are others who, when subjected to historical reflections, might well follow Marshall's successes.

Associate yourself with men of good quality if you esteem your own reputation; for 'tis better to be alone than in bad company.

—George Washington

7

Leadership as an Art

James L. Stokesbury

There is a certain sense of paradox, almost of impudence, in choosing as the opening title for a social science annual the topic, "Leadership as an Art." If one is thrown off balance by this, it is because society's perceptions have changed so radically over the past century. A hundred years ago, no one would have suspected that leadership might be anything other than an art, and impudence would have lain in asserting that there were scientific aspects to it.

Indeed, as late as fifty years ago the social sciences had still not come of age, and the most popular British historian of his time, Philip Guedalla (1923: 149), could dismiss them quite offhandedly as "light-minded young things like Psychology, with too many data and no conclusions, and Sociology, with too many conclusions and no data." In the 1960s, a distinguished American military historian used to tell his classes that the social sciences and statistical method were capable of telling us "all those things that are not worth knowing," a remark which the disgruntled humanist, pushed ever farther back behind the shrinking perimeter of his defenses, teaching Latin in his office or lecturing on Napoleon to an audience that confuses the Weimar with the Roman Republic, is likely to cherish lovingly.

Now the development of computer technology has finally given the social scientist the tools he needs to amass data as never before, and to extract from it conclusions that are necessarily changing our ways of approaching problems. Social science has come of age, and the humanistic protest that "there is more to it than that" sounds increasingly plaintive. Students who used to read the classics now study executive management, and where they once learned how Caesar addressed his men, or Napoleon tweaked his

James L. Stokesbury, "Leadership as an Art," pp. 23–40 in *Military Leadership,* edited by James H. Buck and Lawrence J. Korb, Sage Publications, Inc., 1981.

grenadiers' earlobes when he was pleased with them, they now absorb graphs and mathematical formulae that are supposed to guarantee magic results. It is a sort of acupuncture of the mind: If you put the needle in here, the object will respond by doing whatever it is supposed to do.

There remains, however, a place for art. The essence of science is in mathematics and predictability. It has become more and more feasible to forecast how more and more of any given group will respond to certain stimuli. If the President looks forthright on television, public confidence will strengthen; if he looks tired, or if his makeup is the wrong shade, the stock market will drop so many points. Elections, we are confidently told, depend on that ever-smaller number of mavericks whose reactions simply cannot be predicted.

In a way, history is repeating itself, as it always does, with twists and quirks. In the eighteenth century, at the height of the Enlightenment, critics of society thought that if only they could be rid of the few remaining irrationalities, they would then achieve the perfect society. Old anomalous institutions like the monarchy, and especially the Church, founded on emotion and faith rather than on the dictates of pure reason, had to be swept away, and once they were, all would be for the best in the best of all possible worlds, as Voltaire wrote in his jibe at Leibnitz. Unhappily, when people destroyed the old institutions, they got the Terror and the Napoleonic Wars, and reason turned out to be little better a guide than tradition, or emotion, or history. One suspects a tendency now on the part of the computer analysts to feel much as the philosophers did in their day: If only we could reduce everything to quantifiable factors, then we should have perfection.

Happily, we cannot, and though a great many of the things that matter in life have been shown to be more amenable to quantitative analysis and scientific predictability than was previously thought to be the case, there still remains the province of art. We still respond to the leader, in fact we hear more and more desperate cries for the emergence of one, and the leader, to bridge that last gap between corporate management and true leadership, still depends upon unmeasurables, that is, on art rather than on science. The elements of his gift, or his skill and how he develops it, are qualitative rather than quantitative, and the problem for the humanist describing the leader is that he is trapped by the inadequacies of the language to describe qualities that defy precise definition. A leader, he may say, needs courage, resolution, self-reliance, and on and on. But he can only define any one of these terms by reference to others of them, and in the end he has produced a tautology: The leader is a leader because he can exercise leadership. One can hardly blame the social scientist for finding this less than adequate, and for preferring to work with something he can pin down, i.e., can measure.

One way out of this dilemma is that history does teach by example. If it is no more than vicarious experience, it is also no less than that. It is useful to look at men whose place in history, large or small, has been guaranteed by the passage of time, and to try to extract from their careers, or episodes in them, elements that epitomize the qualities of leadership that men have most prized. In a not-quite-random sampling, consider the careers of the Marquis of Montrose, Suvorov, Robert E. Lee and Henri Philippe Petain. These four all achieved pinnacles of leadership, but they are useful examples in that the external details of their careers had little in common. Each was from a different country, in a different century. Two were losers—most of the time, two were winners—most of the time; two fought in civil wars and two in external wars; two fought more or less unconventional wars, and two conventional. Two were in the pre-, and two in the post-industrial period. Though all are admittedly in the European tradition,that is after all our own, and it is legitimate to suggest in the aftermath of *Shogun* that some of the elements of leadership in other traditions may be so significantly different from ours as to be safely disregarded here.

The Marquis of Montrose

If the Stuart dynasty had been worthy of the devotion it inspired, there would still be a Stuart on the throne of England, and Elizabeth II would be just Mrs. Battenburg. James Graham, Marquis of Montrose, was born in 1612 and educated in Scotland and abroad. As a leading member of the Scottish nobility, he took part in the risings against the introduction of the Anglican prayerbook in Scotland in the 1630s, and was one of the foremost signers of the Solemn League and Covenant. When the Scottish Presbyterians became ever more insistent on their own interpretations of salvation and politics, Montrose drifted openly into the Royalist cause, and in 1644 he came out for Charles I. For the next two years, he routed army after army of Scottish troops, relying on his own brilliance as a tactician and a leader of men. His ultimate inability to hold Scotland for King Charles lay more in Charles's failure, or unwillingness, to support him fully, and Montrose's own lack of resources to overcome the tremendous power of the Campbells, the strongest of the western clans and the most determinedly anti-Stuart, than in any personal failing of his own.

Montrose's tiny army was finally routed in 1646; he himself got away to the Continent, where he remained until after the execution of Charles I. In a last chivalrous gesture, the Marquis returned to Scotland with a forlorn hope; most of his little band was shipwrecked; he himself was betrayed and sold to the Covenanters, and he was hanged in chains in Edinburgh in 1650.

It was a short but glorious career, and ever since its end the story of Montrose has seemed to epitomize all that courage and daring might achieve in the face of great odds. It is the more remarkable in that Montrose had no formal military training, though of course every gentleman of the day, and especially every great lord, was expected to know something of war. Nor did he ever have much in the way of troops. For the most part his army was made up of Irish peasants, often brought over with their families and following their own chiefs, or Scots of the Highland clans who came out for the love of fighting and the hope of booty.

Yet Montrose knew how to get the most from such men; he never asked for more than they could perform, though he asked much indeed of them. He took them into the Great Glen in the midst of winter and harried the Campbell lands when others said it could not be done, and he held his little army together in spite of reverses and the general sinking of the Royalist cause. Nothing typifies the spirit of his leadership more than his performance in his first battle, at Tippermuir. Here, with but 3,000 men, no cavalry, and his musketeers down to one round per man, he met a well equipped army of 5,000 horse and foot. The Covenanters spent several hours in prayers and exhortations, but Montrose's speech to his men was short and to the point, and set precisely the right tone: "Gentlemen! It is true you have no arms; your enemy, however, to all appearance have plenty. My advice therefore is, that as there happens to be a great abundance of stones upon this moor, every man should provide himself in the first place with as stout a one as he can well manage, rush up to the first covenanter he meets, beat out his brains, take his sword, and then I believe, he will be at no loss how to proceed!" (Williams, 1975: 155)

The Irish and the Highlanders did exactly that, and when the survivors of the Covenanters fled back to Perth they had lost over 3,000 men; one of Montrose's men was killed, and a second later died of his wounds.

Such disproportionate figures as that would tend to the conclusion that Montrose's lopsided victory was no more than a fluke and that any reasonably resolute force would have defeated the Covenanters. However, Montrose did it again, at Kilsyth, in August of 1645. Once more outnumbered, by three to two this time, he attacked the overconfident Covenanters as they marched across his front. He lost three men; his enemy something more than 6,000. The clansmen and Irish slaughtered their fleeing foes for eighteen miles before they finally stopped from exhaustion.

Yet Montrose himself was not a bloody-minded man. He did his best to avoid the excesses of seventeenth-century warfare, and gave quarter where he could manage to do so. He remained a high-minded gentleman, courteous to his adversaries when he was not actively engaged in killing them, and was the very archetype of all that later Romantics saw as the virtues of the Cavalier party. He was something of a minor poet, too, and spent the night before his execution composing some appropriate lines. Probably best known, though, are the lines from *I'll Never Love Thee More* which have been attributed to him, and which sum up his career and his character as a leader:

He either fears his fate too much,
Or his deserts are small,
That puts it not unto the touch,
To win or lose it all. (Williams, 1975: 395–396)

Montrose had the conventional upbringing and education of the nobility of his day. His knowledge of warfare was instinctive and intuitive rather than studied, and that indeed remained the norm in the British service until well into the nineteenth century. Except for the scientific arms, engineers, and artillery, the function of British officers was to lead their men and, if necessary, to die well; the bulldog spirit was more important than technical expertise.

This was true of most armies of the eighteenth century, and most soldiers who studied war at all did so because they were interested in it, rather than because such study was a prerequisite for advancement. Knowledge could be an actual impediment in some cases; it was practically that in the career of Alexander Suvorov.

Alexander Suvorov

Born in 1729, the weak and sickly son of a former military officer who transferred into the civil service side of the Russian bureaucracy, Suvorov never wanted to be anything but a soldier. He read voraciously, and pushed his frail body to and beyond its limits. His father, much against his will, enrolled him as a cadet in the Semenovosky Regiment when he was thirteen. That was late for a Russian noble to start his military career—officers were often put on a regiment's list at birth—and Suvorov's rise was extraordinarily slow. He spent years in staff and routine work, and the ordinary chores of garrison duty. Even through the early years of the Seven Years' War he saw no action, though he was present at Kunérsdorf in 1759, where Austro-Russians slaughtered half of Frederick the Great's army.

Not until 1761 did Suvorov see independent action, and from that point on he never stopped. His many years of dull service had given him a great contempt for the scheming courtier-soldiers he saw constantly promoted ahead of him, but an even greater love for the Russian soldier, conscripted for life, punished by the knout and the gauntlet, and consistently abused by his superiors. Suvorov understood such men, and empathized with them. He started making his name as a leader of Cossack irregulars, and his commander noted he was "swift in reconnaissance, daring in battle and cold-blooded in danger" (Longworth, 1965: 26).

After the war, as commander of the Suzdal regiment, he rewrote the drill and tactical manuals and spent his time working up a unit that in spirit and performance resembled Sir John Moore's light infantry more than it did other Russian formations. There was active service in Poland against the armies that tried to reverse the Polish slide toward oblivion, and Suvorov enhanced his growing fame particularly by the siege and taking of the fortress of Cracow.

Real glory came to him over the next twenty years as he was almost incessantly campaigning against the Turks in Catherine the Great's wars to expand Russia southward. His success is the more amazing in view of his constant ill health, and before one of his greatest battles, Rymnik, he was too weak to carry his own sword—but not too weak to lead his men personally on an all-night march that set up the victory.

His brilliance lay not only in intensive study allied to native military genius, but in his leadership qualities. More than any Russian before or perhaps since, he had the touch that appealed to his soldiers. On campaign he ate and slept with them, and was more than content with a pile of straw for a bed. This was a period when many Russian officers could not even address their men, having been brought up speaking French, and often those who could would not deign to do so. Suvorov, by contrast, was the common Russian writ large. In a gathering of officers, he looked like a tough weed among a bed of lilies. Regrettably, his popularity with his soldiers cost him both advancement and patronage, for just as he despised most of his fellow generals, he was hated by them. While Catherine lived he was protected, for she had learned to value his deeds more than his manners, but when she died in 1796, he was dismissed abruptly, and not recalled until Russia joined the Second Coalition against France in 1799. After a brilliant campaign in northern Italy, in which he again showed all the qualities that had made him a great soldier, he was caught up in the general Allied defeat in Switzerland, and forced to lead his starving army over the Alps and back to the Danube. Tsar Paul fired him a second time, refused to see him, and he died in disgrace in 1800.

His spirit lived on in the Russian army, however, and the great Encyclopedia Britannica edition of 1911 (Vol. 26: 173) compared the Russian Army to him in its "spirit of self-sacrifice, resolution, and indifference to losses," adding a remark which we would do well to remember in our own time: "In an age when war had become an act of diplomacy, he restored its true significance as an act of force." In 1941 and 1942, when war was universally recognized as being an act of force, Russian patriotic posters showed the ghostly figure of Suvorov, still leading Holy Mother Russia's sons into battle.

Robert E. Lee

Probably no American soldier has ever epitomized the art of leadership more fully than Robert E. Lee. Washington was often aloof, Jackson erratic for all his brilliance, MacArthur and Patton were both perhaps a little too overtly propagandistic to win the unreserved loyalties of their men, but it is safe to say of Lee that he was truly loved. On the Federal side only George H. Thomas approached Lee in this. McClellan came close for awhile, until his men found out he was so solicitous of them that he refused to risk their lives in battle, an apparently ironic fault which soldiers are quicker to perceive as such than members of less dangerous professions.

Where Suvorov was a fierce old war-horse, and a looter and slaughterer of civilians as well, Lee was every inch a gentleman. Few soldiers have ever fought a civil war more chivalrously; Lee was in the peculiar position of having been offered the command of the army against which he was fighting, and he studiously referred to the Federals as "those people," never as "the enemy."

In spite of a brilliant record in the Mexican War and being offered the command of the Union forces, Lee did not do anything outstanding in the Confederate service until after his appointment to command the Army of Northern Virginia in June of 1862. But the new posting proved a happy mating of leader and material. Both still had much to learn, as the following campaigns showed, but they had less to learn than their opponents, and they learned it faster. The result was to produce as nearly perfect a fighting force as the world is ever likely to see again. Consider the battle of Chancellorsville, universally regarded as Lee's masterpiece. Outnumbered by better than two to one, and virtually surrounded at the outset of the battle, he ended it by nearly surrounding his foes and driving them off the field in full retreat. And that against an army that was itself one of the great ones of military history!

Lee's brilliance as a commander was matched and sustained by his leadership of his men, and the love they bore him. Even in, perhaps especially in, defeat this relationship shone forth. After Pickett's immortal failure at Gettysburg, there was little sense that Lee had been wrong in sending the Confederates against the steady Union center. The famous diorama at West Point which shows the Rebels straggling back from their charge, and their officers reporting to Lee, reflects both his anguish at having sent them on such a mission, and theirs at having failed to do what he asked of them—even if flesh and blood could not do it.

Perhaps the most revealing of all episodes of Lee's career, however, is that of the fight at the Bloody Angle at Spottsylvania Court House. That was nearly a year after Gettysburg, and the shadows were gathering around the Confederacy. U.S. Grant had come out of the West to command the Union armies, and he was, as Lincoln said of him, "a man who knew his arithmetic." It was just before Spottsylvania that he wired back to Washington, "Our losses have been heavy, but so have those of the enemy. I propose to fight it out on this line if it takes all summer." Here was no McClellan, husbanding and pampering his troops to no purpose; here was a man who knew that if you killed enough men in grey and butternut brown, eventually there would be no Confederacy, and that was precisely what he intended to do. While that terrible litany of battles went on through the summer, Lee too came to recognize what fate held in store. As Grant slid south toward Richmond, Lee stopped him in the Wilderness, and entrenched next around Spottsylvania Court House, with his line forming an acute angle.

On the morning of 12 May soldiers of Hancock's II Corps swept like a blue tidal wave over the point of that angle, and the life of the Confederacy hung on a single thread. That morning Robert Lee rode among his soldiers, his sword uplifted, and proposed personally to lead the counterattack. His men would not have it, and shouting "General Lee to the rear" they went forward weeping, screaming, and cursing, to die in his place. For the rest of the day Confederates and Union soldiers fought as bitterly as men have ever done over a rotten little abatis. Lee lost one-fifth of his army, and Grant more than a tenth of his, and students who think that war is a matter of computers, or that Americans do not "know their arithmetic," would do well to study the Civil War.

Later, one day when it was all winding down to its sad finish, Lee lamented what might become of his country, and one of his aides interrupted, "General, for the last two years, these men have had no country; you are their country, and what they have fought for."

*   *   *

In the twentieth century, the tasks of leadership at the highest levels of authority have become strangely complicated. On the one hand the simple growth of the population has made it increasingly difficult for a leader to touch all his potential followers; on the other, the development of modern communications methods has made it easier for a leader to project at least an image of himself to vast numbers of people. That, we may all agree, has been a mixed blessing. We have moved rapidly from the era of the newspaper image, early in the century, when the public followed with bated breath the reports of royalty and nobility visiting this fair or launching that battleship, to the era of the radio, when men as diverse as Franklin Roosevelt and Adolf Hitler discovered the uses of the ether for informing or misinforming their constituencies. And we have moved even more rapidly still to the era of the television set, the all-seeing, all-telling eye that dominates our contemporary scene. If, in the age of mass man, the leader has to reach more people than ever before, he has in the instrument of mass communication an unprecedented means of doing so.

Such problems were in their infancy, and but imperfectly perceived, at the time of the First World War. Until 1914 men were convinced that modern masses could meet and overcome any challenge by the application of modern technology. There was then what now looks like a charmingly naive confidence that anything might be achieved. Had not man recently learned to fly? A few years earlier, when the machine gun was developed, writers had praised the new tool as a means by which the savages and natives of backward territories might be civilized and Christianized the more rapidly. That was the era of Samuel Smiles and self-help, and if you believed you could do better, then by golly you could do better.

That complacent confidence had evaporated by 1917. It had been slaughtered on the "corpsefield of Loos," blown apart on the slopes of Vimy Ridge, and ground into the mud on the Somme and Verdun. In April, when General Robert Nivelle led the French armies once more to defeat in the Second Battle of the Aisne, they finally broke and mutinied. It was for France the greatest crisis of the war, and the government resolved it by the appointment of the one man who typified the army's ideal of leadership, General Philippe Petain.

Philippe Petain

Petain had already made his mark several times over the years, and until fairly recently that mark had always been a black one. As a junior officer he had thoroughly identified with his men in the Chasseurs alpins, much as Suvorov had done in an earlier time. Like his famous predecessor, he was as unpopular with his superiors as he was popular with his men, and one of his fitness reports contained the always-quoted remark, "If this officer rises above the rank of major it will be a disaster for France." His chief problem was not his personality, though; it was his studying of modern tactics which led him to fly in the face of accepted French military dogma. In the late nineteenth century the French, falling behind Germany in all the statistics of great power status, convinced themselves that such statistics meant nothing, and that French spirit was irresistible. They adopted the idea of the all-conquering offensive as an article of religious faith, and Ferdinand Foch became its high priest. Petain was the heretic in the congregation. He believed in the superior power of the defensive, and to all paeans on the attack at all costs he replied with a laconic "Fire kills." By 1914 he was a disgruntled colonel, on the verge of retirement.

The outbreak of the war changed all that, and Petain, twelve years a captain, went from colonel to lieutenant-general in three months. He did well at the Marne, got command of the second Army in mid–1915, and a year later his name was a household word, for when the Germans launched the great Verdun offensive, Petain was sent to stop it.

He did so, at enormous cost in men and material. He instituted a rotation system, and it is estimated that 60 percent of the French army passed through the fighting at Verdun at one phase or another of the battle. He organized the supply system, sending an endless chain of men and materials up the *voie sacree*. When the battle finally ended, the French had lost more than a quarter of a million men, but they had held Verdun, and Petain's name, whatever it might become in another war, was irrevocably linked with this greatest of the Third Republic's victories.

So it was that when the army at last refused duty after Nivelle's vainglorious Aisne offensive—a sort of Fredericksburg writ [at] large—Petain was appointed to the supreme command, and set about to restore order and morale. He did so by the simplest of measures: He showed the soldiers that someone in authority was interested in them. That does not seem like much, but it was far more than most French soldiers had received so far in the war.

British writers charge that after Petain the French army was relatively inactive, and took little offensive part in the war. That is certainly true, but the fact derived more from the enormous wastage of the army before Petain took it over; in terms of generalship he did little but recognize reality. That, indeed, had always been his specialty, and accounted for his prewar unpopularity. As a leader, however, as a restorer of morale, a man who empathized with his troops and won their loyalty and respect, he had few equals in the twentieth century. That accounts in large part for the way in which he was greeted as a savior when he assumed power in 1940. His ultimate tragedy was that he lived too long, and the sad later years of his career should not obscure the enormous impact of his leadership on the soldiers of France in 1916, 1917, and 1918.

A Common Thread

All four of these men, in their own time and since, have been acknowledged as masters of the art of leadership. Do these cursory examinations of their careers reveal any general characteristics, from which it is possible to extract some of the essence of leadership? The answer is both yes and no. No, because there tends to be relatively little in common between them except that they were all soldiers, and, of course, great leaders. But the conditions of war under which Petain labored were not very similar to those of Montrose's day, and the personality of a Robert Lee was not very much like that of Suvorov. There are, however, some elements that can be isolated.

Each of these leaders believed in his men, in their power to rise to the heights of endeavor to which he called them. It is often preached that loyalty is a two-way street; unhappily it is less often practiced. The potential leader cannot demand the unswerving loyalty of his followers unless he is willing to return it. If he sees his men only as instruments to further his own career, he is not going to be very successful. Napoleon once remarked to Metternich that he could use up a million men a month, "for what does a man like me care for such as these," but that was after the legend was established, indeed, that was when Napoleon was already on the way down, and events were to prove he could not use up a million men a month. The leader who says, "You must be loyal to me, but I need think only of my next fitness report" will not go far.

These men also believed in a cause which transcended themselves and their own desires or ambitions. Those causes may in our own day be difficult to discern, but that is more our problem than theirs. Montrose believed both in the right of the Stuarts to rule Britain, and in his own concept of freedom of religion. Suvorov served the dynastic state in the person of Catherine the Great. Robert E. Lee believed in the Confederacy, in fact epitomized what was best in it, and Petain was similarly the embodiment of France, the real France of small villages and infinitely tenacious peasantry—in spite of a reputation for frivolity, the French are among the most dour nations on earth—and he inspired the same attitudes in his men.

It is probable that their followers believed less in these causes than they did in the men who led them. Montrose's Irish and Highlanders followed their own lords to war, and were no doubt but dimly aware of the constitutional principles involved in the English Civil War. Suvorov's peasant soldiers were not asked if they cared to aggrandize Russia when they were dragged off to the army for life. It was the humane treatment, the fact that he was actually interested in them, that made them follow Suvorov, and that made him subsequently a Russian legend, for surely there has not been much of that sort of leadership in Russian history since then. For the most part, leadership as practiced in Russia has been of the remote and awe-inspiring—or indeed fear-inspiring—variety.

Charles de Gaulle (1960: 65), who had some considerable professional interest in the problem, commented on this facet of leadership. He wrote between the wars,

> It is, indeed, an observable fact that all leaders of men, whether as political figures, prophets, or soldiers, all those who can get the best out of others, have always identified themselves with high ideals. Followed in their lifetime because they stand for greatness of mind rather than self-interest, they are later remembered less for the usefulness of what they have achieved than for the sweep of their endeavors.

It is safe to say that de Gaulle and Bernard Montgomery agreed on little, but they both agreed on that. Montgomery (1961:17) thought that one of the prime requisites for leadership was "selflessness, by which I mean absolute devotion to the cause he serves with no thought of personal reward or aggrandizement."

The student is apt to retort that neither de Gaulle nor Montgomery, both of whom were acknowledged as great leaders, particularly lived up to this requirement. Both of them would insist, in rebuttal, that indeed they had. Both saw themselves, however historians have seen them, as essentially self-less men. Here is de Gaulle (1960: 64) again: "Every man of action has a strong dose of egotism, pride, hardness, and cunning. But all those things will be forgiven him, indeed they will be regarded as high qualities, if he can make of them the means to achieve great ends." He would therefore argue that selflessness does not mean self-abnegation; one may be ruthlessly thrusting and ambitious, provided that ambition is directed in the service of something that is perceived as a greater good, and equally provided that the leader has the ability to convey to his followers the importance of that greater good, and not just his own ambition.

Military history is littered with the names of great and good men who were not quite hard enough, and whose disinclination to get their men killed caused only more suffering in the long run; consider again McClellan's solicitousness for his men, which may well have prolonged the Civil War by years, or Ian Hamilton's reluctance to interfere with his subordinate commanders at Gallipoli, which threw away a campaign that might well have been won on the first day. Some writers maintain that one of the few deficiencies of Sir Harold Alexander as a field commander was his preference for the soft word, and it may have cost him the capture of most of the German army south of Rome in May of 1944. Napoleon summed it up when he sent Brune down to clean up the Vendee in 1800; he told his general it was better to kill ten thousand now, than to be too soft and have to kill a hundred thousand later on.

The leader therefore not only has to believe in his men, and have that belief reciprocated; he has to be able to inspire them to risk their lives for some greater end which they may only very dimly perceive, and he has to have himself the courage to demand that they do so. It is of course in this particular that military leadership differs from other kinds.

As we are now nearly a decade away from an active war, there is a tendency, unfortunate but perhaps inevitable in such periods, to regard military leadership as little different from directing, for example, a large company or a political entity. If a man can run a railroad, he ought to be able to run the United States Army, so we say. This, as it happens, is not the case, though the example of Montrose, moving smoothly from civilian to military leadership in his society, might seem to suggest that it was. In such times as these, we try to repress the knowledge that the military obligation, the "profession of arms," in Sir John Hackett's phrase, demands a greater commitment: It demands, in the last analysis, that men agree to die if necessary in fulfilling their tasks. That is rather a different affair from the possibility of losing one's job if one does not do well. The man who raises his right hand and dons a uniform is saying, in so many words, "I shall per-

form a certain task, and if necessary I shall put my life on the line to succeed in it." Not many trade unions, and not many managerial staff, would
be willing to make that sort of statement (though if they were required to
do so, Chrysler might have started making small cars several years ago). If
the military leader has the advantage of trained and disciplined followers,
he also has the disadvantages of the much higher risks of their profession.

This is not, it appears, an unnecessary laboring of the obvious. In recent
years, in spite of having the television bring war into our front rooms, there
has been a very real sense of suppression of this basic fact. People are not
"killed," they are "wasted," or "terminated" in common parlance, and sta-
tisticians succumb to the same impulse that makes undertakers describe
people as having "passed away"; bodies at the funeral home are "resting"
rather than "dead." It may well be that this is a most unfortunate attitude,
and that if there were clearer recognition that someone who is "killed" is
"dead," there would be fewer temptations to resort to war as "an extension
of politics," a mistaken definition which Clausewitz only too belatedly recognized.

The Problem of War

The problem of war, and of leadership, is that if your soldiers are brought
to acknowledge the necessity of achieving their objective or dying in the effort, so are the enemy's. It is that which calls forth the leader's ability to
deal with the unforeseen, "the contingent element inseparable from the
waging of war [which] gives to that activity both its difficulty and its
grandeur" (de Gaulle, 1960: 16). "Whimsy, the irrational or unpredictable
event or circumstance, *Fortuna*" (Record, 1980: 19), these are the things
that are not susceptible to computer analysis, these are what makes war an
art, and therefore leadership an art as well.

There are of course those parts of the trade, or art, that can be studied,
and therefore learned. There have been few great leaders who were not
knowledgeable about the mechanics of the business; you cannot be an inspiring leader if you neglect the logistics that feed your men. They will not
give you their confidence if you forget to bring up the reserve ammunition,
or if you leave them with no way out of an ambush, or even if you consistently schedule two columns to use the same crossroads at the same time.
All of that level of operation is subject to scientific principles, and can be
taught. Any reasonably intelligent person can learn the routine of siting a
battery, or even of administering a battalion. One can go very far on basic
managerial skills, and one cannot do much without them. One of the difficulties, in fact, of dealing with the question of leadership is the tendency
not to distinguish between the aspects of it that relate to making sound mil-

itary decisions, and the aspects that relate to leading men in battle. The last people to insist that science was nothing, art and spirit were all, were the French military advocates of *l'attaque a l'outrance*, the *furia francese*, before World War I, and all they managed to do was kill off the better part of their army in the first couple of weeks of the war, as Petain had all too accurately foreseen. It has been pointed out that if Waterloo was won on the playing fields of Eton, Gallipoli and Singapore were also lost there.

It would therefore again be a mistake to insist on too wide a cleavage between science and art, and to say that either one was all, the other nothing. Every aspect of life has elements of both in it. To repeat the example above, there is an art to siting a battery, but it must be done on scientific principles, as the British discovered when they tried to unlimber within range of the Boer rifle pits at Colenso; they lost 1100 men, and ten out of twelve of their guns, for a Boer loss of less than fifty. The higher elements of leadership remain an art, though the lesser ones can be learned scientifically, can be treated, as it were, by artifice.

Ironically, the better times are, the less artifice works, and the more art is needed. We live in what is undeniably the most prosperous society that has ever existed, with better conditions for more people than has so far been possible in human history. Artifice does not work, because our servicemen are for the most part sufficiently intelligent and sophisticated to see through it. Our society has become so free that preoccupation with freedom as an end in itself has led us to neglect the responsibilities and the obligations that have always been thought to accompany it. No state in history has been able to say to its citizens that they need not, if they do not choose, take any part in defending the unit against the outside world. Most states resorted to conscription of a sort; even Britain, if for two centuries it had no obligatory service, had the press gang when necessary, which was a type of lottery conscription: If you happened to be in the wrong place at the wrong time, you got caught. The United States, however, has only rarely in its history had to resort to a form of conscription that was always far more selective than it was universal. In recent years we have based our security forces on the thesis that enough money will answer our needs, and that if we pay our servicemen sufficiently, they will continue to be servicemen in spite of the siren song of civilian life, a thesis which does not seem, by and large, to be proving correct. The nature of the obligation, once again, and the constraints of military life, are such that even our society does not produce sufficient to pay enough men enough money to fulfill our needs.

To this fact that prosperity breeds a disinclination for the military life must be added the further one that our recent experience has not been such as to enhance the prestige and morale of the military forces. Our position in this respect is summed up, oddly enough, by de Gaulle (1960: 71–72) writing about France after World War I:

The aversion felt for war in general has crystallized around the army. This is an anthropomorphic phenomenon of the same kind as that which makes us dread the dentist even more than the toothache. ... But the mystique of our times must not be allowed to discourage or to humiliate those who wield the sword of France. What better guarantee can be offered to a people gorged with good things, looked at from abroad with embittered resentment, and whose frontiers are so drawn that a single lost battle may put its very capital in jeopardy, than the efficiency of its armed forces.

It is perfectly normal that after a period of unhappy foreign adventuring Americans should prefer to remain at home, that after a long wasting war which was actively opposed by a substantial portion of the population the military services, the most visible target for both fiscal retrenchment and public resentment, should be unpopular. But such attitudes, now hopefully diminishing in the face of returning awareness that there still is a world out there, and that it is not a very friendly one, make the task of leadership, and the exercise of it, all the more difficult.

*   *   *

The more difficult such leadership becomes, the more it requires skill approaching art. One is still left with the problem of precisely what that is, or how to inculcate it into one's potential leaders. But this is by no means a new problem. Ever since society departed, somewhere in the last century, from a stratified system in which certain persons were thought by right of birth to be capable of exercising leadership, men have attempted to grapple with it. Lord Palmerston, when pressed to support the idea of examinations for the civil and military service, wrote to a friend. "Success at an examination is certainly not a decisive proof of Fitness for official employment, because after all, examination is chiefly a test of memory acting upon previous Study, and there are other qualities besides Memory and Studious Habits required to make a Good official Man" (Ridley, 1972: 683).

How to produce the Good official Man, or how to recognize him, has remained one of the besetting problems of our time. If we believe, as our whole history attests we do, in the career open to talent, then talent must be recognizable and rewarded as such. But how to recognize it, and how to cut through the "media hype" that tries to convince us today that a man can walk on water, and the day after he is elected or put in command that he cannot walk at all?

De Gaulle (1960: 127), again, groped for a solution. "Enlightened views and supreme wisdom," he said,

are all a matter of intuition and character which no decree can compel, no instruction can impart. Only flair, intelligence and above all, the latent eagerness to play a part which alone enables a man to develop ability and strength of character, can be of service. It all comes to this, that nothing great will ever be achieved without great men, and men are great only if they are determined to be so.

"Intuition," "character," "flair," "greatness through determination to be great," all these are unsatisfactory to the social scientist as explanations of why men do the things they do. They are, in other words, in the province of art. Leadership remains the most baffling of the arts, and in spite of all the tricks that supposedly make it manageable, it will remain that way. As long as we do not know exactly what makes men get up out of a hole in the ground and go forward in the face of death at a word from another man, then leadership will remain one of the highest and most elusive of qualities. It will remain an art.

References

DeGaulle, C., *The Edge of the Sword* (G. Hopkins, trans.), New York: Criterion, 1960.

Encyclopedia Britannica, "Suvarov" (vol. 26), Cambridge: Cambridge University Press, 1911, pp. 172–173.

Guedalla, P., *Men of War*, London: Hodder and Stoughton, 1923.

Longworth, P., *The Art of Victory*, New York: Holt, Rinehart & Winston, 1965.

Montgomery, B., *The Path to Leadership*, London: Collins, 1961.

Record, J., "The Fortunes of War," *Harper's* (April 1980), pp. 19–23.

Ridley, J., *Lord Palmerston*, London: Panther, 1972.

Williams. R., Montrose, *Cavalier in Mourning*, London: Barrie and Jenkins, 1975.

8

Leaders and Leadership

Gen. S.L.A. Marshall

In that gallery of great Americans whose names are conspicuously identified with the prospering of the national arms in peace and war, there are almost as many types as there are men.

There were a certain few qualities they had to possess in common or their names would never have become known beyond the county line.

But these were inner qualities, often deeply buried, rather than outward marks of greatness that men recognized immediately upon beholding them.

Some almost missed the roll call, either because in early life their weaknesses were more apparent than their strengths, or because of an outward seeming of insignificance, which at first fooled their contemporaries.

In the minority are the few who seemed marked for greatness almost from the cradle, and were acclaimed for leadership while still of tender years.

Winfield Scott, a brigadier in the war of 1812 when brigadiers were few and Chief of Staff when the Civil War began, is a unique figure in the national history.

George Washington, Adjutant of the State of Virginia at 21, is one other military infant prodigy who never later belied his early fame.

The majority in the gallery are not like these. No two of them are strikingly alike in mien and manner. Their personalities are as different, for the most part, as their names. Their characters also ran the length of the spectrum, or nearly, if we are talking of moral habit rather than of conscientious performance of military duty. Some drank their whiskey neat and frequently; others loathed it and took a harsh line with any subordinate who used it.

Reprinted by permission from *The Armed Forces Officer* (Washington, D.C.: Government Printing Office, 1975), pp. 47–57.

One of the greatest generals in American history, celebrated for his fighting scarcely more than for his tippling, would walk from the room if any man tried to tell an off-color story in his presence. One of the most celebrated and successful of our World War II admirals endeared himself to millions of men in all ranks by his trick of gathering his chief subordinates together just before battle, issuing his orders sternly and surely, and then relaxing long enough to tell them his latest parlor story, knowing that finally it would trickle down through the whole command.

In Korea, one infantry division commander was a skilled banjo player. Up at the front, he formed a small orchestra of enlisted men and fitted into it. Between fire fights, they played for troops. The men loved him for it. Later, he became one of the Army's ranking generals and was named to one of its top posts. His name: Arthur G. Trudeau.

Among the warriors in this gallery are men who would bet a month's pay on a horse race. There are duelists and brawlers, athletes and aesthetes, men who lived almost saintly lives and scholars who lived more for learning than for fame.

Some tended to be so over-reclusive that they almost missed recognition; others were hail-fellow-well-met in any company.

Their methods of work reflected these extreme variations in personal type, as did the means they used to draw other men to them, thereby setting a foundation for real success.

Part of their number commanded mainly through the sheer force of ideas; others owed their leadership more to the magnetism of dynamic personality.

In the very few there was the spark of genius. All things seemed to come right with them at all times. Fate was kind, the openings occurred, and they were prepared to take advantage of them.

But the greater number moved up the hill one slow step at a time, not always sure of their footing, buffeted by mischance, owning no exalted opinion of their own merits, reacting to discouragement much as other men do, but finally accumulating power as they learned how to organize the work of other men.

While a young lieutenant, Admiral Sims became so incensed when the United States would not take his word on a voucher that he offered to resign.

General Grant signally failed to organize his life as an individual before a turn of the wheel gave him his chance to organize the military power of the United States in war.

General Sherman, who commanded the Army for almost 15 years, was considered by many of his close friends to be a fit subject for confinement as a mental case just before the Civil War.

General Meade, one of the calmest and most devoted of men in his family relationships, lacked confidence in his own merits and was very abusive of his associates during battle.

Admiral Farragut, whose tenderness as an individual was demonstrated during the 16 years in which he personally nursed an invalid wife, was so independent in his professional thought and action that both in and out of the Navy he was discredited as a "climber." He got into wretched quarrels with his superiors mainly because he felt his assignments afforded him no distinction. The Civil War gave him his opportunity.

General Winfield Scott, as firm a commander as any in our history, plagued the Army with his petty bickering over rank, seniority, and precedent.

Being human, they had their points of personal weakness. A newly appointed ensign or second lieutenant also has chinks in his armor, and sometimes views them in such false proportion that he doubts his own potential for high responsibility.

There is not one perfect life in the gallery of the great. All were molded by the mortal influences surrounding them. They reacted in their own feelings, and toward other men, according to the rise and fall of their personal fortunes. They sought help where it could be found. When disappointed, they chilled like anyone else. But along with their professional talents, they possessed in common a desire for substantial recognition, accompanied by the will to earn it fairly, or else the Nation would never have heard their names.

All in all it is a much mixed gallery. If we were to pass it in review and then inspect it carefully, it would still be impossible to say: "This is the composite of character. This is the prototype of military success. Model upon it and you have the pinnacle within reach."

The same thing would no doubt hold true of a majority of the better men who commanded ships, squadrons, regiments, and companies under these commanders, and at their own level were as superior in leadership as the relatively few who rose to national prominence because of the achievements of the general body.

The same rule will apply tomorrow. Those who come forward to fill these places, and to command them with equal or greater authority and competence, will not be plaster saints, laden with all human virtue, spotless in character, and fit to be anointed with a superman legend by some future Parson Weems. They will be men with ambition and a strong belief in the United States and the goodness of a free society. They will have some of the average man's faults and maybe a few of his vices. But certainly they will possess the qualities of courage, creative intelligence, and physical robustness in more than average measure.

What we know of our great leaders in the current age should discourage the idea that only a genius may scale the heights. Trained observers have noted in their personalities and careers many of the plain characteristics each man feels in himself and mistakenly regards as a bar to preferment

Drew Middleton, the American correspondent, wrote of General Carl "Tooey" Spaatz: "This man, who may be a heroic figure to our grandchildren, is essentially an unheroic figure to his contemporaries. He is, in fact, such a friendly, human person that observers tend to minimize his stature as a war leader. He is not temperamental. He makes no rousing speeches, writes no inspirational orders. Spaatz, in issuing orders for a major operation involving 1,500 airplanes, is about as inspiring as a groceryman ordering another five cases of canned peas."

An interviewer who called on General Ira C. Eaker when he was leading the 8th Air Force against Germany found "a strikingly soft-spoken, sober, compact man who has the mild manner of a conservative minister and the judicial outlook of a member of the Supreme Court. But he is always about two steps ahead of everybody on the score, and there is a quiet, inexorable logic about everything he does." Of his own choice, Eaker would have separated from military service after World War I. He wanted to be a lawyer, and he also toyed with the idea of running a country newspaper. In his off hours, he wrote books on aviation for junior readers. On the side, he studied civil law and found it "valuable mental training."

On the eve of the Guadalcanal landing, General A. A. Vandegrift's final order to his command ended with the stirring and now celebrated phrase "God favors the bold and strong of heart." Yet in the afterglow of later years, the Nation read a character sketch of him that included this: "He is so polite and so soft-spoken that he is continually disappointing the people whom he meets. They find him lacking in the fire-eating traits they like to expect of all marines, and they find it difficult to believe that such a mild-mannered man could really have led and won the bloody fight." When another officer spoke warmly of Vandegrift's coolness under fire, his "grace under pressure," to quote Hemingway's phrase, he replied "I shouldn't be given any credit. I'm built that way."

The point is beautifully taken. Too often the man with great inner strength holds in contempt those less well endowed by nature than himself.

Brilliance of intellect and high achievement in scholarship are an advantage, though in the end they have little or no payoff if character and courage are lacking. Thousands of officers who served in Vietnam, some dubious about the wisdom of the national policy, questioning whether the tight rein on operations made military sense, still believed that "My country right or wrong" is the only course possible for one who has taken the oath.

No, brain trusting and whiz kidding are not what it takes. Of 105 major generals who served in World War I, 56 had failed to score above the middle of their class in mathematics. Of 275 in World War II, 158, or 58 percent, were in the middle group or among the dubs in the same subject. General William C. Westmoreland, who commanded in Vietnam and was later

Army Chief of Staff, had punched practically none of the buttons. As for military schooling, for over 30 years after graduating from West Point, he attended only Cooks and Bakers School and the Airborne School. One of his outstanding subordinates, a two-star general, respected and loved by all who served under him, had joined the service at the age of 15 out of reform school to straighten himself out. By sweat and study, he won his sergeant's stripes at 18 and his commission at 21. He made his resolve and stayed with it, which was the main thing. The solution of every problem, every achievement is, as Justice Holmes said, a bird on the wing; and he added, one must have one's whole will on one's eye on that bird. One cannot be thinking of one's image, or one's place in history—only of that bird.

While there are no perfect men, there are those who become relatively perfect leaders of men because something in their makeup brings out in strength the highest virtues of all who follow them. That is the way of human nature. Minor shortcomings do not impair the loyalty or growth of the follower who has found someone whose strengths he deems worth emulating. On the other hand, to recognize merit, you must yourself have it. The act of recognizing the worthwhile traits in another person is both the test and the making of character. The man who scorns all others and thinks no one else worth following parades his own inferiority before the world. He puts his own character into bankruptcy just as surely as does that other sad sack of whom Thomas Carlyle wrote: "To recognize false merit, and crown it as true, because a long trail runs after it, is the saddest operation under the sun."

Sherman, Logan, Rawlins, and the many others hitched their wagons to Grant's star because they saw in him a man who had a way with other men, and who commanded them not less by personal courage than by patient work in their interest. Had Grant spent time brooding over his own civilian failures, he would have been struck with a disorderly camp and would never have gotten out of Illinois. He was not dismayed by his own short-comings. Later he said: "I doubt that any of my officers ever discovered that I hadn't bothered to study tactics."

The nobility of the private life and influence of General Robert E. Lee and the grandeur of his military character are known to every American school boy. His peerless gifts as a battle leader have won the tribute of cele-brated soldiers and historians throughout the world. Likewise, the deep re-ligiosity of his great lieutenant, Stonewall Jackson, the fiery zeal and almost evangelical power with which he lifted the hearts of all men who followed him, are hallmarks of character that are vividly present in whatever context his name happens to be mentioned.

If we turn for a somewhat closer look at Grant, it is because he, more than any other American soldier, left us a full, clear narrative of his own growth, and of the inner thoughts and doubts pertaining to himself which attended his life experience. There was a great deal of the average man in Grant. He was beset by human failings. He could not look impressive. He had no sense of destiny. In his great hours, it was sweat, rather than inspiration, dogged perseverance, rather than the aura of power, that made the hour great.

Average though he was in many things, there was nothing average about the strong way in which he took hold, applying massive common sense to the complex problems of the field. That is why he is worth close regard. His virtues as a military leader were of the simpler sort that plain men may understand and hope to emulate. He was direct in manner. He never intrigued. His speech was homely. He was approachable. His mind never deviated from the object. Though a stubborn man, he was always willing to listen to his subordinates. He never adhered to a plan obstinately, but nothing could induce him to forsake the idea behind the plan.

History has left us a clear view of how he attained to greatness in leadership by holding steadfastly to a few main principles.

At Belmont, his first small action, he showed nothing to indicate that he was competent as a tactician and strategist. But the closing scene reveals him as the last man to leave the field of action, risking his life to see that none of his men had been left behind.

At Fort Donelson, where he had initiated an amphibious campaign of highly original daring, he was not on the battlefield when his army was suddenly attacked. He arrived to find his right wing crushed and his whole force on the verge of defeat. He blamed no one. Without more than a fleeting hesitation, he said quietly to his chief subordinates: "Gentlemen, the position on the right must be retaken." Then he mounted his horse and galloped along the line shouting to his men: "Fill your cartridge cases quick; the enemy is trying to escape and he must not be permitted to do so." Control and order were immediately reestablished by his presence.

At Shiloh the same thing happened, only this time it was worse; the whole Union Army was on the verge of rout. Grant, hobbling on crutches from a recent leg injury, met the mob of panic-stricken stragglers as he left the boat at Pittsburgh Landing. Calling on them to turn back, he mounted and rode toward the battle, shouting encouragement and giving orders to all he met. Confidence flowed from him back into an already beaten Army, and in this way a field nearly lost was soon regained, with decisive help provided by Buell's Army.

The last and best picture of Grant is on the evening after he had taken his first beating from General Lee in the campaign against Richmond. He was new with the Army of the Potomac. His predecessors, after being whipped by Lee, had invariably retreated to a safe distance. But this time, as the defeated army took the road of retreat out of the Wilderness, its columns got only as far as the Chancellorsville House crossroad. There the soldiers saw a squat, bearded man sitting horseback, and drawing on a cigar. As the head of each regiment came abreast of him, he silently motioned it to take the right-hand fork—back toward Lee's flank and deeper than ever into the Wilderness. That night, for the first time, the Army sensed an electric change in the air over Virginia. It had a man.

"I intend to fight it out on this line" is more revealing of the one supreme quality that put the seal on all of U.S. Grant's great gifts for military leading than everything else that the historians have written of him. He was the essence of the spirit that moderns call "seeing the show through." He was sensitive to a fault in his early years, and carried to his tomb a dislike for military uniform, caused by his being made the butt of ridicule the first time he ever donned a soldier suit. As a junior officer in the Mexican War, he sensed no particular aptitude in himself. But he had participated in every engagement possible for a member of his regiment, and had executed every small duty well, with particular attention to conserving the lives of his men. This was the school and the course that later enabled him to march to Richmond, when men's lives had to be spent for the good of the Nation.

In more recent times, one of the great statesmen and soldiers of the United States, Henry L. Stimson, has added his witness to the value of this force in all enterprise: "I know the withering effect of limited commitments and I know the regenerative effect of full action." Though he was speaking particularly of the larger affairs of war and national policy, his words apply with full weight to the personal life. The truth seen only halfway is missed wholly; the thing done only halfway had best not be attempted at all. Men can't be fooled on this score. They will know every time when the arrow falls short for lack of a worthwhile effort. And when that happens, confidence in the leader is corroded, even among those who themselves were unwilling to try.

There have been great and distinguished leaders in our military Services at all levels who had no particular gifts for administration and little for organizing the detail of decisive action either within battle or without. They excelled because of a superior ability to make use of the brains and command the loyalty of well-chosen subordinates. Their particular function was to judge the goal according to their resources and audacity, and then to hold the team steady until the goal was gained. So doing, they complemented the power of the faithful lieutenants who might have put them in the shade in any IQ test. Wrote Grant: "I never knew what to do with a paper except to put it in a side pocket or pass it to a clerk who understood it better than I did." There was nothing unfair or irregular about this; it was as it should be. All military achievement develops out of unity of action. The laurel goes to the man whose powers can most surely be directed toward the end purposes of organization. The winning of battles is the product of the winning of men. That aptitude is not an endowment of formal education, though the man who has led a football team, a class, a fraternity or a debating society is the stronger for the experience he has gained. It is not unusual for those who have excelled in scholarship to despise those who have excelled merely in sympathetic understanding of the human race. But in the military Services, though there are niches for the pedant, character is at all times at least as vital as intellect, and the main rewards go to him who can make other men feel toughened as well as elevated.

- Quiet resolution.
- The hardihood to take risks.
- The will to take full responsibility for decision.
- The readiness to share its rewards with subordinates.
- An equal readiness to take the blame when things go adversely.
- The nerve to survive storm and disappointment and to face toward each new day with the scoresheet wiped clean, neither dwelling on one's successes nor accepting discouragement from one's failures.

In these things lie a great part of the essence of leadership, for they are the constituents of that kind of moral courage that has enabled one man to draw many others to him in any age.

It is good, also, to look the part, not only because of its effect on others, but because, from out of the effort made to look it, one may in time come to be it. One of the kindliest and most penetrating philosophers of our age, Abbe Ernest Dimnet, has assured us that this is true. He says that by trying to look and act like a socially distinguished person, one may in fact attain to the inner disposition of a gentleman. That, almost needless to say, is the real mark of the officer who takes great pains about the manner of his dress and address, for as Walt Whitman said: "All changes of appearances without a change in that which underlies appearances are without avail." All depends upon the spirit in which one makes the effort. By his own account, U.S. Grant, as a West Point cadet, was more stirred by the commanding appearance of General Winfield Scott than by any man he had ever seen, including the President. He wrote that at that moment there flashed across his mind the thought that some day he would stand in Scott's place. Grant was unkempt of dress. His physical endowments were such that he could never achieve the commanding air of Scott. But he left us his witness that Scott's military bearing helped kindle his own desire for command, even though he knew that he could not be like Scott. Much is said in favor of modesty as an asset in leadership. It is remarked that the man who wishes to hold the respect of others will mention himself not more frequently than a born aristocrat mentions his ancestor. However, the point can be labored too hard. Some of the ablest of the Nation's military commanders have been anything but shrinking violets; we have had now and then a hero who could boast with such gusto that this very characteristic somehow endeared him to his men. But that would be a dangerous tack for all save the most exceptional individual. Instead of speaking of modesty as a charm that will win all hearts, thereby risking that through excessive modesty a man will become tiresome to others and rated as too timid for high responsibility, it would be better to dwell upon the importance of being natural, which means neither concealing nor making a vulgar display of one's ideals and motives, but acting directly according to his dictates.

This leads to another point. In several of the most celebrated commentaries written by higher commanders on the nature of generalship, the statement is made rather carelessly that to be capable of great military leadership a man must be something of an actor. If that were unqualifiedly true, then it would be a desirable technique likewise for any junior officer; he, too, should learn how to wear a false face and play a part that cloaks his real self. The hollowness of the idea is proved by the lives of such men as Robert E. Lee, W. T. Sherman, George C. Marshall, Omar N. Bradley, Carl A. Spaatz, William H. Simpson, Chester A. Nimitz, Harold K. Johnson, Matthew B. Ridgway, Lew Walt, Creighton W. Abrams and John S. McCain, Jr., to mention only a few. As commanders, they were all as natural as children, though some had great natural reserve, and others were warm and much more outgoing. They expressed themselves straightforwardly rather than by artful striving for effect. There was no studied attempt to appear only in a certain light. To use the common word for it, their people did not regard them as "characters." This naturalness had much to do with their hold on other men.

Such a result will always come. He who concentrates on the object at hand has little need to worry about the impression he is making on others. Even though they detect the chinks in the armor, they will know that the armor will hold.

On the other hand, a sense of the dramatic values, coupled with the intelligence to play upon them skillfully, is an invaluable quality in any military leader. Though there was nothing of the "actor" in Grant, he understood the value of pointing things up. To put a bold or inspiring emphasis where it belongs is not stagecraft but an integral part of the military fine art of communicating. System that is only system is injurious to the mind and spirit of any normal person. One can play a superior part well and maintain prestige and dignity, without being under the compulsion to think, speak, and act in a monotone. In fact, when any military commander becomes over-inhibited along these lines because of the illusion that this is the way to build a reputation for strength, he but doubles the necessity for his subordinates to act at all times like human beings rather than robots.

Coupled with self-control, consideration and thoughtfulness will carry a man far. Men will warm toward a leader when they come to believe that all the energy he stores up by living somewhat within himself is at their service. But when they feel that this is not the case, and that his reserve is simply the outward sign of a spiritual miserliness and concentration on purely personal goals, no amount of restraint will ever win their favor. This is as true of him who commands a whole Service as of the leader of a squad.

To speak of the importance of a sense of humor would be futile, if it were not that what cramps so many men isn't that they are by nature humorless as that they are hesitant to exercise what humor they possess. Within the military profession, this is as unwise as to let the muscles go soft or to spare the mind the strain of original thinking. Great humor has always been in the military tradition. The need of it is nowhere more delicately expressed than in Kipling's lines:

> My son was killed while laughing at some jest,
> I would I knew
> What it was, and it might serve me in a time
> When jests are few.

Marcus Aurelius, Rome's soldier philosopher, spoke of his love for the man who "could be humorous in an agreeable way." No reader of Grant's *Memoirs* (one of the few truly great autobiographies ever written by a soldier) could fail to be impressed by his light touch. A delicate sense of the incongruous seems to have pervaded him; he is at his whimsical best when he sees himself in a ridiculous light. Lord Kitchener, one of the grimmest warriors ever to serve the British Empire, warmed to the man who made him the butt of a practical joke. There is the unforgettable picture of Admiral Beatty at Jutland. The *Indefatigable* had disappeared beneath the waves. The *Queen Mary* had exploded. The *Lion* was in flames. Then word came that the *Princess Royal* was blown up. Said Beatty to his Flag Captain, "Chatfield, there seems to be something wrong with our ___ ships today. Turn two points nearer the enemy." Admiral Nimitz, surveying the terrible landscape of the Kwajalein battlefield for the first time, said gravely to his staff: "It's the worst devastation I've ever seen except for that last Texas picnic in Honolulu." There is a characteristic anecdote of General Patton. He had just been worsted by higher headquarters in an argument over strategy. So he sat talking to his own staff about it, his dog curled up beside him. Suddenly he said to the animal "The trouble with you, too, Willy, is that you don't understand the big picture." General Eisenhower, probably more than any other modern American commander, had the art of winning with his humor. He would have qualified under the English essayist Sydney Smith's definition: "The meaning of an extraordinary man is that he is eight men in one man; that he has as much wit as if he had no sense, and as much sense as if he had no wit; that his conduct is as judicious as if he were the dullest of human beings, and his imagination as brilliant as if he were irretrievably ruined."

In Korea, just before the first battle of Pork Chop Hill began, Lt. Thomas V. Harrold heard a loud wailing from the Communist trench and asked his company its meaning.

"They're prayer singing," said an interpreter. "They're getting ready to die."

Said Harrold: "Then I guess we ought to be singing too."

And not a bad idea. The 1st Marine Division, fighting its way back from the Chosin Reservoir in December 1950, was embattled amid the snows from the moment the column struck its camp at Hagaru. By midnight, after heavy loss through the day, it had bivouacked at Kotori, still surrounded, still far from the sea. Maj. Gen. Oliver P. Smith was alone in his tent. It was his bad moment. The task ahead seemed hopeless. Suddenly he heard music. Outside some truckers were singing the Marine Hymn. "All doubt left me," said Smith. "I knew then we had it made."

Concerning leadership within the terms here set forth, the final thought is that there is a radical difference between training and combat conditions.

In training the commander may be arbitrary, demanding, and a hard disciplinarian. But so long as his sense of fair play in handling his men becomes evident to them, and provided they become aware that what he is doing is making them more efficient than their competition, they will approve him, if grudgingly, stay loyal to him, and even possibly come to believe in his lucky star.

They are more likely to do it, however, if he takes a fatherly interest in their personal welfare. But that feeling doesn't have to come naturally to a man for him to win the respect of troops. If he knows his business, they're on his team.

When it comes to combat, something new is added. Even if they have previously looked on him as a father and believed absolutely that being with him is their best assurance of successful survival, should he then show himself to be timid and too cautious about his own safety, he will lose hold of them no less absolutely. His lieutenant, who up till then under training conditions has been regarded as a mean creature or a sniveler, but on the field suddenly reveals himself as a man of high courage, can take moral leadership of the company away from him, and do it in one day.

On the field there is no substitute for courage, no other binding influence toward unity of action. Troops will excuse almost any stupidity; excessive timidity is simply unforgivable. This was the epitome of Captain Queeg's failure in *The Caine Mutiny*. Screwball that he was, and an oppressor of men, his other vices would have been tolerable had he, under fire, proved himself somewhat better than a coward.

9

Leadership

Gen. Matthew B. Ridgway

In discussing the subject of leadership, I am struck by two diametrically opposite concepts. One conceives leadership as an exact science capable of being understood and practiced by anyone. This view is ably developed by Colonel Sherman L. Kiser, US Army, Retired, in his book, *The American Concept of Leadership*. An opposite concept holds that "no amount of learning will make a man a leader unless he has the natural qualities of one." This latter view was that of General Sir Archibald P. Wavell, and is expounded in his published lectures in *Generals and Generalship*. One concept treats leadership as a science; the other as an art.

I incline strongly to the Wavell concept. While recognizing that there are many principles, or truths, pertaining to the exercise of leadership, and while firmly believing that powers of leadership can be greatly increased in any individual through knowledge of these principles and practice in their application, I still think the variables of human nature combined with those of combat, and to a lesser degree with those in peacetime training, make the exercise of leadership far more of an art than a science.

There is, of course, a great deal of bad leadership as well as of good. It, too, deserves study so that its pitfalls may be avoided. But in general, I believe bad leadership is the result either of violation of basic principles, or the lack or failure to develop one or more of the qualities of good leadership. In any event, I want to speak now of the good type of military leadership with some specific reference later to combat leadership of large units—the division, corps, and army.

The chief ingredients of leadership, as I have known it to be exercised by those whose careers I have studied, or under whose command I was privi-

Reprinted by permission from *Military Review*, 46:10 (October 1966), pp. 40–49.

leged to serve, are three. I call them the three C's—character, courage, and competence.

Character is the bedrock on which the whole edifice of leadership rests. It is the prime element for which every profession, every corporation, every industry searches in evaluating a member of its organization. With it, the full worth of an individual can be developed. Without it—particularly in the military profession—failure in peace, disaster in war, or, at best, mediocrity in both will result.

Types of Character

We often use this word "character" carelessly. There are those of notoriously evil character, as well as those of an exemplary one. Yet in its usual acceptation it stands for those magnificent traits which placed George Washington first among his countrymen and, in fact, made him the Father of his Country—the unanimous choice for our first Presidency. It stands for the time-honored code of the officer corps. It stands for self-discipline, loyalty, readiness to accept responsibility, and willingness to admit mistakes. It stands for selflessness, modesty, humility, willingness to sacrifice when necessary, and, in my opinion, for faith in God. Let me illustrate.

During a critical phase of the Battle of the Bulge, when I commanded the 18th Airborne Corps, another corps commander just entering the fight next to me remarked: "I'm glad to have you on my flank. It's character that counts." I had long known him, and I knew what he meant. I replied: "That goes for me, too." There was no amplification. None was necessary. Each knew the other would stick however great the pressure; would extend help before it was asked, if he could; and would tell the truth, seek no self-glory, and everlastingly keep his word. Such feeling breeds confidence and success.

Self-Discipline

Only those who have disciplined themselves can exact disciplined performance from others. When the chips are down, when privation mounts and the casualty rate rises, when the crisis is at hand, which commander, I ask, receives the better response? Is it the one who has failed to share the rough going with his troops, who is rarely seen in the zone of aimed fire, and who expects much and gives little? Or is it the one whose every thought is for the welfare of his men, consistent with the accomplishment of his mission; who does not ask them to do what he has not already done and stands ready to do again when necessary; who with his men has shared short rations, the physical discomforts and rigors of campaign, and will be found at the crises of action where the issues are to be decided?

I know your answer: self-disciplined, self-controlled, and so in control of others, no matter how tough the going—Washington at the Battle of Long Island and at Valley Forge; Grant at Shiloh; Mackenzie of the 4th Cavalry in his epic raid; the junior officer pursuing hostile Indians in subzero weather on our western plains, closing up at dark for a dawn attack, with no fires permitted and only cold rations, if any, before H-hour—much the same many times in Korea, I might add, and I am sure under equally arduous conditions in Vietnam today; the young ship commander named Kennedy, his patrol torpedo boat sunk in action, his crew safely on the beach, then swimming out in shark-infested waters to try to intercept a friendly destroyer and rescue his men.

The world's annals and our own are studded with the names of such men, of all services and all grades. Always ready to assume responsibilities, they could always assign them to others and know they would be willingly accepted. True to themselves and to their conscience, their men sense they will be true to them, giving them full credit, and frankly admitting mistakes and accepting responsibility when they themselves are to blame.

General Washington wrote to Congress from Valley Forge:

> . . . without arrogance or the smallest deviation from truth, it may be said that no history now extant, can furnish an instance of an Army's suffering such uncommon hardships as ours have done, and bearing them with the same patience and fortitude. To see men without clothes to clothe their nakedness, without blankets to lie on, without shoes, by which their marches might be traced by the blood from their feet, and almost as often without provisions as with; marching through frost and snow, and at Christmas taking up their winter quarters within a day's march of the enemy, without a house or hut to cover them till they could be built, and submitting to it without a murmur, is a mark of patience and obedience which in my opinion can scarce be paralleled.

And what Washington did not say—a mark of his own unexcelled leadership.

An eyewitness report of Lee after Pickett's failure stated:

> His face did not show the slightest disappointment, care or annoyance, and he addressed to every soldier he met a few words of encouragement; "All will come right in the end, we'll talk it over afterwards," And to a Brigade Commander speaking angrily of the heavy losses of his men: "Never mind, General, all this has been my fault. It is I who have lost this fight, and you must help me out of it the best way you can."

For leadership through willingness to admit mistakes and instantly to accept responsibility, I think, history can offer few examples to surpass this.

Willingness to Sacrifice

Archibald Rutledge once wrote that there can be no real love without a willingness to sacrifice. Tuck this away in your inner minds. It may pay off in some crisis coming to you in the years now hidden beyond the horizon. Do you love your country and its flag? Do you love the branch in which you are serving, the men with whom you will be privileged to share service and to command? If you do, then you will be prepared to sacrifice for them, if your responsibilities or the situation so demands. The commander of Torpedo Squadron 8 at Midway; the four army chaplains on the torpedoed *SS Dorchester* off Iceland in predawn darkness in February 1942; the many aircraft commanders who have ordered "abandon ship," then stuck overlong to the controls to insure that their last man was out.

Courage, the second "C," could well be treated as a trait of character, as, indeed, it is. Yet it deserves, I believe, a separate category, for I know of not one recipient of history's accolade for battle leadership of enduring fame who was not known for great gallantry.

Physical and Moral Courage

There are two kinds of courage, physical and moral, and he who would be a true leader must have both. Both are products of the character-forming process, of the development of self-control, self-discipline, physical endurance, of knowledge of one's job and, therefore, of confidence. These qualities minimize fear and maximize sound judgment under pressure and—with some of that indispensable stuff called luck—often bring success from seemingly hopeless situations.

Putting aside impulsive acts of reckless bravery, both kinds of courage bespeak an untroubled conscience, a mind at peace with God. An example is Colonel John H. Glenn who was asked after his first rocket flight if he had been worried, and who replied: "I am trying to live the best I can. My peace had been made with my Maker for a number of years, so I had no particular worries."

Examples of physical courage are neither confined to combat nor limited to a stouthearted few, but are common throughout the world among men and women of every color, creed, race, and age, in peace as well as in war. However, examples of moral courage are less well known. They can be considered as proof of true greatness of soul. Where the individual has not measured up, he has generally failed fortune's bid to fame.

To me such incidents most frequently found in war are those where the career of the leader is at stake, and where his actions or decisions will determine the saving or slaughter of many of his men. History is full of these cases. The lure of glory, the fear of being thought afraid, of losing personal power and prestige, the mistaken idea that blind obedience to orders has no alternative—all have been followed by tragic losses of lives with little or no gain.

History often glosses over the countless thousands of lives which have been fruitlessly sacrificed to the pull of power, prestige, and publicity. Haig's Flanders Campaign in 1917 is a conspicuous example. Here, 100,000 men were sacrificed for the gain of 1,000 yards of almost bottomless morass.

It is easy to gamble with other peoples' money, and sometimes easier still with other men's lives, particularly when your own is in no great danger. You remember the commanders' conference prior to one of the big offensives of World War I, when a corps commander—whose command post was miles behind the front—spoke out during a lull in the meeting, saying: "I'd give 10,000 men to take that hill." And a liaison officer from a front-line infantry unit remarked to a brother officer standing beside him in the back of the room: "Generous, isn't he?"

Opposition to Orders

The military services deal harshly, as they should, with failure to carry out orders in battle. The commander present on the scene is entitled to full, instant, and enthusiastic execution of orders by subordinates. Yet when faced with different situations from those anticipated, as well as in the transition from plans to orders, there sometimes comes the challenge to one's conscience, the compelling urge to oppose foolhardy operations before it is too late, before the orders are issued and lives are needlessly thrown away.

Or the leader may be faced with the decision: Shall I take the responsibility of discarding the original mission? Shall I take the initiative and strive for success along different lines? He will have to put those questions to his conscience. "Blind obedience," said Napoleon Bonaparte, "is due only to a superior present on the spot at the moment of action." I concur.

I still support a statement of mine of some years ago:

> It has long seemed to me that the hard decisions are not the ones you make in the heat of battle. Far harder to make are those involved in speaking your mind about some harebrained scheme which proposes to commit troops to action under conditions where failure seems almost certain, and the only results will be the needless sacrifice of priceless lives. When all is said and done, the most precious asset any nation has is its youth, and for a battle commander ever to condone the unnecessary sacrifice of his men is inexcusable. In any action you must balance the inevitable cost in lives against the objectives you seek to attain. Unless the results to be expected can reasonably justify the estimated loss of life the action involves, then for my part I want none of it.

General George C. Marshall, one of the noblest men who has worn an American uniform since Washington, once said of decisions of this kind: "It is hard to get men to do this, for this is when you lay your career, perhaps your commission, on the line."

Twice in my personal experience as a division commander I felt compelled to protest against tactical decisions that were about to be assigned to my 82d Airborne Division.

The first occasion was the planned drop on Rome in September 1943. I have recounted the incident in some detail in my book, *Soldier*. Recently, however, published memoirs of German generals then present in the Rome area have confirmed my views. One passage from the account of that incident illustrates the point I wish to make: "When the time comes that I must meet my Maker, the source of most humble pride to me will not be accomplishments in battle, but the fact that I was guided to make the decision to oppose this plan, at the risk of my career, right up to the Theater Commander."

The drop was not ordered.

The second experience was a proposed attack by the 82d across the Volturno River where the Germans had brought the Allied advance to a halt. The sector chosen involved getting across an unfordable river and, then, after an advance of roughly 1,000 yards across open flat terrain, the attack and seizure of a line of hills, curving away from the river on one flank, then like a bow curving back almost to the stream again on the other flank of the zone of attack, so that the assaulting troops would be under concentrated fire from the front and both flanks.

While the proposal to use the 82d was a high compliment—since it was the weakest numerically, and much the most lightly armed of any of the divisions in the 5th Army—I could only view the proposed operation as a suicide mission that would result in the loss of most of the assaulting troops and, then, with small chance of success. I could not accept such a mission without protest. But first I decided to discuss the plan with General Lucien K. Truscott, Commanding General, US 3d Infantry Division, a field commander conspicuous for competence and gallantry, and an old friend. He said he wouldn't touch it with a 40-foot pole, even with his heavier division. So I spoke my mind, first to the corps commander, under whom the operation was to be mounted—and I recall I used the word "fantastic"—and, finally, to the army commander. The plan was canceled.

In action and out, there is often a thin dividing line between recklessness, boldness, and caution. Even later study of battle records may fail to erase that line, for it is next to impossible to reconstruct the exact picture as it was thrown on the screen of the commander's brain at any particular crisis of combat. Yet experience, your own and that of others which you have absorbed, together with common sense, will be your best guides, and with good luck will see you through.

Physical Fitness

Physical fitness comes under competence, the third of my three basic ingredients of leadership. It plays a great part. My own earlier training at Fort Leavenworth, Fort Benning, Fort Sam Houston with the 2d Division, with the 33d Infantry in the Panama area, and with the airborne paid off in battle—first as a division, then as a corps, and, finally, as an army commander. Because of strenuous and unremitting physical training, I was able to keep up with the best of my troops in the hottest sectors and the toughest terrain and climate.

Let me mention briefly what I think the standards should be for commanders of large units. The division commander should have the physical endurance, stamina, and reserves of his best infantry battalion commanders, because that is where he belongs—with them—a good part of the time; the corps commander, those of his infantry regimental commanders; and the army commander just about the same.

And remember this, since no one can predict today when you may be thrown into combat, perhaps within hours of deplaning in an overseas theater—as happened to thousands in Korea, and as I have no doubt to many in Vietnam—you will have no time to get in shape. You must be in shape all the time.

There is another element in battlefield leadership which I want to mention and illustrate. It is a cardinal responsibility of a commander to foresee insofar as possible where and when crises affecting his command are likely to occur. It starts with his initial estimate of the situation—a continuing mental process from the moment of entering the combat zone until his unit is pulled out of the line. Ask yourself these questions. What are the enemy capabilities? What shall I do, or what could I do, if he should exercise that one of his capabilities which would be most dangerous to me, or most likely to interfere with the accomplishment of my mission?

Personal Presence

As commander of a division or smaller unit, there will rarely be more than one crisis, one really critical situation facing you at any one time. The commander belongs right at that spot, not at some rear command post. He should be there before the crisis erupts, if possible. If it is not possible, then he should get there as soon as he can after it develops. Once there, then by personal observation of terrain, enemy fires, reactions, and attitudes of his own commanders on the spot—by his eyes, ears, brain, nose, and his sixth sense—he gets the best possible picture of what is happening and can best exercise his troop leadership and the full authority of his command. He can start help of every kind to his hard-pressed subordinates. He can urge higher commanders to provide additional fire support, artillery, air, other infantry weapons, and, in the future, perhaps, nuclear strikes.

No other means will provide the commander with what his personal perceptions can provide, if he is present at the critical time and place. He can personally intervene, if he thinks that necessary, but only to the extent that such intervention will be helpful and not interfere with his subordinates. He is in a position to make instant decisions, to defend, withdraw, attack, exploit, or pursue.

If, at this time, he is at some rear command post, he will have to rely on reports from others, and time will be lost, perhaps just those precious moments which spell the difference between success and failure. Notwithstanding the console capabilities of future television in combat, I still believe what I have said is true. In any event, keep this time factor ever in mind. It is the one irretrievable, inextensible, priceless element in war.

Relief of Commanders

The occasion for the relief of commanders may regrettably arise. If it does, there are three points to consider: Is your decision based on personal knowledge and observation, or on secondhand information? What will the effect be on the command concerned? Are you relieving a commander whose men think highly of him—even with affection—regardless of professional competence? And, finally, have you a better man available?

Every man is entitled to go into battle with the best chance of survival your forethought as a leader can provide. What best helps you discharge this responsibility? Sharing things with your men; to be always in the toughest spots; always where the crisis is, or seems most likely to develop; always thinking of what help you can give your commanders who are executing your orders; doing your utmost to see that the best in rations, shelter, first aid, and evacuation facilities are available; being generous with praise, swift and fair with punishment when you have the facts, intolerant of demonstrated failure in leadership on which lives depend, yet making full allowances for human weaknesses and the stresses and strains of battle on individuals.

Know Your Men

Know your men, and be constantly on the alert for potential leaders—you never know how soon you may need them. During my two years in command of the 82d Airborne Division in World War II, I was in close and daily touch with every regimental and most battalion commanders. Before acceding to command of the division, and while I was General Omar N. Bradley's assistant division commander, I had learned to call by name every infantry officer in the division.

Later, by frequent exchange of views with the infantry regimental commanders and the divisional artillery commander, I knew in advance whom they had earmarked for battalion command. I do not recall any instance where I thought the regimental commander had not picked the right man. The payoff came in Normandy. I went in with 12 infantry battalion commanders—four regiments—and I had 14 new ones when we came out, for some battalions lost as many as three commanders during the 33 days we were in that fight.

The qualities of a leader are not limited to commanders. The requirements for leadership are just as essential in the staff officer, and in some respects more exacting, since he does not have that ultimate authority which can be used when necessary and must rely even more than his commander on his own strength of character, his tact and persuasion in carrying out his duties.

Between the commander and his chief of staff in a division or larger unit there should be thorough mutual respect, understanding, and confidence with no official secrets between them. Together they form a single dual personality, and the instructions issuing from the chief of staff must have the same weight and authority as those of the commander himself.

But this does not mean that a commander who delegates such authority to his chief of staff can allow his chief to isolate him from the rest of his staff. If that happens, the commander will soon find himself out of touch, and the chief of staff will be running the unit.

There is a fine balance here. The chiefs of staff sections should know that they always have access to their commander. He should see them and visit their sections with sufficient frequency to understand their problems, to let them know he appreciates their efforts, and that he stands ready to help where he can.

Inform Subordinates

Closely akin to the relationship with staff officers is keeping in close personal touch with your principal subordinate commanders—in the division, with your brigade and separate battalion commanders; in the corps, with your division commanders, their chiefs of staff, and as many of the commanders of attached corps units as you can; and in the army, with corps and division commanders and their chiefs of staff. There is always time for these visits; administrative work can be done at night. By day you belong with your troops.

Keep them informed of your thinking and plans. When you have the concept of an operation first in mind, consult your principal commanders without delay and get their reactions. No matter how sound a tactical plan may be, the chances of successful execution will be greatly increased if you have first secured the willing acceptance by commanders responsible for execution of the missions you plan to assign them. Insure that they receive notice of your decision and the principal details of your plan as approved in ample time to permit them and their subordinates to make their necessary reconnaissances and issue their orders.

These are some of the reasons why I hold that leadership is not a science, but an art. It conceives an ideal, states it as an objective, and then seeks actively and earnestly to attain it, everlastingly persevering, because the records of war are full of successes coming to those leaders who stuck it out just a little longer than their opponents.

Some suggestions for leadership are:

- Read widely and wisely all the history and biography possible. Soak up all the personal experiences you can of battle-tested brother officers. This broadens your understanding of an art of which you can never hope to know all.
- Study thoughtfully the records of past successful leaders and adapt their methods to yours.
- Work hard to keep fit. That little extra stamina may some day pull you out of some deep holes.
- Work hard, in your own way, at being tops at your job.
- Keep the three C's—character, courage, and competence—always before your mind, and with faith in God, be yourself.
- Remember there are many others on your team, and be inwardly humble. Every man's life is equally precious, although all are at the disposal of our country, and the contribution each makes in battle is of equal potential value.

10

The Art of Taking Charge

Lewis Sorley

General Creighton W. Abrams was the quintessential soldier. In three wars—and in peacetime service before, between, and following them—he demonstrated strategic and tactical skill and audacity, exceptional physical bravery and intellectual courage, the capacity to lead men and touch their hearts, diplomatic perceptiveness and ability, and staff dexterity and effectiveness. Abrams was not just the simple personality suggested by his image as a loud, beefy, tough-talking, cigar-chomping combat leader (which he most assuredly was when the occasion demanded), he was also a complex and sophisticated man, equally capable of coolly overseeing Army troops on civil-rights duty during the enrollment of James Meredith in the University of Mississippi or training an armored division to defend NATO.

As a young Army officer, Abrams made a name for himself during World War II in the van of General Patton's Third Army as it swept across Europe. It was Abrams who led the task force that punched into Bastogne and relieved the encircled 101st Airborne Division during the Battle of the Bulge. Patton told a group of reporters: "I'm supposed to be the best tank commander in the Army, but I have one peer—Abe Abrams. He's the world's champion."

Following the war, Abrams served as head of the tactics department at the Armored School at Fort Knox, Kentucky, then spent a year as a student officer at the Army's Command & General Staff College at Fort Leavenworth, Kansas. What happened next, although set in a military rather than business context, is a classic lesson in how to take over a poorly performing organization and raise its standards, production, and morale.

Reprinted by permission of The Conference Board from *Across the Board*, 29:5 (May 1992), pp. 29–35.

After his year in school, Abrams was named commanding officer of the 63rd Tank Battalion, a unit of the 1st Infantry Division on occupation duty in Germany. It was the only tank battalion in the division, in fact the only tank battalion among all of the American forces in Europe, and it was a recently formed outfit, activated less than a year earlier. Some said that the people who made it up had been swept out of the Frankfurt stockade.

The 1st Infantry Division was the special concern of General Clarence Huebner, who had commanded it during World War II and was now the commanding general of all Army forces in Europe. The 63rd Tank Battalion was not making the 1st Division look good, and anything that did not make the 1st Division look good made Huebner mad as hell. He wanted the battalion bucked up, and he wanted it bucked up right now, and to that end he arranged that Abrams be sent to command it.

Abrams was not thrilled by the prospect. He had already commanded a tank battalion for more than two years, and then a larger unit, a combat command. Since then four more years had elapsed, so the battalion command assignment looked like a big step backward. It was a job, Abrams felt, that he had already performed satisfactorily "when it counted. That's the way I looked at it," he later admitted.

The cultural shock of moving to an infantry division from an academic environment was intensified by the fact that, while General Huebner may have wanted Abrams on the job bucking up that troublesome tank battalion, the division commander of the infantry division in which it was situated had no use for tankers. When Abrams arrived it was, in the view of one friend, "the low point in his career."

The mission, then, was not just to whip the battalion into shape, but to educate the division's senior leaders as to the use of tanks. The regimental commanders of the three infantry regiments were, in particular, superb officers and leaders. The way in which Abrams was able to gain their confidence was a telling measure of his abilities. "He's the only man that could have done it," said one of his company commanders. "He's the only man who had the reputation to even be able to talk to them, to get them to listen to him, or to gain any personal respect for this bloody old tank battalion, these noisy, filthy, destructive pieces of equipment that ran over their damn bloody telephone wires that they laid all over the area." The first step, though, was to get the tank battalion up to his standards.

In his first couple of weeks with the battalion, Abrams kept a very low profile. He walked around, greeted people politely, was courteous if gruff. He said nothing. From time to time he would make a few notes. He held no meetings, no formations. Then one day he convened a session that was to become part of the folklore of the outfit. The company commanders and their executive officers were assembled, and Abrams told them that he would like to take a little stroll. "I have a stick here," he said, "and we are going to walk through the battalion area. I will say nothing. But if I raise my stick and point at something, if I see it again I'm going to relieve the company commander."

It took about half a day to complete the walk, even though it was just through the battalion area. There were a lot of things for Abrams to point out, like a tank with the hatches left open and three feet of water in the hull, and a trailer that had no cover and a tire that had obviously been flat for a week or two.

Three days later he retraced his steps. The one thing he found uncorrected was the jeep trailer with a flat tire. Abrams relieved the company commander on the spot. "Then," recalls another company commander, "it became evident to those of us that were privileged to be there that he meant goddamn business. There was no more fooling around. I mean, it just stopped." The shock treatment was essential, according to people who had been serving in the battalion before Abrams came. The battalion had 22 tanks per company. When Abrams arrived, there were 14 operational tanks in the entire battalion, and two of those had no breechblocks for the main gun. It was "a deplorable military outfit when he assumed command," the old-timers agreed.

Next Abrams assembled the whole outfit in the post theater. There he related to them how Sergeant Joseph Sadowski had won the Medal of Honor in his outfit in World War II, winding up with a charge to these soldiers of the postwar Army. (He had some recorded music as an accompaniment, and here at the end the music came up, softly.) "You people are in the same Army, with the same traditions. Remember when you walk through the streets of Chemnitz and Grafenwohr that you walk with Sergeant Sadowski." Then the music came up all the way, and it was "The Star-Spangled Banner." Abrams saluted, and everybody was obliged to jump up and salute with him.

The U.S. Army in Europe was riddled with problems during these years of the late 1940s. In his first few days on the job, Abrams got an abrupt introduction to one of them. It came in the form of a letter from the division commander that said something like this: "The 63rd Tank Battalion, which had previously held the record high for venereal disease of any battalion-size unit in Europe, broke that record in the month of August. This has raised some serious doubts about your qualifications for command." Abrams was incensed by the injustice of it. He had only been in command two days in August.

"I spent a couple of days contemplating a severe rebuke, one that would sizzle right back through the same message centers that the letter had come down through," Abrams said. "Then I got thinking. It is already September, then was going to come October, November, December. Whatever I said about August . . . what was I going to say? I had no place to go. So I got the letter out and looked at it again. This time I looked at the statistics.

Well, I had one company with 90 men in it and 110 new cases in the month of August. So I could see that the problem was real."

At the time, the VD policy in Europe was a punitive one. The incentives were to conceal incidences of infection and avoid treatment. Abrams, studying the matter, became convinced that other outfits had the same problems he had, but that they were covering them up. He decided something had to be done about it.

Abrams took the matter to his men. He told them that for their health's sake they must report themselves. He would have a doctor on duty at Sullivan Barracks, and he would treat anyone who came to see him. But nobody would be punished for seeking treatment. Then he went to work on the morality side, and used that issue to get a chaplain assigned to the battalion, something it had not had before. As a result, said his wife, Julie, "Abe wiped VD off the map, because other outfits, when they realized that this was the way to handle it, stopped fighting it."

The VD problems weren't the worst of it. One Sunday, driving back in a pelting rainstorm from visiting Julie and the children where they were living temporarily at Bad Tolz, Abrams had trouble with the windshield wipers. Pulling off the autobahn and into a big German gasoline station, he got out to see whether he could get some help. Moments later a soldier came running up to him, saluted, and inexplicably blurted out, "It's not my fault, sir!"

What he meant soon became clear. At the German service station Abrams found a two-and-a-half-ton truck from his own outfit. It was loaded with five-gallon cans of gasoline that, investigation established, some people in the battalion were selling to the Germans. In fact, they were moving about 100,000 gallons a month. One thing led to another, and Abrams also determined that they were selling food that was supposed to be going to feed soldiers. By the time the whole thing unraveled he had sent some people to Fort Leavenworth—not the school, but the Federal penitentiary.

Later Abrams related those experiences in a talk at West Point, including the apparently innocent way in which the illegal acts got started. Somebody needed a new windshield for a vehicle, and the supply system was a long time coming up with one, but the Germans would put one in for the exchange of five gallons of gas. Then it turned out they would put one in and give you some marks for two five-gallon cans. And so on down the proverbial slippery slope. Remember that part of the Cadet Prayer where it talks about choosing "the harder right instead of the easier wrong," Abrams said, because "it is very difficult . . . for a fellow to wind up being mostly honest. If he ever achieves that situation, I can guarantee you that it is going to be a temporary one."

Abrams believed that one good way of keeping the Army honest was by example from above. And, whatever the desired goal, showing was always better than telling. On road marches he wanted every man out pulling maintenance each time he called a halt. So, recalled one of his officers, Abrams would "come out of the turret with his crash helmet on and a cigar sticking out of his mouth, with a sledgehammer hitting the end connectors on the track . . . and tightening the bolts, checking the oil."

At Sullivan Barracks they dedicated a new chapel, but chapel attendance wasn't very good. There might be only 12 or 16 people at a service. Abrams called in his company commanders for a meeting, and he told them that, by God, he was going to do something about it, but he would not reveal what. The next Sunday the company commanders formed up their units. "Catholics and Jews fall out," they commanded. As for the rest, it was "Left face. Forward march." And off to the chapel. Simpler times then. When they got to the chapel, they heard a choir. There had never been a choir. And in front of the choir, carrying the crucifix, leading the processional to "Onward Christian Soldiers," marched Abrams. "The next Sunday," said young George Patton, son of Abrams's old commander and a lieutenant in the battalion, "there was standing room only, because everyone wanted to see Abe carrying the crucifix."

Abrams worked directly with his company commanders, giving them a full-time tutorial in the art and science of effective command. He held meetings amounting to seminars, in which he would bring up anticipated problems, then lead a discussion of how to deal with them. And he made it fun. "We just looked forward to those meetings," said "Hap" Haszard. "He would put on a performance."

Abrams made sure that his young officers were not inhibited in these discussions. In fact, stimulated by his challenges, they argued with him constantly. Usually, he would let them persuade him to do it their way. Maybe that way was not always as good as the way he would have done it, but— having argued so strongly for their own solutions—they were committed to making them work. Abrams, of course, knew this full well.

He didn't cut individual officers any slack, either. Once young Patton, who had broken a leg on a ski trip and had it in a cast, slipped down on the ice while Abrams was in the process of chewing him out. Abrams finished what he had to say before helping Patton regain his feet. The incident became part of the folklore. There's an art to correcting people without losing their goodwill. Abrams had the gift.

When it came to integrity, Abrams saw absolutely no room for compromise. One day he came by to see Warrant Officer Miller, the battalion supply officer. "Do you have any tent pegs?" Abrams asked. Miller said they did. "How about parts for the cots, the springs?" They had those, too, said Miller. Both items were in the self-service bins, and all anybody who needed them had to do was stop by and pick them up. From there Abrams went through one of the companies. Some bunks were missing springs, and there weren't enough tent pegs. Abrams asked the company commander why there were shortages. "They don't have them over at S4," the officer replied. Abrams fired him on the spot.

Haszard was driven to coin a word to explain his commander's outlook: "Abe never talked about ethics—he just exampled it." There was one thing Abrams did say about it, though, and many who served with him remembered it: "Nobody on the face of the earth can take honesty away from anybody; he's got to give it up himself."

As a major event drew near, Abrams would make preparation for it a learning experience for his young officers. One such occasion was a period of field duty at Baumholder, a training area that was being taken over from the French. Nothing was put out in writing, but each day Abrams would make his way through the battalion. "How's your mess truck?" he might ask Haszard in one company. "Going to be ready to feed the troops in the training areas at Baumholder?" Naturally, Haszard would get busy on the state of the mess truck. Next door in another company Abrams might ask, "How's your maintenance setup for the field? How are you going to operate at Baumholder?" That company commander would get hot on his maintenance arrangements.

Over the course of three months, Abrams took them through every detail of getting ready for a major field exercise. On the morning of the day appointed for departure, at the specified hour, still without a thing having been put in writing, Abrams came up on the radio and told the battalion to move out. They did. "And there," said Haszard, "was Abe, in his own tank, leading the way."

When Abrams first arrived in Germany the battalion had been loaded with a lot of deadwood. It had gotten its personnel entirely by levies on other outfits and, not surprisingly, had not been sent much talent as a result. Within a few months, however, several outstanding young officers from the recently graduated West Point class of 1948 joined the battalion. Under Abrams's tutorial hand they developed rapidly. The next year more talent came in from that year's West Point class, and there were some strong graduates of ROTC as well, so the talent level was going up dramatically. Abrams knew what to do with it. At least four of the young officers went on to become generals, and one wound up with four stars. For all of them Abrams had made it challenging, exciting, and fun. "I didn't go on leave for two years," said Ennis Whitehead, one of the class of '48 officers, "because I was afraid I'd miss something."

In order to see all the officers together at least once a day, Abrams instituted a morning coffee call at which attendance was mandatory. This took place in the officers' club, beginning at 10 A.M., and lasted a strict 20 minutes. It gave Abrams a chance to have a look at people, put out the word on anything he wanted everyone to hear directly from him, and expose them as a group to his personality.

One day one of the newest officers in the battalion, a young second lieutenant, arrived late for the coffee call. What is more, he arrived absolutely covered with grease. There was grease on his face, grease in his ears, grease up one side and down the other of him. When he burst through the door, everyone else already assembled, the first person to spot him was his battalion commander.

Abrams stared across the room at his young subordinate, taking in both the hour and his appearance, then shouted, "Look at that! Just look at that!" There was about a three-beat pause while everyone held his breath, expecting the fellow's head to roll the very next moment. "Goddamn it, that's the way a second lieutenant should look at 10 o'clock in the morning!" Abrams finished, elevating the man from culprit to paragon in the instant. It was his familiar technique of making an example in front of the rest of the outfit of someone who was doing what he wanted done.

Tank outfits involve a lot of physical labor. Ammunition and gasoline have to be humped, and tank maintenance is hard work and never-ending. The 63rd Tank Battalion was equipped with the M26 tank. No one, suggested Haszard, could say with a straight face that automotively it was a decent piece of equipment. It was, in fact, damnably hard to keep running. With its water-cooled engine came myriad fan belts, and they were constantly breaking. But Abrams would not allow anyone to criticize the equipment. If anyone did, they had to answer to him. Inevitably, they lost that argument, not because he would not listen to what they had to say, but because he knew so much more about the tank, about its capabilities and maintaining it and compensating for whatever drawbacks it might have, that he won every point. "He stressed that the equipment was good, as good as the soldier, as good as the officer, as good as any of us."

Of course, Abrams knew there were problems with the tank. But he also knew that if war came that was what his soldiers were going to go into battle with. And he knew they had to have the confidence that they could make it perform if they were going to fight effectively. Giving their soldiers that confidence, he taught his officers, was where they needed to spend their effort, not on condemning the equipment.

Abrams had a saying that expressed his outlook on soldiers: "No one really wants to do it wrong." This had its effect. He loved maneuvers, and played them just as aggressively and just as enthusiastically as he had conducted his real battles. They were sort of the graduation exercises for all the training, and he took them seriously. On the other hand, maneuvering in Germany, a rather small and fairly densely populated country, had the potential for doing a lot of damage to roads, crops, and property. Abrams was very sensitive to this, according to his company commanders.

Thus on one maneuver, when the area designated for his battalion's overnight bivouac turned out to be filled with sugar beets, he got his commanders together and carefully instructed them to place their units in big square formations around the edges of the fields. Then he warned them, "Now, if tomorrow morning when I come back here and you have departed and you have bruised even the first leaf on one of these beets, then you will be summarily relieved."

Ever so delicately the tank companies eased out of the position the next morning. Then they got into the maneuver for the day. Hap Haszard had his tank company rolling down the road when a spotter aircraft overhead reported a whole "aggressor" regiment just over the ridge line to his left. Abrams came up on the radio: "Hap, you know what you're doing, don't you?" Haszard had no doubt: "Roger that." Abrams was concise: "Move out." Haszard wheeled his company left on line and crested the ridge in a rush. Down below, in a peach orchard, was the "enemy" unit. And all down the intervening slope were beets.

Haszard didn't see a peach orchard. He didn't see beets. All he saw was the objective. So he roared right on down in company line, a wild cavalry charge, right through the beets, right through the peaches, right through the enemy. When the umpire arrived he declared they had won the battle, and he waved off the aggressor unit, requiring it to retreat in defeat. "What a triumph!" Haszard thought happily. Then, as he started coming down to earth, he looked back and saw 22 sets of track marks rolling through the beets.

Not until after the maneuver was over did Haszard see Abrams again. It was back at home station, when he had gotten his company closed in and buttoned up, by which time it was about 1 A.M. On the way home, Haszard decided to stop by the club and see if he could get a drink. To his surprise, Abrams was there. "Get a beer. Come join me," he said. "Oh, Jesus!" thought Haszard. When they were sitting down together, Abrams proceeded. "I just wanted to ask you a couple of questions, Lieutenant. Do you recall the morning of such and such when I came down to visit you in that beet field?" "Yes, sir." "Do you recall what I said?" "Yes, sir—summarily relieved."

"You disobeyed my orders. I watched that attack of yours. I want you to know right now that you caused 50,000 deutsche marks' worth of maneuver damage in that one exercise. Do you realize that?" "Yes, sir."

"Well, I want to tell you that it was worth every goddamn cent of it. Now, that does not give you license to interpret my orders. You best be very careful in the future. But in that instance, as I view it, the commander on the ground made the decision, and it was the right one." End of conversation.

In May 1951, after nearly two years of running the battalion, Abrams got a new assignment. Although still a lieutenant colonel, he was given command of one of the standout units in Europe, the 2nd Armored Cavalry Regiment, part of the United States Constabulary. Six weeks after assuming command, he was promoted to full colonel.

There were more promotions ahead, many more, and they put Abrams in some tough jobs at critical times. Back in Germany on a later assignment, he commanded the 3rd Armored Division during the Berlin crisis. On duty in the Pentagon, he was sent to oversee Army operations in a succession of civil-rights crises throughout the South. As Army Vice Chief of Staff, by then wearing four stars, he carried the load of the Army's buildup for the Vietnam War. Then he was himself sent to Vietnam where, after a year as deputy, he commanded U.S. forces for four more long and hard years. Finally, he was brought home to be Chief of Staff and undertake the rebuilding of a much larger institution, this time the entire Army, that was badly in need of restoration of standards, morale, and self-regard.

Once again the force of his personality, the depth of his commitment, his refusal to compromise on principle, his love and compassion for the soldiers under his command, his skill as a mentor and teacher, and his vision of what could be were the keys to turning things around. Even though death took Abrams prematurely in 1974, only two years into that final assignment, one measure of his success is that the leaders of today's Army credit him with the reforms and initiatives that, carried forward by his successors, produced victory in Operation Desert Storm.

11

The Greatest Man
Churchill and Truman Ever Met

Albert R. Hunt

In a time when anniversaries from the monumental to the mundane are celebrated, today marks one of the more important, if little noticed, in modern American history: It was 55 years ago that George Catlett Marshall became Army chief of staff.

For the next dozen years Gen. Marshall, as chief of staff, secretary of state and secretary of defense, left a legacy rivaled by few public servants in this century: He built and shaped the military machine that won World War II; launched the economic plan that put postwar Europe back on its feet, and reinforced the supremacy of civilian control when he recommended the firing of Gen. Douglas MacArthur. Dwight Eisenhower, Winston Churchill, Harry Truman and countless others considered him the greatest man they'd ever met.

It's unclear whether this man of such vision and integrity would have been able to adapt to the exigencies of contemporary politics and statecraft. But Forrest Pogue's magnificent four-volume biography of Gen. Marshall should be required reading for today's practitioners.

When George Marshall took over as chief of staff on Sept. 1, 1939, there were two stark realities: Hitler's powerful army had overrun Poland that day and was on the verge of dominating the continent of Europe to an extent not seen since Napoleon; and the U.S. Army numbered fewer than 200,000 soldiers, ranking behind 16 other nations. In less than five years Gen. Marshall built an army of 8.3 million, the most powerful fighting machine the world had ever seen.

As secretary of state and later as secretary of defense, Gen. Marshall was President Truman's right hand; no one played a larger role in constructing the policy that contained the menace of communism. The author of the Marshall Plan was the first military man to win the Nobel Peace Prize in peacetime.

The issues were so awesome, and Gen. Marshall's involvement so central, that he made major mistakes. He didn't adequately anticipate a Japanese attack on Pearl Harbor in 1941; arguably, along with Gen. Eisenhower and others, he underestimated Soviet intentions in 1945; and he was on the wrong side of the debate over recognizing Israel in 1948. But as big as these miscalculations are, they are dwarfed by his contributions.

The Marshall vision and sense of duty never were deterred by the prevailing political winds. It's easy to forget what a herculean task he performed in building the Army, overcoming initial public resistance. In 1938 a majority of the House voted for a constitutional amendment to require a national referendum before the U.S. could go to war. In 1941, less than four months before Pearl Harbor, the extension of the draft passed by one vote; without Gen. Marshall's enormous influence on Capitol Hill it would have failed decisively.

The aftermath of World War II ushered in another new world order; despite the Soviet threat there was a strong tendency to look inward. But Gen. Marshall and President Truman not only proposed the multibillion-dollar rescue of Europe but persuaded a Republican Congress to approve it.

Gen. Marshall, an unusually secure man, spotted bright subordinates and then delegated huge responsibilities. In the Army, Gens. Eisenhower, Omar Bradley, Matthew Ridgway and George Patton all were Marshall men. The Army chief of staff had no use for yes men. At the end of his first week, Gen. Bradley once recalled, he summoned his top aides and expressed strong disappointment: "You haven't disagreed with a single thing I have done all week."

He was a military leader with a special sensitivity. When some expressed surprise that an Army general won the Nobel Peace Prize, he noted in his acceptance speech that "the cost of war is constantly spread before me, written neatly in many ledgers whose columns are gravestones. I am greatly moved to find some means or method of avoiding another calamity of war." Working with industrialists and Congress he made sure that his army was the best supplied and best cared for in the world.

This son of the Virginia Military Institute lacked the charisma of MacArthur or even Eisenhower, but he possessed a powerful presence that commanded trust and respect. Churchill, notoriously condescending to military commanders, quickly realized that George Marshall was different. Although he eschewed conventional politics he was a superb politician. During the war he was at the epicenter of an extraordinary collection of powerful personalities and egos—Churchill and Roosevelt, the Machiavellian commanders in chief with their own notions of military strategy, and in his own Army, MacArthur and Patton. Yet the single domineering military figure was George C. Marshall.

He loathed self-promotion. An oft-quoted Marshall dictum is that there's no end to what can be accomplished if you credit others; it's not clear whether he actually said it, but he certainly practiced it.

The most remarkable example of his character was when the time came to choose the supreme Allied commander for the invasion of Europe; most everyone, from Churchill to the entire American military establishment, thought Gen. Marshall the perfect choice. Yet when President Roosevelt pressed him for a recommendation, Gen. Marshall, with a devout belief in civilian control, refused to lift a hand on his own behalf, insisting the president must be free to make the choice. FDR said he would sleep better with Gen. Marshall in Washington; Gen. Eisenhower thus led what became the Normandy invasion. Gen. Marshall never expressed any regret and reveled in his subordinate's success.

Yet as Forrest Pogue says, George Marshall was humble only "if you use the term correctly. He was quite aware of his ability to run the Army and the war better than anyone else." And he was secure enough not to react when he was viciously attacked by Joe McCarthy and the Republican right in the early 1950s.

Would Gen. Marshall succeed as easily today? Mr. Pogue suspects not, worried that he would despise television's penchant for the instantaneous passions of the moment, the ever-reliance on polls, and the constant negative drumbeat about public service.

Whether it's politicians or generals or athletes, there is an irresistible temptation to suggest we don't make them like we used to. In that vein, it's good to remember that in 1888 Lord Bryce wrote his famous essay about American politics entitled "Why Great Men Are Not Elected President." America, over the next 60 years, then proceeded to elect Teddy Roosevelt, Woodrow Wilson, Franklin Roosevelt and Harry Truman.

Perhaps there's a George Marshall on the horizon. Let's hope so.

PART THREE

Followership: Requisite for Effective Leadership

Learn to obey before you command.
                              —Solon

In the study of leadership, followers are all too often taken for granted. There are critical interdependencies between leader and followers that cannot be ignored. These interdependencies are essential to mission accomplishment as well as the leader's success.

Followers' expectations continue to change. Social, economic, technological, and international environments have resulted in a better educated and more sophisticated constituency for leadership. Superior education, technical skills, and access to information are no longer available only to leaders or the aristocracy. They are available to everyone. As a result, there is a very narrow gap between the abilities of leaders and followers. Leaders must more actively engage followers in organizational activities.

Leaders come from the ranks of followers. Few leaders can be successful without first learning the skills of followership. Aristotle's *Politics*, Plato's *Republic*, Homer's *Odyssey*, and Hagel's *Phenomenology of Mind* affirm the mastery of followership as the sine qua non of leadership. Hence, the contemporary study of leadership must examine followership and leader development as they affect organizational success. Followership is, in effect, a prerequisite for effective leadership.

Most of us are followers more often than we are leaders. Even when we have subordinates, we still have those above us. Followership dominates our lives and our organizations, but a preoccupation with leadership often constrains us from truly appreciating the nature of the follower.

Qualities that make effective followers are paradoxically the same qualities found in effective leaders. What distinguishes effective followers from effective leaders is the role they play. Effective followers and leaders easily move from one role to the other. In many organizations, the leadership role is the path to success and the one that is most focused on for development and rewarded. That is unfortunate because most organizations need good followers more than they need emerging leaders. A few organizations such as the military recognize the importance of the role of follower.

The term "subordinate" is often stereotyped in an unfavorable way. Many organizations prefer to use words like "associates," "partners," "team members," or "colleagues." However, other words make little difference because it is how the leader treats others that really counts. We have observed disrespectful treatment of team members and partners just as we have witnessed caring concern for subordinates.

Regardless of the nomenclature, followers do not want to be treated as inferior. They want leaders to help define direction, create a path to the future, and give feedback on progress. There is no reason to suggest that theirs is somehow a lesser role. The truth is that every leader is also a follower. Thus, a major tenet of developing effective leadership is understanding and experiencing effective followership.

Implications for Leadership

Because leadership consists of getting things done through others, followership is critical to the leader's effectiveness. One cannot be an effective leader if he or she is not (or has not been) an effective follower. The experience of following gives leaders perspective and enables them to share vision, communicate with empathy, treat people as individuals, and empower others to achieve shared goals and objectives. It is through followership that one learns self-knowledge and self-confidence—the personal elements of leadership development.

The responsibility for developing followers rests with the leader. Leaders must encourage participation in the creation of goals and objectives, allowing ideas to be modified and owned by everyone. Separating the individual—"I"—from leadership creates "we," building a true sense of shared leadership and followership.

In many ways, leaders serve followers. This may differ from many models of leadership, but it is one that we believe. Effective leaders create opportunities, help followers obtain resources, delegate to those best able to make the best decisions, and vigorously support the actions taken. Often, this means that leaders watch while others do things differently than they would. Helping people learn by allowing them to make mistakes takes true courage and results in organizational learning. This is how leaders develop effective followers who, in turn, are learning the key elements of effective leadership.

Some people evaluate leaders on the basis of who they have around them. We see many leaders who like to be the smartest, most decisive, and most powerful of those in the group. They thrive on having followers revere them. Unfortunately, the unit becomes completely dependent upon such leaders for access to resources and for goal achievement. In these situations, everything happens because of the leader. Truly effective leaders surround themselves with people who are bright, who are critical thinkers, and who are independent. Decisions are made at the organizational level having the best information. Followers are given the means and the responsibility to do the job. Innovation is prized. Therefore, leaders are best evaluated on the basis of organizational success and how well they develop their followers.

Consider how much training you have had in followership. Can you translate leadership development into the behaviors necessary to be an effective follower? We believe that effective followership involves communicating openly, participating on the front end before decisions are made, expressing loyalty to the organization, handling conflict in terms of what is best for the organization, having the courage to express one's opinion, and supporting the final decision regardless of whether one agrees with that decision. Effective leadership is dependent upon how well the leader develops his or her followers.

On Followers and Followership

Robert Kelley provides an excellent framework with "In Praise of Followers" (Chapter 12). He describes the characteristics of effective followership as being the same as effective leadership, suggesting a redefinition of both roles. With good leaders setting an example of followership, independent critical thinking and self-management can be developed in leader and follower alike. Evaluating people on their followership qualities adds to the appraisal dimensions with which we are familiar. With the military restructuring for changing times, Kelley's piece has important implications for creating flatter, leaner organizations designed to encourage the development of followership and leadership.

Potter, Rosenbach, and Pittman present their conceptual model of followership in "Leading the New Professional" (Chapter 13), a piece written especially for this book. They describe effective followers as partners in an enterprise who are committed to high performance and healthy relationships with their leaders. The authors agree that organizations that keep pace with the rapidly changing global environment are characterized by leaders who encourage partnerships as well as followers who seek to be partners.

In "The Ten Rules of Good Followership" (Chapter 14), Col. Phillip Meilinger presents a set of techniques and ideas that are very powerful. He is convinced that good followership is no less important than effective leadership. His rules are straightforward: Do not blame the boss; do not fight the boss; use initiative; accept responsibility; tell the truth and do not quibble; do your homework; be prepared to implement your own suggestions; keep the boss informed; fix problems as they occur; and put in an honest day's work. Meilinger reinforces the fact that we are all subordinate to someone and learning how to serve those who lead us is an important responsibility. By following these rules, we will be better prepared to lead.

Finally, we present "Followers Make Good Leaders Good" (Chapter 15) by Warren Bennis. He proposes that effective leaders encourage and reward dissent. Followers must speak out with candor, for their intellect and insights are critical to organizational and unit effectiveness. The ultimate irony, Bennis notes, is that the follower who is willing to speak up demonstrates the initiative of effective leadership.

> *Each of us is led, some of us are leaders. The competence we demand in our leaders must be our model when we lead. Where are you?*
> —General Glenn K. Otis

12

In Praise of Followers

Robert E. Kelley

We are convinced that corporations succeed or fail, compete or crumble, on the basis of how well they are led. So we study great leaders of the past and present and spend vast quantities of time and money looking for leaders to hire and trying to cultivate leadership in the employees we already have.

I have no argument with this enthusiasm. Leaders matter greatly. But in searching so zealously for better leaders we tend to lose sight of the people these leaders will lead. Without his armies, after all, Napoleon was just a man with grandiose ambitions. Organizations stand or fall partly on the basis of how well their leaders lead, but partly also on the basis of how well their followers follow.

In 1987, declining profitability and intensified competition for corporate clients forced a large commercial bank on the east coast to reorganize its operations and cut its work force. Its most seasoned managers had to spend most of their time in the field working with corporate customers. Time and energies were stretched so thin that one department head decided he had no choice but to delegate the responsibility for reorganization to his staff people, who had recently had training in self-management.

Despite grave doubts, the department head set them up as a unit without a leader, responsible to one another and to the bank as a whole for writing their own job descriptions, designing a training program, determining criteria for performance evaluations, planning for operational needs, and helping to achieve overall organizational objectives.

They pulled it off. The bank's officers were delighted and frankly amazed that rank-and-file employees could assume so much responsibility so successfully. In fact, the department's capacity to control and direct itself virtually without leadership saved the organization months of turmoil, and as the bank struggled to remain a major player in its region, valuable management time was freed up to put out other fires.

What was it these singular employees did? Given a goal and parameters, they went where most departments could only have gone under the hands-on guidance of an effective leader. But these employees accepted the delegation of authority and went there alone. They thought for themselves, sharpened their skills, focused their efforts, put on a fine display of grit and spunk and self-control. They followed effectively.

To encourage this kind of effective following in other organizations, we need to understand the nature of the follower's role. To cultivate good followers, we need to understand the human qualities that allow effective followership to occur.

The Role of Follower

Bosses are not necessarily good leaders; subordinates are not necessarily effective followers. Many bosses couldn't lead a horse to water. Many subordinates couldn't follow a parade. Some people avoid either role. Others accept the role thrust upon them and perform it badly.

At different points in their careers, even at different times of the working day, most managers play both roles, though seldom equally well. After all, the leadership role has the glamour and attention. We take courses to learn it, and when we play it well we get applause and recognition. But the reality is that most of us are more often followers than leaders. Even when we have subordinates, we still have bosses. For every committee we chair, we sit as a member on several others.

So followership dominates our lives and organizations, but not our thinking, because our preoccupation with leadership keeps us from considering the nature and the importance of the follower.

What distinguishes an effective from an ineffective follower is enthusiastic, intelligent, and self-reliant participation—without star billing—in the pursuit of an organizational goal. Effective followers differ in their motivations for following and in their perceptions of the role. Some choose followership as their primary role at work and serve as team players who take satisfaction in helping to further a cause, an idea, a product, a service, or, more rarely, a person. Others are leaders in some situations but choose the follower role in a particular context. Both these groups view the role of follower as legitimate, inherently valuable, even virtuous.

Some potentially effective followers derive motivation from ambition. By proving themselves in the follower's role, they hope to win the confidence of peers and superiors and move up the corporate ladder. These people do not see followership as attractive in itself. All the same, they can become good followers if they accept the value of learning the role, studying leaders from a subordinate's perspective, and polishing the followership skills that will always stand them in good stead.

Understanding motivations and perceptions is not enough, however. Since followers with different motivations can perform equally well, I examined the behavior that leads to effective and less effective following among people committed to the organization and came up with two underlying behavioral dimensions that help to explain the difference.

One dimension measures to what degree followers exercise independent, critical thinking. The other ranks them on a passive/active scale. The resulting diagram identifies five followership patterns. (See Figure 12.1.)

Sheep are passive and uncritical, lacking in initiative and sense of responsibility. They perform the tasks given them and stop. Yes People are a livelier but equally unenterprising group. Dependent on a leader for inspiration, they can be aggressively deferential, even servile. Bosses weak in judgment and self-confidence tend to like them and to form alliances with them that can stultify the organization.

Alienated Followers are critical and independent in their thinking but passive in carrying out their role. Somehow, sometime, something turned them off. Often cynical, they tend to sink gradually into disgruntled acquiescence, seldom openly opposing a leader's efforts. In the very center of the diagram we have Survivors, who perpetually sample the wind and live by the slogan "better safe than sorry." They are adept at surviving change.

In the upper right-hand corner, finally, we have Effective Followers, who think for themselves and carry out their duties and assignments with energy and assertiveness. Because they are risk takers, self-starters, and indepen-

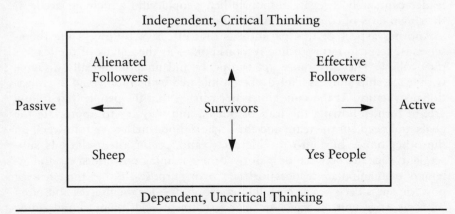

FIGURE 12.1 Five Followership Patterns

dent problem solvers, they get consistently high ratings from peers and many superiors. Followership of this kind can be a positive and acceptable choice for parts or all of our lives—a source of pride and fulfillment.

Effective followers are well-balanced and responsible adults who can succeed without strong leadership. Many followers believe they offer as much value to the organization as leaders do, especially in project or task-force situations. In an organization of effective followers, a leader tends to be more an overseer of change and progress than a hero. As organizational structures flatten, the quality of those who follow will become more and more important. As Chester I. Barnard wrote 50 years ago in *The Functions of the Executive*, "The decision as to whether an order has authority or not lies with the person to whom it is addressed, and does not reside in 'persons of authority' or those who issue orders."

The Qualities of Followers

Effective followers share a number of essential qualities:

- They manage themselves well.
- They are committed to the organization and to a purpose, principle, or person outside themselves.
- They build their competence and focus their efforts for maximum impact.
- They are courageous, honest, and credible.

Self-Management.   Paradoxically, the key to being an effective follower is the ability to think for oneself—to exercise control and independence and to work without close supervision. Good followers are people to whom a leader can safely delegate responsibility, people who anticipate needs at their own level of competence and authority.

Another aspect of this paradox is that effective followers see themselves—except in terms of line responsibility—as the equals of the leaders they follow. They are more apt to openly and unapologetically disagree with leadership and less likely to be intimidated by hierarchy and organizational structure. At the same time, they can see that the people they follow are, in turn, following the lead of others, and they try to appreciate the goals and needs of the team and the organization. Ineffective followers, on the other hand, buy into the hierarchy and, seeing themselves as subservient, vacillate between despair over their seeming powerlessness and attempts to manipulate leaders for their own purposes. Either their fear of powerlessness becomes a self-fulfilling prophecy—for themselves and often for their work units as well—or their resentment leads them to undermine the team's goals.

Self-managed followers give their organizations a significant cost advantage because they eliminate much of the need for elaborate supervisory control systems that, in any case, often lower morale. In 1985, a large midwestern bank redesigned its personnel selection system to attract self-managed workers. Those conducting interviews began to look for particular types of experience and capacities—initiative, teamwork, independent thinking of all kinds—and the bank revamped its orientation program to emphasize self-management. At the executive level, role playing was introduced into the interview process: how you disagree with your boss, how you prioritize your in-basket after a vacation. In the three years since, employee turnover has dropped dramatically, the need for supervisors has decreased, and administrative costs have gone down.

Of course not all leaders and managers like having self-managing subordinates. Some would rather have sheep or yes people. The best that good followers can do in this situation is to protect themselves with a little career self-management—that is, to stay attractive in the marketplace. The qualities that make a good follower are too much in demand to go begging for long.

Commitment. Effective followers are committed to something—a cause, a product, an organization, an idea—in addition to the care of their own lives and careers. Some leaders misinterpret this commitment. Seeing their authority acknowledged, they mistake loyalty to a goal for loyalty to themselves. But the fact is that many effective followers see leaders merely as coadventurers on a worthy crusade, and if they suspect their leader of flagging commitment or conflicting motives they may just withdraw their support, either by changing jobs or by contriving to change leaders.

The opportunities and the dangers posed by this kind of commitment are not hard to see. On the one hand, commitment is contagious. Most people like working with colleagues whose hearts are in their work. Morale stays high. Workers who begin to wander from their purpose are jostled back into line. Projects stay on track and on time. In addition, an appreciation of commitment and the way it works can give managers an extra tool with which to understand and channel the energies and loyalties of their subordinates.

On the other hand, followers who are strongly committed to goals not consistent with the goals of their companies can produce destructive results. Leaders having such followers can even lose control of their organizations.

A scientist at a computer company cared deeply about making computer technology available to the masses, and her work was outstanding. Since her goal was in line with the company's goals, she had few problems with top management. Yet she saw her department leaders essentially as facilitators of her dream, and when managers worked at cross-purposes to that vision, she exercised all of her considerable political skills to their detriment. Her immediate supervisors saw her as a thorn in the side, but she was quite effective in furthering her cause because she saw eye to eye with company leaders. But what if her vision and the company's vision had differed?

Effective followers temper their loyalties to satisfy organizational needs—or they find new organizations. Effective leaders know how to channel the energies of strong commitment in ways that will satisfy corporate goals as well as a follower's personal needs.

Competence and Focus.   On the grounds that committed incompetence is still incompetence, effective followers master skills that will be useful to their organizations. They generally hold higher performance standards than the work environment requires, and continuing education is second nature to them, a staple in their professional development.

Less effective followers expect training and development to come to them. The only education they acquire is force-fed. If not sent to a seminar, they don't go. Their competence deteriorates unless some leader gives them parental care and attention.

Good followers take on extra work gladly, but first they do a superb job on their core responsibilities. They are good judges of their own strengths and weaknesses, and they contribute well to teams. Asked to perform in areas where they are poorly qualified, they speak up. Like athletes stretching their capacities, they don't mind chancing failure if they know they can succeed, but they are careful to spare the company wasted energy, lost time, and poor performance by accepting challenges that coworkers are better prepared to meet. Good followers see coworkers as colleagues rather than competitors.

At the same time, effective followers often search for overlooked problems. A woman on a new product development team discovered that no one was responsible for coordinating engineering, marketing, and manufacturing. She worked out an interdepartmental review schedule that identified the people who should be involved at each stage of development. Instead of burdening her boss with yet another problem, this woman took the initiative to present the issue along with a solution.

Another woman I interviewed described her efforts to fill a dangerous void in the company she cared about. Young managerial talent in this manufacturing corporation had traditionally made careers in production. Convinced that foreign competition would alter the shape of the industry, she realized that marketing was a neglected area. She took classes, attended seminars, and read widely. More important, she visited customers to get feedback about her company's and competitors' products, and she soon knew more about the product's customer appeal and market position than any of her peers. The extra competence did wonders for her own career, but it also helped her company weather a storm it had not seen coming.

Courage.   Effective followers are credible, honest, and courageous. They establish themselves as independent, critical thinkers whose knowledge and judgment can be trusted. They give credit where credit is due, admitting mistakes and sharing successes. They form their own views and ethical standards and stand up for what they believe in.

Insightful, candid, and fearless, they can keep leaders and colleagues honest and informed. The other side of the coin of course is that they can also cause great trouble for a leader with questionable ethics.

Jerome LiCari, the former R&D director at Beech-Nut, suspected for several years that the apple concentrate Beech-Nut was buying from a new supplier at 20% below market price was adulterated. His department suggested switching suppliers, but top management at the financially strapped company put the burden of proof on R&D.

By 1981, LiCari had accumulated strong evidence of adulteration and issued a memo recommending a change of supplier. When he got no response, he went to see his boss, the head of operations. According to LiCari, he was threatened with dismissal for lack of team spirit. LiCari then went to the president of Beech-Nut, and when that, too, produced no results, he gave up his three-year good-soldier effort, followed his conscience, and resigned. His last performance evaluation praised his expertise and loyalty, but said his judgment was "colored by naivete and impractical ideals."

In 1986, Beech-Nut and LiCari's two bosses were indicted on several hundred counts of conspiracy to commit fraud by distributing adulterated apple juice. In November 1987, the company pleaded guilty and agreed to a fine of $2 million. In February of this year [1988], the two executives were found guilty on a majority of the charges. The episode cost Beech-Nut an estimated $25 million and a 20% loss of market share. Asked during the trial if he had been naive, LiCari said, "I guess I was. I thought apple juice should be made from apples."

Is LiCari a good follower? Well, no, not to his dishonest bosses. But yes, he is almost certainly the kind of employee most companies want to have: loyal, honest, candid with his superiors, and thoroughly credible. In an ethical company involved unintentionally in questionable practices, this kind of follower can head off embarrassment, expense, and litigation.

Cultivating Effective Followers

You may have noticed by now that the qualities that make effective followers are, confusingly enough, pretty much the same qualities found in some effective leaders. This is no mere coincidence, of course. But the confusion underscores an important point. If a person has initiative, self-control, commitment, talent, honesty, credibility, and courage, we say, "Here is a leader!" By definition, a follower cannot exhibit the qualities of leadership. It violates our stereotype.

But our stereotype is ungenerous and wrong. Followership is not a person but a role, and what distinguishes followers from leaders is not intelligence or character but the role they play. As I pointed out at the beginning of this article, effective followers and effective leaders are often the same people playing different parts at different hours of the day.

In many companies, the leadership track is the only road to career success. In almost all companies, leadership is taught and encouraged while followership is not. Yet effective followership is a prerequisite for organizational success. Your organization can take four steps to cultivate effective followers in your work force.

1. Redefining Followership and Leadership. Our stereotyped but unarticulated definitions of leadership and followership shape our expectations when we occupy either position. If a leader is defined as responsible for motivating followers, he or she will likely act toward followers as if they needed motivation. If we agree that a leader's job is to transform followers, then it must be a follower's job to provide the clay. If followers fail to need transformation, the leader looks ineffective. The way we define the roles clearly influences the outcome of the interaction.

Instead of seeing the leadership role as superior to and more active than the role of the follower, we can think of them as equal but different activities. The operative definitions are roughly these: people who are effective in the leader role have the vision to set corporate goals and strategies, the interpersonal skills to achieve consensus, the verbal capacity to communicate enthusiasm to large and diverse groups of individuals, the organizational talent to coordinate disparate efforts, and, above all, the desire to lead.

People who are effective in the follower role have the vision to see both the forest and the trees, the social capacity to work well with others, the strength of character to flourish without heroic status, the moral and psychological balance to pursue personal and corporate goals at no cost to either, and, above all, the desire to participate in a team effort for the accomplishment of some greater common purpose.

This view of leadership and followership can be conveyed to employees directly and indirectly—in training and by example. The qualities that make good followers and the value the company places on effective followership can be articulated in explicit follower training. Perhaps the best way to convey this message, however, is by example. Since each of us plays a follower's part at least from time to time, it is essential that we play it well, that we contribute our competence to the achievement of team goals, that we support the team leader with candor and self-control, that we do our best to appreciate and enjoy the role of quiet contribution to a larger, common cause.

2. Honing Followership Skills. Most organizations assume that leadership has to be taught but that everyone knows how to follow. This assumption is based on three faulty premises (1) that leaders are more important than followers, (2) that following is simply doing what you are told to do, and (3) that followers inevitably draw their energy and aims, even their talent, from the leader. A program of follower training can correct this misapprehension by focusing on topics like:

- Improving independent, critical thinking
- Self-management
- Disagreeing agreeably
- Building credibility
- Aligning personal and organizational goals and commitments
- Acting responsibly toward the organization, the leader, coworkers, and oneself
- Similarities and differences between leadership and followership roles
- Moving between the two roles with ease

3. Performance Evaluation and Feedback. Most performance evaluations include a section on leadership skills. Followership evaluation would include items like the ones I have discussed. Instead of rating employees on leadership qualities such as self-management, independent thinking, originality, courage, competence, and credibility, we can rate them on these same qualities in both the leadership and followership roles and then evaluate each individual's ability to shift easily from the one role to the other. A variety of performance perspectives will help most people understand better how well they play their various organizational roles.

Moreover, evaluations can come from peers, subordinates, and self as well as from supervisors. The process is simple enough: peers and subordinates who come into regular or significant contact with another employee fill in brief, periodic questionnaires where they rate the individual on followership qualities. Findings are then summarized and given to the employee being rated.

4. Organizational Structures That Encourage Followership. Unless the value of good following is somehow built into the fabric of the organization, it is likely to remain a pleasant conceit to which everyone pays occasional lip service but no dues. Here are four good ways to incorporate the concept into your corporate culture:

• In leaderless groups, all members assume equal responsibility for achieving goals. These are usually small task forces of people who can work together under their own supervision. However hard it is to imagine a group with more than one leader, groups with none at all can be highly productive if their members have the qualities of effective followers.

• Groups with temporary and rotating leadership are another possibility. Again, such groups are probably best kept small and the rotation fairly frequent, although the notion might certainly be extended to include the administration of a small department for, say, six-month terms. Some of these temporary leaders will be less effective than others, of course, and some may be weak indeed, which is why critics maintain that this structure is inefficient. Why not let the best leader lead? Why suffer through the tenure of less effective leaders? There are two reasons. First, experience of the leadership role is essential to the education of effective followers. Second, followers learn that they must compensate for ineffective leadership by exercising their skill as good followers. Rotating leader or not, they are bound to be faced with ineffective leadership more than once in their careers.

• Delegation to the lowest level is a third technique for cultivating good followers. Nordstrom's, the Seattle-based department store chain, gives each sales clerk responsibility for servicing and satisfying the customer, including the authority to make refunds without supervisory approval. This kind of delegation makes even people at the lowest levels responsible for their own decisions and for thinking independently about their work.

• Finally, companies can use rewards to underline the importance of good followership. This is not as easy as it sounds. Managers dependent on yes people and sheep for ego gratification will not leap at the idea of extra rewards for the people who make them most uncomfortable. In my research, I have found that effective followers get mixed treatment. About half the time, their contributions lead to substantial rewards. The other half of the time they are punished by their superiors for exercising judgment, taking risks, and failing to conform. Many managers insist that they want independent subordinates who can think for themselves. In practice, followers who challenge their bosses run the risk of getting fired.

In today's flatter, leaner organization, companies will not succeed without the kind of people who take pride and satisfaction in the role of supporting player, doing the less glorious work without fanfare. Organizations that want the benefits of effective followers must find ways of rewarding them, ways of bringing them into full partnership in the enterprise. Think of the thousands of companies that achieve adequate performance and lackluster profits with employees they treat like second-class citizens. Then imagine for a moment the power of an organization blessed with fully engaged, fully energized, fully appreciated followers.

13

Leading the New Professional

Earl H. Potter III,
William E. Rosenbach, and
Thane S. Pittman

For the past several years corporate America has been engaged in redefining the relationship between employers and employees. Born on the crest of the wave of "downsizing" companies, the "new employee contract" describes an independence for employees who can no longer depend on lifelong employment in the same organization. While cynics suggest the new contract is nothing more than a convenient way for corporate leaders to shed the bonds of loyalty to their employees, scholars and many leaders see the possibility of a new kind of partnership with employees as offering the best hope for flexible, competitive organizations that will be able to meet the challenges of the future.

Throughout U.S. industrial history the military services have offered models of organization and leadership. Innovation in the corporate sector has often followed change led by the military. From the use of psychological testing for selection to the racial integration of military units in the 1950s, change leadership has resulted from creative problem solving by U.S. military leaders. However, in the past two decades, corporate America has often taken the lead. No initiative better makes this point than the adoption of total quality management (TQM) practices by the military. So successful has this adoption been that Tom Peters, writing in *In Search of Excellence*, and Margaret Wheatly, author of *Leadership and the New Science*, repeatedly draw on military examples of creative and flexible leadership. The flow of ideas from military to corporate organizations and back has been one of the most powerful learning systems in this country throughout this century.

The new employee contract offers another learning opportunity. The irony of this lesson, however, is that it may well take us "back to the fu-

ture" to the time of the "citizen-soldier" who knowingly gave up some freedom to accept the discipline of service. The New Professional is enlisting in
a time when rapid change is the order of the day and the expectation that
organizational members will have a voice in their own affairs is at an all-
time high. Leading the New Professional will require that military leaders
create conditions in which followers can accept discipline and still exercise
initiative. The only way this can be done is if the soldier, sailor, or marine
understands the shared responsibility for making this new role work. The
new employee contract for the military will be a new definition of professionalism that unites leader and follower in a partnership that both understand and choose.

The New Professional

Whether we ask successful leaders to describe their best bosses or to describe the ideal follower, we get essentially the same description. What effective leaders and followers tell us is that the best relationship between a
leader and follower looks and feels like a partnership. Each understands the
perspective of the other, and both recognize that they can be successful in
the long term only if they share success. Each is flexible and willing to
switch between the roles of the leader and follower, performing the role
that best facilitates achieving the goals of the group or organization.

It may be possible, in the short term, for followers to play it safe and do
only what they are told. However, organizations cannot succeed in today's
ambiguous, complex, and rapidly changing global environment if they use
only part of their talent; followers who play it safe are contributing only
part of their talent. To achieve and maintain a competitive advantage, organizations must have leaders who work in partnership with followers to
bring all of their resources to the tasks at hand.

The recent movie *Crimson Tide* brings the notion of partnership to life.
Denzel Washington, in the role of the executive officer, Commander
Hunter, and Gene Hackman, in the role of Captain Ramsey, the commanding officer of the nuclear submarine USS *Alabama,* come into conflict when
Commander Hunter refuses to concur that a "Flash" message, ordering
missile launch, is authentic. The disagreement over what steps to take in the
confusion is loud and public; the events that follow lead Commander
Hunter to relieve his commanding officer. The climax seems to come when
the broken communications equipment is repaired and the message contro-
verting the "fire" order is received. To the inexperienced eye, the courage of
the executive officer is rewarded and the belligerent captain is humiliated.
Such stuff plays well with an American audience distrustful of leaders.

At the court martial that follows as epilogue, however, we are surprised
to learn that although both are technically exonerated, both are also

faulted for failing to work together effectively. From the moment that his new executive officer reported aboard, Captain Ramsey tested Commander Hunter, challenging commitment, understanding, and style. Commander Hunter, for his part, responded professionally but with a streak of independence grounded in openly different values that troubled his skipper. The two never developed trust and understanding. It is clear that neither understood the responsibility to do so. The theme is the same in *The Caine Mutiny* and even *Mutiny on the Bounty*, but there is a new twist.

Earlier studies of the issue of loyalty and command turn on the concept of discipline and good order. In modern times, understanding the perspective of "the other" is added. This theme in fiction is echoed by experience and validated by current research. The U.S. Navy, with the support of management consultants from McBer and Company, has described what it takes to "be the best." Two of the five "requirements" described by Whiteside in a report for the Bureau of Personnel are mid-level leaders who "support top leadership" and "raise issue with top leadership." Discipline is still essential, but understanding allows intermediate leaders to act independently in the best interests of the command, and tough critical thinking brings the best minds to the task of continually improving the effectiveness of any unit. The challenge for leaders, then, is to teach the skills of effective followership and to create the conditions that encourage followers to seek partnership in service to the mission of the organization. The New Professional in today's service must be a full partner—sharing in the responsibility for success and sharing in the rewards of success won through the combined efforts of her or his team. The model that follows offers a tool that should help leaders assess their own strategy for developing effective followers and offers followers a tool for planning their approach to followership.

A Model for Evaluating Followers as Partners

Partners and Other Followers

Our basic assumption is that no one gets up in the morning and goes to work with the intent to fail. Everyone who can survive in the workplace gives what he or she believes will be at least enough effort to keep the job. Likewise, leaders do not intend to purposefully alienate the people on whom they depend. Yet experience and prevailing wisdom have seldom taught followers that those who take the personal initiative to strengthen the relationship with their leaders will be more effective. In fact, efforts to build an effective relationship with the boss are more often understood by both parties as ingratiation and advantage seeking rather than a sincere effort to build an effective partnership. This view may be accurate when the follower pursues a better relationship with the boss without a commitment to high performance. However, the most effective followers are intent on high performance and recognize that they share the responsibility for the quality of the relationship they have with their leaders. More than that, however, they know that they cannot be fully effective unless they work in partnerships that require both a commitment to high performance and a commitment to develop effective relationships with partners (including their boss) whose collaboration is essential to success in their own work.

Taken together, these two dimensions, performance initiative and relationship initiative, define four types of followers who are familiar to military leaders: the subordinate, the contributor, the politician, and the partner.

Follower Styles

Subordinate.   The subordinate is the "traditional" follower who does what he or she is told. This follower is competent at a satisfactory level but is not one to whom the organization looks for leadership or to whom challenging assignments are given. The subordinate keeps a job and may rise in a seniority-driven organization but demonstrates neither a sensitivity to relationships nor a commitment to high performance. The subordinate is the only kind of valued follower in hierarchical organizations that operate only with orders from the top and obedience from the bottom. In organizational settings where this is desired behavior, "good" followers will exhibit these characteristics even when they are fully capable of and even desirous of behaving like individuals described in other quadrants of this analysis. Such is also the likely style of a somewhat or completely disaffected follower who is not interested in giving anything extra or whose job is not one of his or her primary concerns.

Contributor.   This type of follower behaves in an exemplary way, that is, works hard and is known for the quality of his or her work. This person rarely seeks to understand the perspective of the boss, however, and generally waits for direction before turning to new challenges. Although this person is thorough and creative in obtaining resources, information, and skills that are needed to do the job, the interpersonal dynamics of the workplace are not a primary concern. These individuals can develop into full partners by gaining skills and perspectives on the relationship initiative dimension. Alternatively, their valued inclinations can be accommodated and their work value maximized by allowing them to focus on that at which they excel and feel comfortable, removing or minimizing aspects of the job that call for interpersonal relationships with the boss.

Politician.   The politician gives more attention to managing relationships than to maximizing performance. This person "possesses" valued interpersonal qualities that are often misdirected or misunderstood. Followers such as these are unusually sensitive to interpersonal dynamics and are valuable for their ability to contribute when interpersonal difficulties have arisen or might arise. They can provide valuable assistance to the leader because they are willing and able to give insights into group relationships. However, often these followers neglect the defined aspects of their jobs in favor of the more relationship-oriented or political aspects of their relationship with the boss. This is a particular problem when others rely on them for job performance. Politicians can become full partners by focusing on job performance, learning how to balance these two concerns, or they can be accepted as they are and given responsibilities that call primarily for the skills and inclinations they possess.

Partner. The partner is committed to high performance and effective relationships. In fact, the energy given to the development of relationships serves the purpose of gaining the kind of understanding that leads to plans and actions that anticipate new directions and contributions that serve unmet needs. Organizations that anticipate and keep pace with change in the global environment are characterized by leaders who encourage partnership and followers who seek to be partners. (See Figure 13.1.)

Follower Behaviors

These four types of followers can be identified by describing their behavior in terms of two dimensions—performance initiative and relationship initiative—that each have four subscales.

Performance Initiative

Effective partners are committed to high performance. They understand that their future depends on the future of the organization and are not con-

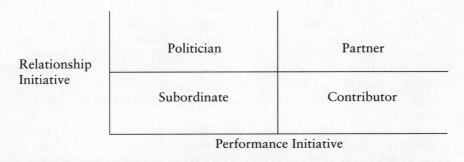

FIGURE 13.1   Follower Styles

tent to simply do what they were asked to do yesterday. At the low end of this scale, one still finds satisfactory performers. At the high end, one finds experts who lead in their fields and whose contributions strengthen the bottom-line performance of the organization. The following subscales describe performance initiative:

Working with Others.   One is able to balance personal interests with the interests of others, discovers common purpose, and draws upon interpersonal skills to support the development of an effective team. One coaches, leads, mentors, shares expertise, and collaborates to accomplish the mission.

Embracing Change.   One is committed to continuous quality improvement, seeks to reduce wasted time and energy, anticipates orders, and leads by example. One acts as a change agent by anticipating and embracing change.

Doing the Job.   One knows what is expected and strives to be the best. Work is an important and integral part of one's life. Satisfaction is derived from applying the highest personal standards.

Self as a Resource.   One understands oneself as a valuable and limited resource and takes care to protect that asset for the future. Such a person avoids both stagnation and burn-out.

Relationship Initiative

Effective partners understand that they share the responsibility for the relationship that defines the partnership. At the low end of this dimension, people take the relationship that they are given. At the high end they work to increase openness and understanding in order to gain a perspective that can inform their choices as a partner. The following subscales describe relationship initiative:

Building Trust.   One works with the intent to build the kind of trust that leads others to give honest feedback, share plans and doubts, and rely on one. Such a person earns the leader's confidence.

Courageous Communication.   One tells the truth when others may not like to hear it in order to serve the goals of the organization and, in the end, those others who have been resistant to the truth. Such a person seeks honest feedback from others and takes risks with self-disclosure.

Identifying with the Leader.   One is loyal to the person whose success is tied to one's own. This person identifies with the leader and takes satisfaction from the leader's success.

Adopting the Leader's Vision.   One understands the limits of personal perspective and seeks to know the perspective of the leader and others in order to work with them effectively. This person has a clear understanding of priorities.

Growing Professionals

Creating the conditions that lead followers to partnership requires first that leaders know what they are looking for in their followers. The model we have described offers this picture. Creating the right conditions for effective followership next requires a clear understanding of practical steps that invite followers to partnership. This example may help readers think about the steps they might take.

The unit inspection is the archetypal military ritual—the symbol of high standards and discipline. For many service members, it is an occasion when someone with a lot of power surveys a lot of people with less power for the purpose of discovering discrepancies that the less powerful must correct. The experience usually carries some anxiety and ends most often with relief. Good officers pride themselves in a reputation for tough inspections. In general, one would not describe the inspection as a partnership—but what if it were?

Everyone involved in the inspection would understand that the purpose was to help all come up to the high standards to which they all aspired. The results of the inspection would provide information that would help the leaders and followers improve. The overall results of the inspection would be seen as information for the commanding officer concerning how effective he or she and other leaders of the command were at teaching the standards. Failure to perform would lead to problem solving in order to discover the underlying reasons for nonperformance, and every member of the command would take pride when all members of the command achieved the highest standards.

If reading this brief scenario causes you to object that this picture could not be real, remember the elite units you have known. Then remember the other inspections you have experienced. When the responsibility for quality and high performance is vested in the hands of the few, it is heavy work. When every member of a command understands and seeks to perform to the same high standards, the load lightens considerably. This is a simple example, but the climate of command is the result of many such "simple" interactions.

The experienced military professional might observe that "sharp" followers never experience anxiety during an inspection. They are good and they know it—and that is the point. Good followers take responsibility for their own performance, seeking to learn the expectations they must meet in the simple and complex tasks they must perform. But good followers had to learn the attitudes and skills that support their independent initiative. The challenge of leadership is to develop in the modern military professional the habit of effective followership; if this challenge is met, the follower will be an effective partner.

References

Boccialetti, Gene. *It Takes Two: Managing Yourself When Working with Bosses and Other Authority Figures*. San Francisco: Jossey-Bass, 1995.

Cohen, Allan R., and Bradford, David L. *Influence Without Authority*. New York: Wiley & Sons, 1990.

Chaleff, Ira. *The Courageous Follower*. San Francisco: Berrett-Koehler, 1995.

Herman, Stanley M. *A Force of Ones: Reclaiming Individual Power in a Time of Teams, Work Groups and Other Crowds*. San Francisco: Jossey-Bass, 1994.

Kelley, Robert E. *The Power of Followership: How to Create Leaders People Want to Follow and Followers Who Lead Themselves*. New York: Doubleday, 1991.

Kouzes, James M., and Posner, Barry Z. *Credibility: How Leaders Gain and Lose It, Why People Demand It*. San Francisco: Jossey-Bass, 1993.

Noer, David M. *Healing the Wounds: Overcoming the Trauma of Layoffs and Revitalizing Downsized Organizations*. San Francisco: Jossey-Bass, 1993.

Organ, Dennis W. *Organizational Citizenship Behavior: The Good Soldier Syndrome*. Lexington, MA: D.C. Heath, 1988.

Ryan, Kathleen D., and Oestreich, Daniel K. *Driving Fear Out of the Workplace: How to Overcome the Invisible Barriers to Quality, Productivity and Innovation*. San Francisco: Jossey-Bass, 1991.

Sashkin, Marshall, Rosenbach, William E., and Sashkin, Molly G. *Development of the Power Need and Its Expression in Management and Leadership with a Focus on Leader-Follower Relations*. Paper presented at the Twelfth Scientific meeting of the A. K. Rice Institute, Washington, D.C. May 12, 1995.

Whiteside, D. E. *Command and Excellence: What It Takes to Be the Best*. Department of the Navy, Washington, D.C.: Leadership Division, Naval Military Personnel Command, 1995.

14

The Ten Rules of Good Followership

Phillip S. Meilinger

I often discover articles written by great leaders—generals, politicians, even businessmen—that list the properties and attributes of good leadership. These lists are usually similar, noting the importance of intelligence, physical and moral courage, stamina, compassion, and so forth. These characteristics are not only fairly general, but they seem to fall into the *great leaders are born, not made* category.

Moreover, the entire subject of leadership principles always strikes me as a bit grandiose because the authors are usually great men or women who have performed impressive deeds. Although they provide useful advice for those chosen few who will someday command troops in battle or direct the operations of large organizations, what about the rest of us? It occurred to me that there is a subject more relevant to all men and women, regardless of rank or duty position, throughout the military services—followership!

How *does* one become a good follower? This is a responsibility no less important than that of leadership. In fact, it enables good leadership, yet is often ignored. As we dedicate ourselves to service to nation, it is likely most of us will be followers more often than we will be leaders.

For my part, I have over 23 years of military experience taking orders, implementing policy guidance and serving as an intermediate supervisor. Here are my *Ten Rules of Good Followership* gleaned from those years.

Do Not Blame the Boss. Do not blame your boss for an unpopular decision or policy—your job is to support, not undermine. It is insidiously easy to blame an unpopular policy or decision on your superior. "I know this is a dumb idea and a pain for everyone, but that is what the boss wants, sorry." This may garner some affection from your subordinates (al-

Reprinted by permission from *Military Review,* 74:8, (August 1994), pp. 32–37.

though even the lowest one-striper is wise enough to eventually see through such ploys), but it is certainly showing disloyalty to your superior.

Unquestionably, the desire for popularity is strong, but it may have unpleasant side effects that can weaken unit cohesion. One colleague I served with several years ago indulged in periodic gripe sessions with his subordinates in which he would routinely criticize the commander and his decisions in front of the youngest troops. When asked why he was undermining the boss, he replied sanctimoniously that his integrity would not allow him to lie. He thought the policies were idiotic and he had a duty to tell his people how he felt. He said he was exercising "good leadership" by telling the truth as he saw it. Rubbish!

Leadership is not a commodity to be bought at the price of followership. If a subordinate asks you whether or not you agree with a particular decision, your response should be that the question is irrelevant. The boss has decided and we will carry out his orders. That is what good subordinates are expected to do. Loyalty must travel both up and down the chain of command.

Do Not Fight the Boss. Fight with your boss if necessary, but do it in private. Avoid embarrassing situations and never reveal to others what was discussed. Chronologically, this rule should come first, but I felt the above principle so important it deserved priority. Before the decision is made, however, you will generally have the opportunity to express your opinion to the boss. Speak honestly and frankly. Do not be a yes man. There is always a tendency to tell the boss what you think he or she wants to hear. Resist the temptation. In fact, if you have strong reservations about an issue under discussion, you have an obligation to express them. Fight for your people and your organization, but do not roll over on principles or issues that you believe are detrimental to the unit's mission accomplishment.

As a rule of thumb, you should be willing to revisit an issue three times. Do not give up after the first discussion or even the second if you are in earnest (not considered here are decisions that are illegal or immoral; there are other avenues to resolve those issues). Remember, do this in private. A weekly staff meeting is not the time to challenge the boss, because human nature will take over and your stance may be seen as a threat, making the boss dig in his heels. However, if you are able to sway a decision or deflect a policy, it will be natural to boast to your troops about it. Once again, you may have just won points for yourself but at the expense of your superior.

Use Initiative. Use initiative—make the decision and then run it past the boss. No one likes to work for a micro-manager. We all believe we are smart enough and mature enough to get the job done without someone hovering around and providing detailed guidance. There is another side to that coin. One reason commanders become micro-managers is because they see their subordinates standing by and waiting for specific instructions.

They then feel obliged to provide them. You can short-circuit this debilitating spiral by showing initiative, accomplishing the task and then backbriefing the boss on what you did. Very few people actually like to be bombarded with problems that require them to devise solutions. Even the most "hands-on" supervisors would generally prefer that someone present them with a workable plan and ask for their ratification. Help the boss out by taking a load off his mind. A word of warning here, though: you may have to know your boss fairly well before you begin showing too much initiative. There is a fine line between seizing the moment to get something done and becoming a "loose cannon." You do not want to gain a reputation for the latter. In sum, always try to provide answers and not questions. As trust and understanding develop between you and the boss, begin acting on those answers once you have arrived at them. Then tell the boss what you have done. Initiative is something I always look for in subordinates, but as the next rule notes, it is often in short supply.

Accept Responsibility.   Accept responsibility whenever offered. When I was in basic training, an instructor gave me what he thought was sage and sane advice—do not volunteer for anything. It took me several years to realize his suggestion was worthless. The military, or any top-flight organization, cannot work effectively or continue to grow and evolve unless it is composed of risk takers willing to assume responsibility. This can be difficult because no one wishes to risk failure or embarrassment. Most of us have experienced self-doubt and received healthy doses of humility along the way that often caused us to hold back when a challenge was offered. I used to worry about feeling unworthy whenever given a new task and would ask, "Will I measure up?" Then I read the memoirs of former Air Force chief of staff and war hero General Curtis LeMay. His comment that he had never been given a job that he felt qualified to handle put my mind at rest. Nonetheless, the fear of failure is real and must be overcome.

While working at the Pentagon in 1990 during the Persian Gulf crisis, there was a flurry of activity as we scrambled to devise a suitable response to Saddam Hussein's aggression. During those hectic days, I often saw leadership and responsibility lying on the table waiting to be picked up by anyone who wanted it. I was amazed at how few people were willing to walk over and grasp it. The reasons given were plausible: "It's not my job," "That's above my pay grade" or "I'm not an expert in that area," but they were rationalizations, not reasons. The call to glory came, but few were listening. Be a risk taker, accept responsibility, volunteer.

Tell the Truth and Do Not Quibble.   Your boss will be giving advice up the chain of command based on what you say. Mighty oaks from little acorns grow. The same could be said for major miscalculations that were based on minor indiscretions. Another unfortunate human reaction is to hide or cover up mistakes before they are discovered by others. When asked if you accomplished a certain task, wrote a point paper, made a phone call, reserved a conference room—and you have not done so—the temptation is great to respond affirmatively, curse softly and hurriedly complete what you had forgotten to do earlier.

Such instances of deceit are minor and not likely to cause misfortune, but it is not hard to imagine how similar white lies can easily become magnified. Take the example of an alert aircraft that is being checked out following a minor maintenance problem. You "fudge" by reporting the aircraft as mission capable in order to avoid telling the commander you are not ready to respond to an alert condition. Your nightmare begins if an alert is declared before that aircraft is ready. In organizations as large and multi-layered as the military services are today, each level must scrupulously adhere to the truth. If each supervisor exaggerates unit achievements or capabilities even a little, the combined error of the message will be enormous by the time it reaches the boss. We have all seen examples of this phenomenon, but the most publicized recently are those regarding procurement programs for new weapon systems where wishful thinking and sloppy reporting allowed things to get out of control. Because those at all levels bent the truth or told the boss what he wanted to hear, great harm was done to the nation and the military's reputation.

Do Your Homework.   Give your boss all the information needed to make a decision. Anticipate possible questions. Being a good staff officer is harder than it looks—do your homework. When given a problem to solve by the boss, you must become an expert on the subject before you attempt to propose a course of action. Read up on the issue, talk to the offices that will be affected by the decision, pulse your network of friends and co-workers to gain insights—in short, do your homework! Most important, think through the implications of the problem, what it means and whom it affects, not just now but down the road. Anticipate the type of questions your boss will ask and prepare suggested answers. Be creative here. Ask the second- and third-level questions, not just the obvious ones. Remember, if your boss will be taking this proposal to his boss, you must prepare him properly to avoid his being embarrassed (guess who pays for that). You might find it surprising how often your supervisor will rely on you to actually make policy.

Upon arriving for a tour at the Pentagon, I was told my task would be "to lead the generals." Few flag rank officers have the time to study closely all of the dozens of issues they are confronted with each day. Consequently, they will expect you to become the subject matter expert and propose the appropriate courses of action. More often than not they will listen to your recommendation.

Suggestion Implementation.   When making recommendations, remember who will probably have to implement them. This means you must know your own strengths and limitations. Once you have finished studying a problem in depth and are about to make a recommendation you want the boss to ratify, remember that you will likely be tasked to implement your own suggestion. After all, who can better carry out a policy than the person who just became an expert on it? In other words, do not propose solutions that are impracticable. It is one thing to recommend a course of action that is designed for an ideal world, but quite another to suggest something that is workable under prevailing circumstances and constraints. This does not imply that you always look for easy fixes or latch on to the lowest common denominator. Yet, there is a calculus you must make that will reveal whether the ideal solution is worth the effort or if a 90-percent solution might be more efficient. Be prepared to brief the perfect answer, but note how much extra it will cost. At the same time, bear in mind your own role in this process, as it is crucial to have a clear understanding of your weaknesses as well as your strengths. Some people are originators, while others are organizers. Some are drivers, others are facilitators. Some work better in groups, others perform more successfully alone. Know who you are and put yourself in positions that maximize your strengths while masking your limitations. This will make you a more successful subordinate.

Keep the Boss Informed. Keep the boss informed of what is going on in the unit. People will be reluctant to tell him or her their problem and successes. You should do it for them and assume someone else will tell the boss about yours. One thing you will notice as you advance in rank and responsibility is that people will be less inclined to talk to you. As a result, what you hear about the unit may be heavily filtered. Staying informed on the true state of affairs is a constant but essential challenge. Subordinates who routinely drop the boss notes or mention tidbits in passing can really help a boss stay in touch.

Most of us feel a bit uneasy about blowing our own horn to the boss. If something important happens in our life or career, we are embarrassed to tell anyone for fear it will sound self-serving. Similarly, we hesitate to mention our troubles, because it sounds like we are complaining. Humility is an attractive virtue. That is when we need to take care of each other. Tell the boss about your co-workers' successes and assume they will reciprocate for you. This type of mutual support helps build esprit and cohesion within a unit. At the same time, remember that the boss needs to know everything that is going on—the bad as well as the good. If there are problems in the unit, do not let the boss be last to know. Most difficulties can be short-circuited and solved quickly if the boss knows about them. Keep him informed.

Fix Problems as They Occur. If you see a problem, fix it. Do not worry about who gets the blame or praise. Army Chief of Staff General George C. Marshall commented that there was no limit to the amount of good people could accomplish as long as they did not care who received the credit. Although this rule might look similar to my earlier calls for initiative and accepting responsibility, my point here is to stress selflessness. When you see something has gone wrong or is about to go wrong, fix it. Too often we notice a bad situation developing and shake our heads and mumble "it's not my problem." It is our problem. Do not get wrapped around the axle wondering if you are directly affected by the problem or if you stand to benefit from its solution. We all serve for the greater good, so every time difficulties are straightened out, we, our unit and the service are better off.

As you can tell by now, I am an optimist who truly believes that good deeds will eventually be rewarded. The military, in particular, is an equal opportunity society that recognizes and responds to merit. It is not necessary to have the attitude of one major league baseball player of whom it was said "he'd give you the shirt off his back; then call a press conference to announce it to the world."

The essence of military life is teamwork. Do your job quietly, confidently and professionally, and trust your colleagues to do likewise. But if you do come across a problem, just go ahead and take care of it. We are all in this together.

Put in an Honest Day's Work.   Put in more than an honest day's work, but never forget the needs of your family. If they are unhappy, you will be too, and your job performance will suffer accordingly. Americans believe in hard work. It is a matter of great pride for us that we have a strong work ethic and are among the most productive societies in the world. The military is certainly no exception.

It has always been an honor for me to be associated with military men and women, of all ranks and services, because I am constantly amazed at how hard working, conscientious and dedicated they are. That is a high standard to maintain and why I exhort all of you to give more than an honest day's labor, but be careful not to become a "workaholic" and let your job become your life. Certainly, there will be times in war, crisis situations or during inspection visits when you will have to double your work efforts. Do not make a habit of this and do not let your subordinates either. There was a popular T-shirt a few years back that stated: "If mama ain't happy, ain't nobody happy." That's the way it was in my house growing up and still is. In addition, if things are miserable at home, you will probably bring those troubles to the office. Your family is married to the service every bit as much as you are. They, too, must pick up and move, change jobs and schools, leave friends behind and start over with each new assignment. That periodic turmoil exacts a price from them. Make sure you pay your family back for all they have done for you and your career. Remember, families are forever.

There are my 10 rules of good followership. All of us are subordinate to someone, and learning how to serve our boss well is an important responsibility. If we can master this task, and master it well, then we in turn will be better leaders when the challenge comes. After all, even our greatest military leaders started at the bottom. We must learn to follow before we can lead. I hope you find these thoughts useful in your own professional journey.

15

Followers Make Good Leaders Good

Warren Bennis

It is probably inevitable that a society as star-struck as ours should focus on leaders in analyzing why organizations succeed or fail. As a long-time student and teacher of management, I, too, have tended to look to the men and women at the top for clues on how organizations achieve and maintain institutional health. But the longer I study effective leaders, the more I am persuaded of the under-appreciated importance of effective followers.

What makes a good follower? The single most important characteristic may well be a willingness to tell the truth. In a world of growing complexity, leaders are increasingly dependent on their subordinates for good information whether the leaders want to hear it or not. Followers who tell the truth, and leaders who listen to it, are an unbeatable combination.

Movie mogul Samuel Goldwyn seems to have had a gut-level awareness of the importance of what I call "effective backtalk" from subordinates. After a string of box-office flops, Mr. Goldwyn called his staff together and told them: "I want you to tell me exactly what's wrong with me and M.G.M., even if it means losing your job."

Although Mr. Goldwyn wasn't personally ready to give up the ego-massaging presence of "yes men," in his own gloriously garbled way he acknowledged the company's greater need for a staff that speaks the truth.

Like portfolios, organizations benefit from diversity. Effective leaders resist the urge to people their staffs only with others who look or sound or think just like themselves, what I call the doppleganger, or ghostly-double, effect. They look for good people from many molds, and then they encourage them to speak out, even to disagree. Aware of the pitfalls of institutional unanimity, some leaders wisely build dissent into the decision-making process.

Organizations that encourage thoughtful dissent gain much more than a heightened air of collegiality. They make better decisions. In a recent study, Rebecca A. Henry, a psychology professor at Purdue University, found that groups were generally more effective than individuals in making forecasts of sales and other financial data. And the greater the initial disagreement among group members, the more accurate the results. "With more disagreement, people are forced to look at a wider range of possibilities," Ms. Henry said.

Like good leaders, good followers understand the importance of speaking out. More important, they do it. Almost 30 years ago, when Nikita Khrushchev came to America, he met with reporters at the Washington Press Club. The first written question he received was: "Today you talked about the hideous rule of your predecessor, Stalin. You were one of his closest aides and colleagues during those years. What were you doing all that time?" Khrushchev's face grew red. "Who asked that?" he roared. No one answered. "Who asked that?" he insisted. Again, silence. "That's what I was doing," Mr. Khrushchev said.

Even in democracies where the only gulag is the threat of a pink slip, it is hard to disagree with the person in charge. Several years ago TV's John Chancellor asked former Presidential aides how they behaved on those occasions when the most powerful person in the world came up with a damned fool idea. Several of the aides admitted doing nothing. Ted Sorenson revealed that John F. Kennedy could usually be brought to his senses by being told, "That sounds like the kind of idea Nixon would have."

Quietism, as a more pious age called the sin of silence, often costs organizations—and their leaders—dearly. Former President Ronald Reagan suffered far more at the hands of so-called friends who refused to tell him unattractive truths than from his ostensible enemies.

Nancy Reagan, in her recent memoir, *My Turn*, recalls chiding then-Vice President George Bush when he approached her, not the President, with grave reservations about White House chief of staff Donald Regan.

"I wish you'd tell my husband," the First Lady said. "I can't be the only one who's saying this to him." According to Mrs. Reagan, Mr. Bush responded, "Nancy, that's not my role."

"That's exactly your role," she snapped.

Nancy Reagan was right. It is the good follower's obligation to share his or her best counsel with the person in charge. And silence—not dissent—is the one answer that leaders should refuse to accept. History contains dozens of cautionary tales on the subject, none more vivid than the account of the murder of Thomas à Becket. "Will no one rid me of this meddlesome priest?" Henry II muttered, after a contest of wills with his former friend.

The four barons who then murdered Becket in his cathedral were the antithesis of the good followers they thought themselves to be. At the risk of being irreverent, the right answer to Henry's question—the one that would have served his administration best—was "No," or at least, "Let's talk about it."

Like modern-day subordinates who testify under oath that they were only doing what they thought their leader wanted them to do, the barons were guilty of remarkable chutzpa. Henry failed by not making his position clear and by creating an atmosphere in which his followers would rather kill than disagree with him. The barons failed by not making the proper case against the king's decision.

Effective leaders reward dissent, as well as encourage it. They understand that whatever momentary discomfort they experience as a result of being told from time to time that they are wrong is more than offset by the fact that reflective backtalk increases a leader's ability to make good decisions.

Executive compensation should go far toward salving the pricked ego of the leader whose followers speak their minds. But what's in it for the follower? The good follower may indeed have to put his or her job on the line in the course of speaking up. But consider the price he or she pays for silence. What job is worth the enormous psychic cost of following a leader who values loyalty in the narrowest sense?

Perhaps the ultimate irony is that the follower who is willing to speak out shows precisely the kind of initiative that leadership is made of.

PART FOUR

Climate, Culture, and Values

And in the end, through the long ages of our quest for light, it will be found that truth is still mightier than the sword. For out of the welter of human carnage and human weal the indestructible thing that will always live is a sound idea.
—General Douglas MacArthur

The leadership climate is one where followers have set expectations for their leaders and the leader demands certain responses from his or her followers. When we say there is effective leadership, we mean there is a climate that supports the leader and the actions that result from shared decisions. Simply put, the leader's personality sets the tone and creates the climate. If the leader is a good communicator, there will be openness and candor in organizational information exchanges. When a leader has integrity, the organization will reflect strong values. A leader who works hard and sets high expectations will create a climate where people give their best and know what it takes to be superior. When leaders stand by their people and allow them to make mistakes, which are seen as learning experiences, the organization will be known for risk taking and innovation.

Just walking about an organization, an astute observer gets a sense of the leadership climate. How people treat each other and what they say tell us a great deal about the leader and the responses of the followers. In a sense, this is the "personality" of the organization. Successful organizations reflect optimism and confidence. Organizations in trouble communicate fear and uncertainty. The style of leadership sets the stage for organization climate.

There is a unique culture in the military as well as in each of the armed forces. Characterized by tradition, the mores, norms, and socialization reflect a unique set of social patterns that are at once a strength and a shortcoming. Organizational culture is a set of shared assumptions, beliefs, and values that form the basis for individual and collective behaviors. Perhaps the best articulation of the special culture of the military are those famous words *duty, honor, and country.* Men and women entering the military know that it will be different from the lives they left. Those who are in the military know that they are set apart from the rest of society.

Leadership in the military is bound by a defined chain of command. Although not unlike corporate organizations, the military places more emphasis on rank in the work setting (and often in social environments); thus one cannot escape that there are special responsibilities that go along with being a leader in the military. There is a culture that is communicated through stories, rituals, and symbols, and it is one that is implicit as well as explicit.

Self-knowledge is based upon values; self-confidence is the behavioral outcome of knowing and believing in one's values. Our values play a large part in determining the type of follower or leader we are. Leaders reveal their values in the way they make decisions, the way they work with people, the choices they make in routine and unusual situations, and the people and actions they reward. Thus, good leadership is marked by a congruency between actions and words. People know our values by observing the consistency of what we do with what we say.

Leaders must understand their values *and* the values of their followers. We find, for example, that generational differences create some interesting problems. Ranking officers and senior noncommissioned officers often hold to values such as always giving one's best, accepting any assignment out of duty, welcoming competition, and striving constantly for the top command positions. Some of the junior officers and younger noncommissioned officers may, with equal fervor, seek the minimum acceptable standards of performance (while meeting those standards quite well), expect assignments that provide a desirable quality of life, prefer cooperation over competition, and be content to remain in a particular job or rank throughout their careers.

It is important to recognize that there are distinct groups within the military that represent subcultures with a unique pattern of values and philosophy that is not inconsistent with the dominant values and philosophy of the military. In contrast, countercultures have a pattern of values and philosophy that outwardly rejects those of the larger military organization. For example, the first week of President Clinton's presidency (1993), the press was filled with arguments over whether homosexuals should be allowed to state their sexual preference and still serve in the military. Some argued it was time to be more inclusive; others were shocked and morally outraged. Each side claimed the other was a minority counterculture.

Whereas the continued existence of countercultures is damaging to organizations, very large organizations, including the military, import potentially important subculture groups from our larger society. The leadership implication is in the relevance the subgroups have to the organization as a whole. At one extreme, leaders can merely accept the subcultures and work within the confines of the larger culture. At the other extreme, leaders can value diversity but systematically work to block the transfer of societal-based subcultures into the fabric of the organization.

If one set of values is accepted to the exclusion of others, there may be high turnover and conflict. More important, it will be difficult to create a sense of ownership in shared goals; it will be impossible to build cohesive teams. We need to understand and appreciate a diversity of values, molding unit structures and processes in ways that permit individuals to work together—no matter the gender, age, or cultural background. Values that differ from our own are neither bad nor good; they are just different and should be recognized as such. Critics lament the "good old days" when a person's values were predictable. We believe that effectiveness can be achieved in a variety of ways and that allowing people to live their values will permit them to contribute in meaningful ways.

The articles that follow provide some guidelines for climate, culture, and values. The common theme is that although what we say makes a difference, our actions clearly communicate our values and set the climate and culture of the organization we lead. Study the issues and reflect upon your values—what they are and how you live them. By examining your own actions, you may get a better insight as to how you might be more effective as a leader.

Setting Standards

In "The Credibility Factor: What People Expect of Leaders" (Chapter 16), James Kouzes and Barry Posner note that successful leadership depends more on the followers' perceptions of the leader than the leader's own perceptions. Honesty, competency, vision, and inspiration are the four characteristics that make up a leader's credibility. The authors suggest that credibility is earned over time but always remains fragile. Five fundamental actions help build credibility: knowing your constituents, standing up for your beliefs, speaking with passion, leading by example, and conquering yourself. Kouzes and Posner affirm that self-confidence comes from two sources: knowledge and integrity.

Sergeant First Class Douglas Ide presents a view from a senior noncommissioned officer that is quite similar to the one expressed in the previous article. In "Lessons on Leadership" (Chapter 17), courage, candor, competence, and commitment are described as the basic leadership traits. SMA Richard Kidd is interviewed about his perspectives on leadership. He believes that the leader must set the example with his or her actions. Trust is the key and is ratified by example. By example, values are communicated. Leadership is recognizing the responsibilities one has to the others in the unit or organization.

The importance of ethical behavior in climate and culture is outlined in Major Reed Bonadonna's piece, "Above and Beyond: Marines and Virtue Ethics" (Chapter 18). He notes that most modern military ethics are rule centered. However, Bonadonna's preference is for virtue ethics, and he suggests that there are probably three criteria in making decisions of ethical importance: the rules, the consequences, and our own traits. Virtue ethics have more relevance because they are adaptable to different situations, they have the ability to apply motive, and they can stimulate us to do more than what is defined as our duty.

Lt. Col. Karen Dunivin addresses contemporary issues in her "Military Culture: Change and Continuity" (Chapter 19). With a framework of U.S. military culture, she compares the traditional model with an evolving model. Inclusion replaces exclusion, egalitarianism replaces separatism, and tolerance replaces hostility. Dunivin notes that conservatism, moralism, combat, and the masculine warrior elements remain the same in both models. With most social change in the military externally imposed, she notes that an evolving model is challenging the military with women in combat and homosexuals in the military (issues we address in Part 5). Dunivin advances that the military must challenge the male-only paradigm and the traditional combat-only identity. Her ultimate concern is that the military retain its culture within the social framework in which it exists rather than becoming a counterculture.

Finally, Lt. Gen. Walter Ulmer updates his original essay, "Leaders, Managers, and Command Climate" (Chapter 20). He defines climate in terms of the leader's example and the standards of performance expected in the group or organization. How well people adapt to the climate can be evaluated by peer and subordinate ratings as well as traditional performance evaluations. Ulmer believes that the command climate can be changed by altering the leadership and managerial habits of senior officers, for they are the ones who set the standards of performance. It is still the combination of leadership and management that moves from routine good intentions to routine best practice that will make a difference. He advocates credible standard methods for evaluating command climate to enhance leader development.

A small mind is obstinate. A great mind can lead and can be led.
                                                              —Alexander Cannon

16

The Credibility Factor:
What People Expect of Leaders

James M. Kouzes
and Barry Z. Posner

What you have heard about leadership is only half the story. Leadership is not only about leaders, but about followers, or better yet constituents. Successful leadership depends far more upon the constituent's perception of the leader than upon the leader's own perceptions. Constituents determine when someone possesses the qualities of leadership.

Unfortunately, most writings about leadership ignore the constituent. We know what Lee Iacocca, Harold Geneen, Donald Trump, Roger Smith, Harvey Mackay and other executives say about leadership. But what do their constituents have to say about the subject?

What Do People Admire in Leaders?

Honesty in Leaders

In every survey we conducted, honesty was selected more often than any other leadership characteristic. Honesty is the most essential requirement for leadership. After all, if we are willingly to follow someone, whether it be into battle or into the boardroom, we first must assure ourselves that the person is worthy of our trust. But how is something as subjective as honesty measured? Whatever leaders may say about their integrity, honesty, or ethical practices, constituents will judge leaders by their deeds.

Adapted with permission from Kouzes, James M. and Posner, Barry Z., *The Leadership Challenge: How to Get Extraordinary Things Done in Organizations.* Copyright © 1987 Jossey-Bass Inc., Publishers.

People consider leaders honest when the leaders do what they say they are going to do. Agreements not followed through, false promises, coverups, and inconsistency between word and deed are all indicators that an ostensible leader is not honest.

Competency Ranks High

The leadership attribute chosen next most frequently is competence. To enlist in another's cause, we must believe that person is capable and effective. If we doubt the leader's abilities, we are unlikely to enlist in the crusade.

Leadership competence does not necessarily refer to the leader's technical abilities in the core technology of the business. The abilities to challenge, inspire, enable, and encourage must also be demonstrated if leaders are to be viewed as capable.

The competence we look for also varies with the leader's position and the condition of the organization. For example, the higher the rank of the leader, the more people demand to see abilities in strategic planning and policymaking. At the line function level, where subordinates expect guidance in technical areas, these same abilities will not be enough.

We have come to refer to the kind of competence needed by leaders as *value-added competence*. Functional competence may be necessary, but it is insufficient. The leader must bring some added value to the position.

A Forward-Looking Vision

Over half of our respondents selected "forward-looking" as one of their most sought-after leadership traits. People expect leaders to have a sense of direction and a concern for the future of the organization.

Senior executives affirm their managerial colleagues' requirement of vision for leadership. A study we conducted of 284 senior executives found "developing a strategic planning and forecasting capability" as the most critical concern. These same senior managers, when asked to select the most important characteristics in a CEO, cited "a leadership style of honesty and integrity" first, followed by "long-term vision and direction."

Forward-looking does not mean possessing the magical power of a visionary. The reality is far more down to earth; it is the ability to set or select a desirable destination for the organization.

It is the vision of a leader—the magnetic north—that sets the course. A leader's "vision" is, in this way, similar to an architect's model of a new building or an engineer's prototype of a new product. It is an ideal image of a unique future for the common good.

The Inspirational Quotient

It is not enough for our leaders to dream about the future. They must be able to communicate the vision in ways that encourage us to sign on for the duration.

Some people react with discomfort to the idea that "inspiring" is an essential leadership quality. They say, "I don't trust people who are inspiring"—no doubt in response to past crusaders who led their followers to death or destruction. Other executives are skeptical of their ability to inspire others and, therefore, dismiss the quality as unnecessary.

In the final analysis, it is essential that leaders inspire our confidence in the validity of the goal. Enthusiasm and excitement signal the leader's personal commitment to pursuing that dream. If a leader displays no passion for a cause, why should others care?

The Credibility Factor

Put together, these four characteristics offer clear insight into the foundation of leadership from the constituent's perspective. These characteristics are generally the basis of what social scientists and communications experts refer to as "credibility." What we found in our investigation of admired leadership qualities was that, more than anything, we want leaders who are credible.

When we believe a leader is credible—when we believe he or she is honest, competent, has a sense of the future and personal conviction about the path—then we somehow feel more trusting and secure around that leader. And more willing to commit and work hard to achieve a shared vision.

Credibility, however, is extremely fragile. It takes years to be earned, growing through persistent, consistent, patient exhibition of the four most admired leadership qualities. Yet credibility can be lost with one thoughtless remark, inconsistent act, or one broken agreement.

Actions Speak Louder Than Words

Leadership is a unique and special bond between leaders and their constituents. The development of this relationship requires our constant attention. Credibility is earned, not conferred by title or position. The following are five fundamental actions we have found that help build credibility:

1. *Know Your Constituents*. Building any relationship begins with getting to know those we desire to lead. Find out what is important to your constituents. Only in this way can you show them how their interests can be served by aligning them with yours.

A recent study points out that the ability—or inability—to understand other people's perspectives is the most glaring difference between successful and unsuccessful managers. How do you get to know the aspirations of others? There's no substitute for spending time with and listening to your constituents.

2. Stand Up for Your Beliefs. In our culture we tend to appreciate people who clearly take a position. We resolutely refuse to follow people who lack confidence in their own decisions. People feel stress when confused about what you stand for; not knowing what you believe leads to conflict, indecision, and political rivalry.

There is, however, a danger in always standing on principle. It can make you rigid and insensitive, precisely the attributes that lead to derailment and termination. The key to escaping rigidity is to remain open to others and to new information.

3. Speak with Passion. To gain the commitment of others you must communicate your excitement about the dream. If the leader is a wet match, there will be no spark to ignite passion in others. Effective leadership means delivering the message in a way that lives and breathes. Napoleon is reported to have said, "If you want to lead the people, you must first speak to their eyes." Paint word pictures. Tell stories. Relate anecdotes. Weave metaphors. Enable others to see, hear, taste, smell, and feel what you experience. Martin Luther King, Jr. taught the world that when the dream lives inside others, it lives forever.

4. Lead by Example. Leaders are role models. We look to them for clues on how we should behave. We believe their actions over their words, every time.

If you ask others to observe certain standards, then you need to live by the same rules. That is exactly what we were told many times by exemplary leaders: You can only lead by example.

Leadership is not a spectator sport. Leaders don't sit in the stands and watch. But hero myths aside, neither are leaders in the game substituting for the players. Leaders coach. They show others how to behave, on and off the field. You demonstrate to others what is important by how you spend your time, by the priorities on your agenda, by the questions you ask and the people you see.

5. Conquer Yourself. Jim Whitaker was the first American to reach the summit of Mt. Everest. He learned from his experience that "You never conquer a mountain. Mountains can't be conquered," he told us. "You conquer yourself—your hopes, your fears."

The real struggle of leadership is internal. Do you understand what is going on in your organization and the world in which it operates? Are you prepared to handle the problems the organization is facing? Can you make the right decision? Where should the organization be headed? These and more make up the internal struggle of leadership.

This everyday struggle places enormous stress upon the leader. We will not place our confidence in someone who appears weak, uncertain, or lacking in resolve. People need to sense that the leader's internal struggle—if they know it to exist—has been fought and won.

What Is a Leader to Do?

The self-confidence required to lead has at its core two sources: knowledge and integrity.

Conquering yourself means learning about yourself—your skills and inadequacies, beliefs and prejudices, talents and shortcomings. Self-confidence develops as you build on strengths and overcome weaknesses.

Self-confidence also comes with worldliness. The leader is usually the first to encounter the world outside the boundaries of the organization. The more the leader knows about that world, the easier it is to approach it with assurance. Thus, you should seek to learn as much as possible about the forces that affect your organization, be they political, economic, social, moral, or artistic.

With knowledge of the inner and outer worlds comes an awareness of the competing value systems, of the many different ways to run an organization. The internal resolution of these competing beliefs is what leads to personal integrity. A leader with integrity has one self, at home and at work The late industrialist, John Studebaker, stated it clearly: "To have integrity, the individual cannot merely be a weathervane turning briskly with every doctrinal wind that blows. The individual must possess key loyalties and key convictions which can serve as a basis of judgment and a standard of action."

There is no well-cut path to the future, only wilderness. Strongly held beliefs compel leaders to take a stand and go out in front. Credibility begins with a credo. If, as a leader, you are to have the self-confidence needed to step out into the unknown, you might begin each day by looking in the mirror and asking yourself, "Just what do I stand for?"

17

Lessons on Leadership

SFC Douglas Ide

Courage, candor, competence and commitment. Known as the "four Cs," these are the basic leadership traits that every U.S. Army officer and non-commissioned officer learns early in a career.

SMA Richard Kidd would add one more to the list, though: caring. "They're all Cs anyway," he said with a smile during a recent interview.

Talk to the Army's top enlisted soldier about soldiers and leadership. and the word "caring" pops up again and again. Kidd feels that caring is at the heart of good leadership.

"A leader has to embody all of those things," said Kidd. "That means that they know their job, they're going to be honest about the things they do, and that they have the courage to drive on and do the things that have to be done. I have found that soldiers will do an awful lot for you, for the Army and for the nation, if they feel that someone cares for them. And it's got to be sincere. That's not something you can fake."

Though Kidd has cultivated his opinions over a 32-year Army career, he came by them early on through two junior leaders: a platoon sergeant and a captain.

Sgt. Lee Santerre, one of Kidd's first platoon sergeants, "embodied what we now say a leader should be," he said. "The other platoon sergeants were some of those who would tell you what you should do, kind of the 'Don't do what I do, do what I tell you to do.' He came in and said, 'Here's what we should do.' Everything was we," said Kidd. "He set the example, he led in everything we did."

Capt. Charles H. Fry was a former special forces NCO whom Kidd served under in Vietnam. Kidd was amazed at how the captain understood soldiers.

Reprinted with permission of the author and *Soldiers,* the official magazine of the U.S. Army, 50:2 (February 1995), pp. 18–20.

"He knew the pressure they were under. He knew how to push them to the very limits of their abilities, physically and mentally. Yet he understood how they felt and he was in the middle of it and they knew he cared."

That the two came early in Kidd's career was no fluke. Kidd believes that the junior-level leader is one of the most important in the Army.

"You can lose a young soldier very early on," he said. "Soldiers have left the Army because their leader never took the time just to pat them on the back and say, 'I appreciate what you're doing. We sure could use you. It'd be nice if you'd stay in our great Army because you're doing a great job.'"

Soldiers often leave the Army because they feel that somebody wanted to "get the most out of them, but didn't care about them as individuals," Kidd said.

That's why Kidd is a strong proponent of leadership training early in a soldier's career, both through the NCO Education System and through the example set by more senior leaders. Soldiers are told to find a good leader and then emulate that leader, said Kidd. That means there must be good leaders to emulate. Good leaders breed good leaders: it's a continual evolutionary process, he said.

"As you grow and progress in rank, you wind up being in charge of other leaders," said Kidd. "One of the ways that we challenge the more junior leaders is to put another example up in front of them of how to handle more leadership, how to handle more responsibility, how to be a mentor for somebody."

While soldiers should look to their leaders for guidance, leaders need look no further than their own soldiers for a measure of what kind of leader they are, said Kidd.

"They are a manifestation of your leadership abilities. They will demonstrate what your leadership capabilities are," said Kidd. "I forget exactly how the saying goes, but I've always remembered what it meant, and that is: you're never really a leader until you are confirmed by those you lead.

"You can be put in a leadership position, you can go to a leadership school, and after that someone may call you a leader," Kidd continued. "But if the people you lead have not confirmed you as their leader, you're not truly one."

The key to that confirmation, Kidd said, is trust. Soldiers must trust that leaders know what they are doing, he said. Soldiers must trust that leaders will stand up for them, that leaders will give their all before asking soldiers to do so, and that leaders will share soldiers' experiences.

"Trust is essential to a good leader," Kidd said. Soldiers have said that they would follow a leader "into hell and back, and be glad" that they were asked to go, said Kidd, because they trusted that leader.

Leaders cultivate that trust by setting the example, said Kidd. "When you come in and tell a group of soldiers, this is the standard, this is the way we're going to do things, you yourself live those standards. If you espouse certain values. you should live those values."

But not just any values. "If they're not good values, then the trust won't work either," Kidd said. "It's not just that you come in with any kind of trait and live up to it. It has to be something that people hold in high esteem. People value honesty. They value integrity. They value competence and courage and all those kinds of things."

Soldiers will also test a leader before committing that trust, said Kidd. "I think you can count on it," he said. "And they should, because anything worth following, anything worth believing in and putting your total trust and confidence in, should be able to stand up to a test. You now have that position, you have that responsibility. You have to live up to it."

One of the biggest challenges to continually "living up to it," said Kidd, is never losing the proper focus. "That's probably a fine line. Are you truly doing what's best for the nation, what's best for the Army, what's best for your unit, what's best for your soldiers and their families? Are you taking all of that into consideration, or are you looking at what makes you as an individual look the best?

"You have to look at that every time you do something," continued Kidd. Part of making any decision, he said, is thinking what effect it will have on soldiers and their families. "If you didn't even give that any thought, then you may be looking at just what makes you, as an individual, look good."

Kidd uses education as an example. He tells leaders that continuing their education is important, as long as it's "not at the expense of soldiers and their families. As a leader, they are your first priority," he said. "You owe that to them. You owe your first responsibility to them and their families, as well as your own family."

That's an important point, said Kidd, because leaders affect people's lives. "As you grow in leadership, you actually start to understand the magnitude of the responsibility that you have for developing soldiers in a profession that represents your nation and the Army, and one that can be life-threatening," said Kidd.

"I think that as you internalize that, your understanding of leadership grows immensely. It becomes clear that leadership goes back to some of the things you learned as a child, as you were coming up, and that is: treat others as you would have them treat you, be responsible to your god and country. It goes back to things that are very basic."

Leaders go through a time when they understand leadership as just making people do what other people have told them to, said Kidd. Eventually, they progress to an understanding of their responsibilities in helping their soldiers grow, and in looking out for them and their families.

"The main purpose of being a leader is to be someone who cares enough to bring the group together to accomplish a mission successfully, to allow people to grow, to allow people to be safe and to allow them to be able to take care of their families," said Kidd. "This is, really, basically caring enough about people to make sure that they have a good life, and that in the case of combat they will be able to survive. That may not make sense to some, but it sure makes sense to me."

18

Above and Beyond:
Marines and Virtue Ethics

Maj. Reed R. Bonadonna

Past articles in the *Gazette* (Aug 92, Sep 92) have reflected a growing interest in military ethics. My contribution to this discussion will be to outline a practical, military ethic that combines aspects of the three major ethical theories. In this blending of ethical approaches the greatest emphasis will be on a venerable approach to ethics that has had a recent resurgence among philosophers—virtue ethics. My main point will be that such an approach provides a means of resolving the apparent conflict between the "ethics" and the "military" of military ethics. This effort at resolution is necessary, I believe, if we are to maximize our potential as ethical agents.

Virtue ethics have a long history, going back to Aristotle, with glimmerings in Socrates and Plato. Aristotle created a catalog of valuable traits, each of them representing a "golden mean" between less desirable extremes. He warns us to avoid particularly the most attractive extreme. (Some people, for example, may be tempted by parsimony, others by profligacy, both of which deviate from the desirable mean of liberality.) Not all of the virtues are given the same importance. Aristotle also says that we acquire the virtues by practicing them, thereby gaining the habit of virtue. As we might expect of the philosopher who first said, "Man is a political animal," Aristotle's idea of virtue is strongly attached to the social context, to the individual's role in society. But Aristotle's good man is not valued only because he serves the state. He seems to have viewed the virtuous individual as an important product of the society from which he comes. Virtue, to Aristotle, is not just a means to good ends, but an end in itself.

Reprinted by permission from Marine Corps Gazette, 78:1 (January 1994), pp. 18–20.

In more recent times, Aristotelian virtue ethics were eclipsed by two competing ethical theories: rule-centered or deontological ethics, (thanks mostly to Immanuel Kant) and utilitarian, teleological ethics, which were originated by Jeremy Bentham and developed by John Stuart Mill. The first of these says, "Do x because it corresponds to rule y." Utilitarian ethics says, "Do x whenever it will bring about the greatest good for the greatest number."

The people who write about military ethics, mostly philosophers and social scientists, are generally in agreement that utilitarian ethics don't work well in the military setting. Michael Walzer says in *Just and Unjust Wars* that soldiers are often not in a position to judge the "justice and proportionality" of their actions in war. His view is echoed by Sidney Axinn, who lays great stress on *The Law of Land Warfare* (published as FM 27–10) in his recent book *A Moral Military*. These writers believe that an outcome-centered approach may lead all too easily to military expediency as the sole guide to actions in war.

Most modern military ethics are rule centered. We can see why this is the case. The military's job is warfare, and rules give us something solid to cling to in the movement and confusion, the "friction" to use Clauswitz' term, of war. Rules may be codified, published, and (perhaps most important) enforced. Rule-centered ethics seem to be the most unambiguous of the three approaches. But, as straightforward as they may appear, rules may in practice be hard to apply. The debates over the code of conduct that followed the war in Vietnam and the release of the USS Pueblo crew give some indication of this. More important, rule-centered military ethics seem to be better at preventing us from acting poorly than they are at encouraging us to act well.

I have said that my own preference is for virtue ethics. Let me try to explain why. When making decisions of ethical importance we are probably guided by all three criteria: the rules, the consequences, and our own traits. (The idea of blending traits and principles is familiar to Marines from our instructions in leadership.) In practice, decisions of ethical importance are often made on utilitarian grounds, with rules serving as a kind of "fail safe." But virtue ethics may be said to provide both the underpinnings for these decisions and to pick up where the other approaches leave off. I make this claim for virtue ethics for three reasons: (1) their adaptability to situations, (2) their ability to provide a motive (and not just a rationale) for ethical behavior, and (3) their ability to impel us to doings that are supererogatory, i.e., more than duty. I will discuss these advantages one at a time, and attempt to concentrate on their applicability to the military context.

I have already alluded to the rigidity of rule-centered ethics and to the difficulties we encounter with utilitarian ethics. War appears to provide situations where attempts to apply rules or to predict outcomes will be especially difficult or even futile. Actions which involve target engagement, the treatment of enemy prisoners of war, fairness to subordinates, cohesiveness (How much do we forgive in a comrade?) are the difficult stuff of military ethics. Decisions that invoke these issues must also often be made very quickly. Especially in the most difficult situations, it seems to me, the question becomes: "What kind of person do I want to be, and what would such a person do?" Indeed, there may be no time to ask even this question. The answer will have been determined in advance by the personal traits that the individual has acquired up to the moment of crisis.

The second advantage of virtue ethics addresses an objection often raised to all ethics, which is that they tell us how to be good, but provide no incentive to be good. But virtue ethics have us acquiring the habit of virtue by the commission of good actions. The performance of good actions in the face of adversity may never be easy, but we may be better able to face adversity and not abandon our values if we have successfully done so in the past. Certainly the reverse, that we may be demoralized by acting against our own beliefs, can be true. So the reason for the virtuous person to act on his or her virtues might be the sense that something is being created and strengthened (one's own character) with each good action. We have "something to show" for our good action (a courageous one, for example): the increased ability to face future difficult situations and do so honorably. Aside from questions about its validity, there appears to be a pragmatic justification for virtue ethics. We are perhaps more likely to act rightly if we subscribe to virtue ethics, since this will permit us to see good acts as self-perpetuating and, in that sense, self-interested.

The last feature of virtue ethics is the one on which I would like to concentrate. The ethical situation of the military person is not just the fulfilling of minimal obligations like the avoidance of war crimes. Soldiers have been forces for good and, even in the destructive milieu of war, they have often been good people. Ethicists have most often expressed the ethical phenomenon in the military setting as an act of omission: refusing or declining to act on ethical grounds. But, if we accept the premise that some wars are necessary and even just, then military acts of commission (obeying orders, moving, and shooting) may also have moral value. "Military" and "ethics" are not necessarily terms in conflict.

This opens the question, which I have mostly set aside until now, of the value content of ethics. Ethics are not only about the process of arriving at decisions; their essence is value. The cardinal, or moral, virtues are the basis of this value in virtue ethics; these are justice, wisdom, courage, and temperance. To these we might add the theological virtues of faith, hope, and charity. Even when rules are hard to apply and outcomes difficult to foresee the effort to act out of these virtues, and develop them within ourselves, can provide a moral guide.

Virtue ethics cannot be codified in the same way as rule-centered ethics, or put into a narrative, cause and effect form like utilitarian ethics. They are more difficult to depict, so perhaps harder to teach and learn, than the other approaches. Virtues practiced in public set an example, of course; so does the record of the past. Examples of virtue may be found in the figures, both fictional and nonfictional, who people the accounts of war and military life that we are encouraged to read as part of our professional education. Some of the best for this purpose are novels and memoirs. Harry Brown's *A Walk in the Sun* contains the words: "War, without virtue in itself, breeds virtue." His book goes on to show us how this may take place. *If I Die in a Combat Zone* by Tim O'Brien is a long consideration of the nature and value of courage. This work contains references to classical philosophy, as does Michael Norman's *These Good Men*. Norman was in Vietnam with Company G, 2d Battalion, 9th Marines. His efforts to organize a reunion of the survivors of his platoon lead to a consideration of human virtue in adversity.

Of course, when we read for ethical instruction we must do so with a very critical eye. The author's beliefs and assumptions must be interrogated carefully. We must also ask how the author's time was different from our own, since, alongside the continuities of human life, some important things do change. Two works which may help to focus the critical faculty in this subject are *How Should I Live?* by Randolf Feezell and Curtis Hancock and *On Moral Fiction* by John Gardner. Feezell and Hancock are philosophy professors, but their book, which outlines the main trends of ethics, is written in a very accessible style. Gardner's book is a novelist's attempt to understand and explain the ethical underpinnings of fiction. I would be remiss if I did not mention *The Ethics of War* by Barrie Paskins and Michael Dockrill. Theirs is the only book I have found that applies virtue ethics to warfare.

Possible future missions for the Corps, and I am thinking of peacekeeping in particular, would seem to have the potential for foregrounding ethical concerns at the level of the individual Marine and small unit leader. The idea of virtue may also be helpful to our thinking on the higher levels of Marine Corps policy. Many Marines find themselves in a difficult position when the issue of the ban on homosexuals is raised. Most Marines are opposed to any changes, but our position is not always clear to civilians, who are likely to take a utilitarian, or a "rights" centered (Kantian), position in the debate. Part of this difficulty may lie in our perception (to which the Commandant alluded while the issue was being debated in Congress) that to be a Marine isn't just to engage in certain types of actions, nor simply to follow rules. Doing "Marine things" is an expression of a certain type of character. The acts themselves, we recognize, are often largely symbolic. Why have airplane mechanics do close order drill? Such rituals are important, (even if, as in the case of my example, they are rare) because they are expressions and inculcators of soldierly virtue. Such activity is involved in a view of life which most Marines feel is incompatible with that held by the late 20th century American homosexual. This homosexual view could perhaps be described in the terms of virtue ethics as both intemperate and unwise.

Such a characterization may be inaccurate or mistaken, but to declare it simply irrelevant is to divorce military service from one of its significant concomitants: the instilling of character, not only as a means to an end, but as an end desirable in itself.

19

Military Culture:
Change and Continuity

Lt. Col. Karen O. Dunivin

Social scientists commonly use three interrelated concepts—ideal types, models, and paradigms—to study and explain social phenomena (e.g., poverty, crime, culture, and change). This article uses these theoretical concepts to examine both change and continuity in the American military culture.[1] At the risk of oversimplification, the article 1) briefly describes the three concepts; 2) applies each to the current American military culture; and 3) examines how the military's dominant "paradigm" conflicts with its evolving "model" of culture. First, it is important to establish the conceptual framework of analysis.

Theoretical Concepts

An "ideal type" is an abstract definition of some phenomenon in the real world, focusing on its typical characteristics.[2] As abstractions of reality, ideal types do not fit any single case in the real world exactly. Dictionary definitions are ideal types. For example, Webster's dictionary defines "family" as,

> A fundamental social group in society consisting esp. of a man and woman and their offspring; . . . A group of people sharing common ancestry; . . . All the members of a household living under one roof.[3]

This definition, or ideal type, describes a family's typical characteristics to some degree, but it does not necessarily fit the experience of any single family perfectly. In sum, ideal types define social phenomena and thus instill some sense of order in our complex and dynamic social world.

When we conjure up mental pictures of these ideal types, and speculate how well they fit reality, we build "models." Models organize complex ideal types so we can simplify and understand social phenomena.[4] For example, what is the "correct" model of family in America? Is it the traditional model of a married man and woman with their biological offspring? Or a single parent with his/her child(ren)? Or a childless heterosexual or homosexual couple? Each form represents alternative models of the American family. From our construction of family models, we can speculate what shape (i.e., new model) the family may take under certain conditions such as war, divorce, unwed pregnancies, or homosexual couples.

Finally, a "paradigm" is the underlying collection of broad, often unstated, assumptions, beliefs, and attitudes that shape our ideal types and models.[5] A paradigm is a particular perspective or view of the world. As the foundation for our values, attitudes, and notions, paradigms are important because they influence the kinds of ideal types and models we create to explain social phenomena. For example, the American family model is influenced by society's dominant Judeo-Christian religious paradigm. We tend to create and evaluate family models based on common notions and beliefs about monogamous marriage. If we lived in another society, we might use a polygamous marriage paradigm to construct family models.

Unfortunately, analysts use paradigms and models interchangeably, failing to distinguish between the two. For instance, recent defense models propose new U.S. military missions and roles as the world order shifts from a bipolar Cold War to unpredictable regional conflicts throughout the world.[6] While analysts create defense models (often calling them paradigms), they tend to ignore the underlying paradigm (i.e., beliefs and attitudes) that shape the development of their new defense models. It is important to understand that a paradigm and model may not be complementary, the focus of this study.

In summary, these theoretical constructs—ideal types, models, and paradigms—are a useful, analytical way to study and think about complex social phenomena, including culture. With this brief description of the analytical framework, we can apply each concept to military culture.

U.S. Military Culture

Typically, scholars create models to simplify and explain military organization, culture, and social change.[7] However, models are only one-third of the explanatory equation, as noted. Using the three conceptual tools, this article examines the American military culture and explains the emerging conflict between its dominant paradigm and evolving model as it undergoes major social change.

Ideal Type

For this study, "culture" (an ideal type) is defined as, "a way of life that is learned and shared by human beings and is taught by one generation to the next."[8] While cultures differ in form, all cultures possess certain qualities. Specifically, culture is 1) learned from previous generations; 2) broadly shared by members; 3) adaptive to the conditions in which people live; and 4) symbolic in nature—agreed-on symbols help people create order and make sense of their world.[9]

Although military culture is a unique way of life, it fits the definition of "culture" and possesses these four qualities. Military culture is learned (via socialization training such as boot camp); broadly shared by its members (e.g., saluting); adaptive to changing conditions (e.g., integration of blacks); and symbolic in nature (e.g., rank insignia and language jargon make sense only within a military context). To fully comprehend and appreciate military culture one must understand its underlying paradigm.

Paradigm

Military culture is characterized by its combat, masculine-warrior (or CMW) paradigm. First, the military's core activity, which defines its very existence and meaning, is *combat*.[10] Military structures and forces are built around combat activities—ground combat divisions, fighter air wings, and naval aircraft carrier battle groups. The Services organize and train themselves around their combat roles, distinguishing between combat arms and support activities. Since the primary role of the military is preparation for and conduct of war, the image of the military is synonymous with the image of combat.[11]

The second element of the military's cultural paradigm is the *masculine-warrior* image. As an institution comprised primarily of men, its culture is shaped by men. Soldiering is viewed as a masculine role—the profession of war, defense, and combat is defined by society as men's work.[12] Thus, a deeply entrenched "cult of masculinity" (with accompanying masculine norms, values, and lifestyles) pervades military culture.[13] In *Bring Me Men and Women*, Stiehm wrote,

> . . . how can one distinguish between male culture and military culture, and how can one make female culture legitimate in a military setting?[14]

In summary, the combat masculine-warrior paradigm is the essence of military culture. This paradigm persists today even with the presence of "others" (e.g., women and gays) who do not fit the stereotypical image of combatant or masculine warrior.[15] Given this entrenched CMW world view, we can examine two concurrent models of military culture.

Model

Table 19.1 depicts a continuum of military culture. The traditional model is characterized by conservatism: a homogeneous male force, masculine values and norms, and exclusionary laws and policies. At the other end of the spectrum is an evolving model that is characterized by egalitarianism: a socially heterogeneous force, diverse values and norms, and inclusionary laws and policies. Of course, military culture does not fit either model perfectly. However, the evolving model alerts us to emergent trends within military culture.

As theoretical constructs, these models are open to debate. Some may argue that the military is tolerant (or too tolerant) of force diversity and inclusionary policies.[16] Others may contend that the military remains a socially conservative culture that opposes most social change.[17] While there are different opinions of where military culture is along the continuum, the models illustrate change in military culture. First to consider is the traditional model.

Traditional Model of Military Culture

As a reflection of its traditional CMW paradigm, the military has adopted a complementary traditional model of culture (Table 19.1). The military espouses conservative, moralistic ideology as reflected in its ethics and customs. For example, each service academy's honor code ("We will not lie, cheat or steal [nor tolerate those among us who do]") guides the ethical development of cadets and midshipmen in preparation for their service as

TABLE 19.1   U.S. Military Culture

Cultural Variable	Traditional Model	Evolving Model
Ethics/Customs	Conservatism, Moralism	Conservatism, Moralism
Enculturation	Combat	Combat
Laws/Politics	Masculine Warrior	Masculine Warrior
Force Structure	Exclusion	Inclusion
Attitudes	Homogeneity	Heterogeneity
Majority/Minority	Separatism	Egalitarianism
Interactions	Hostility	Tolerance

"officers and gentlemen." It is assumed that officers are honest, trustworthy, and male. Typically, military culture assumes a moralistic tone as well. For instance, service members who oppose gays in the military often argue that homosexuality is a sin, quoting the Bible.

These ethics and customs are supported by conservative laws and policies. Under the Uniform Code of Military Justice (UCMJ), service members may be punished and/or discharged from service for conduct including sodomy, "behavior unbecoming an officer" (e.g., adultery or financial irresponsibility), and fraternization (e.g., friendship between officers and enlisted members).

In addition, the laws and policies tend to be exclusionary, reinforcing its CMW paradigm. For example, previous laws segregated blacks in units commanded by white officers, limited the number of servicewomen in uniform, and prohibited women from performing duties aboard combat ships or aircraft. As an extension of such laws, military policies have excluded women from combat-related roles including flying, infantry, armor, and sea duty.

The military often justifies exclusionary laws and policies on the grounds of preserving combat effectiveness. Proponents argue that combat effectiveness and unit cohesion are best achieved in homogeneous combat units. As a former Marine Corps Commandant noted, "If you want to make a combat unit ineffective, assign women to it."[18]

The exclusionary, universal masculine model of warrior (with its hidden assumption of male normalcy and female deficiency) has evaluative overtones.[19] For example, DoD's Under Secretary of Defense for Personnel and Readiness, Edwin Dorn, in testimony before Congress, noted that combat exclusion laws and policies that restrict women's assignments lead some members to perceive women as inferiors:

> The combat exclusion reflects and reinforces widespread attitudes about the place of women in the military . . . Put bluntly, women may not be regarded as 'real' soldiers until they are able to do what 'real' soldiers do, which is to kill and die in combat.[20]

Finally, the conservative culture promotes enculturation, attitudes, and interactions that complement its CMW paradigm. As a socializing institution, the military reinforces masculine norms and values.[21] In particular, combat arms provide men the opportunity to demonstrate their masculinity, and the warrior role is one way to prove one's manhood. As Arkin and Dobrofsky observed,

> The military operationalizes the equation of masculinity-warrior, not through the process of anticipating maturity but with a more efficient aggressive condi-

tional model of creating the masculine male. Recruits end up internalizing much of the ethos of masculinity.[22]

This "masculine mystique" is evident during basic training when traditional images of independent, competitive, aggressive, and virile males are promoted and rewarded.[23]

In a "cult of masculinity" with a core principle of exclusion, women and homosexuals are viewed as outsiders and deviants in a man's world. Their presence and participation (especially in war) challenge the ancient paradigm of the combat, masculine warrior.[24] As noted in a recent editorial,

> Logically, there is no argument against allowing women to pilot combat aircraft. The real problem lies not with the abilities of women, but in the minds of men such as Gen. Merrill McPeak, Air Force chief of staff. Two years ago, in testimony before Congress, General McPeak admitted that if ordered to choose between an inferior male pilot and a much better female pilot, he would choose the male. 'I admit it doesn't make much sense, but that's the way I feel about it,' he said. In other words, for General McPeak the issue is not job performance or ability, or even military effectiveness. The existence of female combat pilots would simply offend his sense of proper gender roles.[25]

Separatist attitudes (i.e., "they"ism) along with hostile interactions (e.g., sexual harassment or gay bashing) often emerge. Perhaps the most notable manifestations of the "cult of masculinity" are illustrated by two recent incidents: 1) Tailhook '91; and 2) the debate over gays in the military. In both incidents, the attitudes of and interactions among some service members reflect virtual intolerance of "others" who contradict the military's fundamental CMW world view.

In summary, the traditional model of military culture is characterized by an underlying combat, masculine-warrior paradigm, with complementary ethics/customs, laws/policies, force structures, enculturation, attitudes, and interactions. Traditionally, the military has recruited, trained, and rewarded soldiers that embody its CMW ideology—a homogeneous force comprised primarily of white, single, young men who view themselves as masculine warriors. However, times are changing.

Evolving Model

First and foremost, the military still embraces its CMW paradigm. Even with dramatic social change in America and the expansion of military missions and roles beyond traditional combat activities (e.g., disaster and humanitarian relief operations), the military still views itself as the primary instrument of national power whose combat mission, performed by masculine warriors, characterizes its very existence and meaning. Consequently, military ethics and customs still tend to be conservative and moralistic, as described earlier.

The military continues to promote its combat, masculine-warrior image, as evidenced by the Marine slogan, "Every man a rifleman." Similarly, airplanes on display at the Air Force Academy are combat aircraft (e.g., F-l5s, B-52s, F-111s, A-l0s). You will not find cargo or air refueling airframes at this "proving ground." In addition, the sculpted inscription above the archway leading to the Air Force academy reads "BRING ME MEN." Although female cadets have been present nearly two decades, the bold pronouncement continues to send a message to cadets and visitors alike. It also serves as a symbolic reminder of a masculine tradition of days past, and perhaps days present. Finally, it demonstrates an institution's reluctance to shift from a cult of masculinity to cultural diversity.

While we see continuity in the military's CMW paradigm, other dimensions of military culture are changing to some extent, as portrayed by the evolving model (Table 19.1). Laws and policies are more inclusionary, reflecting greater acceptance of "others." For instance, in his Executive Order in 1948, President Truman ordered the "equality of treatment and opportunity for all persons in the armed forces without regard to race, color, religion, or national origin."[26] In addition, laws barring women from duties aboard combat aircraft and ships were repealed by Congress in 1991.[27] And the services have begun to assign women to combat aircraft and ships.

Proponents of inclusionary laws and policies cite social equality and military effectiveness as reasons for change. Dorn observed, "There appears to be a consensus in the United States that the armed forces should be a reflection of the society."[28] In other words, the military should mirror society's social demographic makeup (regional, economic, racial, ethnic, and gender diversity) as well as its core values (e.g., equality and civil rights). Furthermore, these proponents of inclusion advocate full utilization of ability. To them, excluding whole groups of "others" (e.g., women) from combat diminishes the pool of talent available for our nation's defense.

In response to social pressures, the services began revising their exclusionary policies. In 1948, the military began integrating its racially segregated units. In 1971, the military rescinded its policy that involuntarily separated pregnant women; in 1976, the service academies admitted women; in 1993, the Navy proposed opening all jobs, including combat roles, to women. Finally, in April 1993, former Secretary of Defense Les Aspin rescinded exclusionary military policy by directing the services to open assignments in combat aircraft and aboard combat ships to women.[29] As a result, the military's force structure is more heterogeneous in terms of race, ethnicity, and sex. Today, the military is a socially diverse force whose women and minorities perform many nontraditional jobs heretofore performed primarily by white men.

While the transformation to a pluralistic culture is painful at times (e.g., Tailhook '91), some recent signs suggest an improved social climate, at least in the work place. For example, the services conduct training to sensitize soldiers about racial, ethnic, and women's issues. In addition, the services have a zero-tolerance policy which punishes racist and sexist offenders (one could argue how well the services enforce these policies).

Recent survey data suggest changing attitudes as well. A 1992 Roper poll of over 4,400 service members showed that,

> nearly three out of four service people believe combat assignments should go to 'the best-qualified person, regardless of gender.'[30]

Anecdotal evidence also indicates that service members are acutely aware of prejudice in the work place. For the most part, soldiers conscientiously ensure that their words or actions are not construed as racist or sexist. Thus the Services and their members are taking steps to minimize polarization.

Consequently, both institutions and individuals seem more tolerant of "others" as partners in national defense. For example, the recent policy allowing women in combat reflects changing ideas about "combat" as a gender-exclusive role performed only by men. Some egalitarian attitudes also are emerging. As Major C. R. Myers, a male Marine Harrier jet pilot, noted:

> The military has a natural resistance to change; it's a male-dominated kingdom afraid to admit a few . . . that don't necessarily fit the mold. African Americans of past decades probably remember their entry into the military as a less than joyful event, yet they succeeded. . . . To think that women and gays in combat can't do the same is to deny the principle that all men (and women) are created equal. . . . If a woman or gay person is the most qualified candidate, let her or him in.[31]

Is this observed change permanent or temporary? Most social change within the military has been externally imposed. For example, the integration of blacks resulted from Truman's executive order. Women's inclusion at the service academies resulted from strong feminist pressure and legislative mandate.[32] Finally, the increased presence of minorities and women in the military since the early 1970s evolved from external forces: civil rights laws, the women's rights movement, more women entering the labor force, and the creation of the All-Volunteer Force. The military's pattern of incrementalism (e.g., slowly loosening restrictions that exclude "others") demonstrates its equivocation toward social change.[33]

In summary, although military culture still embraces its CMW paradigm with complementary ethics, customs, and socialization processes, other dimensions of military culture—inclusionary laws/policies, diverse force structures, and improved attitudes and interactions—reflect some social change. However, the evolving model of military culture contradicts the fundamental CMW paradigm.

Conflict Between Paradigm and Model

In a recent interview, former Secretary of Defense Aspin remarked that he asks three questions when facing a tough issue: 1) what is the fight really about; 2) who will win and who will lose; and 3) what are the true implications?[34] We apply each question to assess military culture as it undergoes major social change.

What's the Fight Really About? The present "battle" is between the military's evolving model of culture, which is out of sync with its underlying combat, masculine-warrior paradigm. Current social change challenges the very heart of the military because it undermines the military's core CMW paradigm. As previously noted, paradigms are important because they shape the kinds of models we create. In the case of military culture, the CMW paradigm influences how the military views soldiering and how it organizes, equips, and trains its soldiers. However, in order to survive and thrive, cultures and institutions must adapt to changing conditions—the evolving model of military culture reflects this evolutionary adaptation to ongoing social change.

The recent debates over women in combat and homosexuals in the military epitomize this "battle." While the evolving military culture (as expressed by inclusionary laws and policies) has accepted women to some degree, there remains strong opposition to declared homosexuals in uniform. This attitude is not surprising in the context of its paradigm. The military defines itself as a combat, masculine-warrior organization—a characterization that, by the military's definition, excludes women and homosexuals. As long as the military retains its CMW world view, it will resist integrating women and especially gays (whom the military perceives as stereotypical effeminate homosexual men) into its combat arms because both groups are viewed by many as anomalies who do not fit the military's image (or paradigm) as masculine combatants. This "battle" will continue—major social change will evolve, and problems (e.g., sexism and gay bashing) will persist because the evolving model contradicts the underlying paradigm.

Although the current "battle" is between the military's CMW paradigm and an evolving cultural model, the long-term "war" is over the military's paradigm. Will the military retain its conservative CMW paradigm as it wants? Or will the military succumb to external pressures and adopt an equality view of soldiering? Only time will tell. Until the military and society embrace a mutually shared cultural paradigm—whether CMW, equality, or some combination—clashes will persist. External forces will pressure the military to adopt social change; liberals will push for equality for all service members. In response, the military will resist social change that challenges its core CMW paradigm, the raison d'etre for its existence. In summary, the military will accept some social change (as evidenced by the recent inclusion of women in combat), but it will draw a line in the sand on certain issues (e.g., declared homosexuals in its ranks) and resist that which threatens its CMW paradigm.

Who Will Win and Who Will Lose?   That depends on one's perspective. From the military's point of view, its entrenched CMW paradigm, enculturated over generations, has served the military and nation well, producing superb soldiers who win wars. Drawing from a combat, masculine-warrior paradigm, traditionalists stress that the military's core activity remains combat, and the military should not be a laboratory for social experimentation.[35] Two marines recently emphasized this point:

> The institutional values that once defined a proud force are rapidly being eroded by inroads into its culture by feminist and homosexual-interest groups who view the military as a platform for their politically correct agendas.[36]

Such traditionalists cite combat readiness and unit cohesion as essential to success and thus resist social change (e.g., integration of women or homosexuals) that may destroy combat effectiveness, degrade cohesion and morale, or create an ill-trained, unprepared "hollow" force. These traditionalists conclude that both the military and nation will lose if sweeping social change subsequently destroys the military's cohesion and readiness to fight and win.

Conversely, liberals advocate an ideology of equality and denounce the military's practice of exclusion. They believe that social change is both mandatory and manageable. For example, in testimony before the Senate Armed Services Committee, Lawrence Korb (a former Assistant Secretary of Defense) noted that the inclusion of gays is not that disruptive,

> I find no convincing evidence that changing the current policy would undermine unit cohesion any more than the other social changes that society has asked the armed forces to make over the past 50 years.[37]

According to Korb, training and strong leadership can minimize any disruption. Interestingly, the RAND report on the military's homosexual policy made similar observations.[38]

Drawing from a paradigm of equality, liberals note that the military, as a servant of society, must reflect societal core values and culture or be labeled an anachronism. Without paradigm evolution, the military runs that risk—divorcing itself from society. In turn, the military may lose public confidence, respect, and support (e.g., funding, resources, recruits).

Like conservatives, liberals also are concerned with military effectiveness. However, these activists cite military effectiveness as justification for social change. They contend that when the military excludes whole groups of "others" (e.g., women and gays), the pool of talent is reduced, which undermines combat readiness and effectiveness. In their view, the military and nation lose because military forces do not include the most talented soldiers for crucial but difficult jobs, including combat.

What are the True Implications? While the focus has been upon the evolving model of military culture (Table 19.1) and its incongruence with the dominant CMW paradigm, the real issue is the underlying paradigm—is the military undergoing a cultural paradigm shift?[39] As it moves toward the twenty-first century, will the military be a proactive agent of inevitable social change or a reactive guardian of conservatism and the status quo? Its cultural paradigm is the key.

In order to accommodate current social change (e.g., women in combat arms), the military must adopt an ideology of inclusion and reduce its practice of exclusion. In short, it must alter its CMW paradigm. First, the military must rethink its traditional combat identity.[40] As demonstrated by recent military operations, including disaster relief (Hurricane Andrew) and humanitarian support (Somalia), the military is not merely an instrument of war. Thus, the military must adopt an identity that encompasses warfighting, peacekeeping, and disaster relief roles.

Second, the military must alter its prevailing view of warrior as a male-only vocation. In the emerging pluralistic, egalitarian military, combat includes soldiers (e.g., gays and women) who do not fit the traditional mold of "masculine warrior." Their very existence and success challenge the military's traditional notion of warrior. Therefore, the military must begin to view the warrior as a soldier whose job extends beyond combat and whose ability transcends gender or sexual orientation.[41]

Dramatic alteration of the military's paradigm is very difficult—it is tough to change an institution's fundamental beliefs and attitudes, which are enculturated by generations of soldiers. If President Clinton is to successfully institute the social change he proposes, he may have to implant "new thinkers" in the military who embrace broader visions and paradigms.

Conversely, the military may successfully retain its CMW paradigm (and resist current social change), *if* society supports this paradigm. For example, does mainstream America believe that: 1) homosexuality is morally wrong; and 2) the military is a unique institution that may discriminate against individuals in order to field an effective fighting force? Recent survey data seem to support these beliefs. In a 1991 national survey, 71 percent of the respondents said that homosexual relations between adults are "always wrong."[42] Moreover, a 1993 Gallup national poll showed 53 percent of respondents agreed with the statement, "President Clinton should not change military policy to allow gays to serve."[43] These studies suggest some societal support for the retention of the military's CMW paradigm.

However, if the military retains its CMW paradigm and moves in a cultural direction contrary to that of its egalitarian society, it could become an isolated counterculture—an alienated warrior class divorced from the society it defends. Some military leaders do not support such divergence, including the Air Force's General McPeak, who commented, "We simply must not permit today's debates about . . . social issues to divide us from the society we serve."[44]

Conclusion

While cultural change is inevitable, its outcome is uncertain. Futuristic novelist Michael Crichton noted in *Jurassic Park*, "All major changes are like death . . . you can't see to the other side until you are there."[45] As a result of this uncertainty, military culture entails both change and continuity. There is change, as evidenced by the military's evolving model of culture, but there remains continuity in its traditional combat, masculine-warrior paradigm.

As the military undergoes social evolution, we will not know the final outcome until later. But that does not mean we must wait idly. Theoretical constructs such as ideal types, models, and paradigms provide an objective, analytical framework that we can use to study culture and change in institutions such as the military.

These analytical constructs also provide a means of assessment for military leaders. As shown by recent charges of racism, sexism, and hazing, military culture is not immune to dysfunction. Using this analytical framework, leaders can conduct internal reviews of military culture (e.g., identify potential cultural conflicts, examine effects of exclusion upon individuals and military effectiveness, and develop potential courses of action for change as the military moves toward greater cultural diversity). Such objective self-analysis allows the military to be proactive (versus reactive) in its management of social change.

Notes

AUTHOR'S NOTE: *Views, opinions, and findings contained in this paper are mine and should not be construed as an official position, policy, or opinion of the De-*

partment of Defense. I thank colleagues Steve Sellman Jane Arabian, and Tom Ul-rich for their constructive comments on an earlier draft of this manuscript.

1. This analysis of "culture" is at the macro, institutional level, examining core values, norms, beliefs, attitudes, and behaviors common to all of the military services. Although the Army, Navy, Marine Corps, and Air Force are culturally unique, they are subcultures of the military institution. Thus, this analysis is applicable to each service because elements of military culture described in this paper are found in each service, division, wing, squadron, company, and platoon.

2. See William C. Levin, *Sociological Ideas* (Belmont, CA: Wadsworth Publishing Company, 1991), 23. Max Weber (*The Theory of Social and Economic Organization*, eds. and trans. A. M Henderson and Talcott Parsons [New York: Macmillan, 1946]) "invented" the concept of "ideal type" to explain bureaucracies.

3. Webster's II, *New Riverside University Dictionary* (Boston: Houghton Mifflin Company, 1988), 463.

4. Levin, *Sociological Ideas,* 25–26.

5. *Ibid.,* 26–27; Thomas Kuhn, *The Structure of Scientific Revolutions* (Chicago, IL: University of Chicago Press, 1962); Thomas Kuhn, "Second Thoughts on Paradigms," in Frederick Suppe, ed., *The Structure of Scientific Theories* (Urbana, IL: University of Illinois Press, 1974).

6. Recently, each service revised its roles and missions to mirror the priorities of a changed world. For instance, Air Force missions reflect less emphasis on nuclear arms with the reduced nuclear threat from Russia. The Army unveiled a new doctrine that emphasizes contingency operations in regional "hot spots" around the world. (See Vince Crawley," Johnny-On-The-Spot Army," *European Stars & Stripes,* 7 June 1993, 1; Barton Gellman, "Army's New Doctrine Manual Sees High-Tech, Distant Battles," *Washington Post,* 15 June 1993, 19.)

7. See, for example, Morris Janowitz, *The Professional Soldier* (New York: Free Press, 1960); Charles C. Moskos, "From Institution to Occupation: Trends in Military Organization," *Armed Forces and Society,* 4 (1977): 41–50; Karen 0. Dunivin, "Gender and Perceptions of the Job Environment in the U. S. Air Force," *Armed Forces and Society,* 15 (1988): 71–92.

8. Levin, *Sociological Ideas*: 399.

9. *Ibid.,* 117–119.

10. See Frank R. Wood, *U.S. Air Force Junior Officers: Changing Professional Identity and Commitment* (Ph.D. diss., Northwestern University, 1982), 10. See also David R Unruh, "Characteristics and Types of Participation in Social Worlds," *Symbolic Interaction,* 2 (1979): 115–130. Although a military may not be engaged in war, its core activity remains combat. For example, combat readiness through training is an important peacetime activity.

11. See Melissa S. Herbert, "From Crinoline to Camouflage: Initial Entry Training and the Marginalization of Women in the Military," *Minerva,* 11 (1993): 41–57.

12. See, for example, Martin Binkin and Shirley S. Bach, *Women and the Military* (Washington, D.C: The Brookings Institution, 1977); Cynthia Enloe, *Does Khaki Become You?* (London: South End Press, 1983): 7–15.

13. Charles C. Moskos, Jr., *The American Enlisted Man* (New York: Sage, 1970); Michael L. Rustad, *Women in Khaki* (New York: Praeger, 1982); Enloe, *ibid.*

14. Judith H Stiehm, *Bring Me Men and Women* (Berkeley, CA: University of California Press, 1981): 65–66.

15. Although masculinity and homosexuality are not mutually exclusive, the military paradigm narrowly views combat, masculine warriors as heterosexual, masculine men.

16. Brian Mitchell, *Weak Link: The Feminization of the American Military* (Washington, DC: Regnery Gateway, 1989).

17. Judith H Stiehm, *Arms and the Enlisted Woman* (Philadelphia, PA: Temple University Press, 1989).

18. General Robert Barrow, quoted in William L Stearman's "With Women Aboard, The USS Stark Might Have Sunk," *Washington Times,* 16 June 1993, G–3.

19. Carol Tavris, *The Mismeasure of Women* (New York: Simon & Schuster, 1992), 309.

20. Edwin Dorn, quoted in Grant Willis' "Advocates of Gays, Women, Blacks Nominated for Personnel Post," *Air Force Times,* 12 April 1993, 3.

21. See, for example, Lois B. DeFleur and Rebecca L. Warner, "The Impact of Military Service on Women's Status: A Neglected Area of Inquiry," in Nancy H. Loring (ed.), *Women in the United States Armed Forces* (Chicago, IL: Inter-University Seminar on Armed Forces and Society, 1984), 1–16; Karen O. Dunivin, *Adapting to a Man's World: U.S. Air Force Female Officers* (Ph.D. diss., Northwestern University, 1988), 34.

22. William Arkin and Lynne R Dobrofsky, "Military Socialization and Masculinity," *Journal of Social Issues,* 34 (1978): 155.

23. See, for example, Joseph H. Pleck, "The Male Sex Roles: Definitions, Problems and Sources of Change," *Journal of Social Issues,* 32 (1976): 155–164; Martha A. Marsden, "Sex-Role Attributes, Mental Health, and Job Satisfaction Among Enlisted Army Women in Traditional and Nontraditional Military Units," in Loring, *Women in the United States Armed Forces*: 173–180.

24. See, for example, Stiehm, *Bring Me Men and Women;* Rustad, *Women in Khaki;* Enloe, *Does Khaki Become You?*

25. "Let Women Into Combat," *Atlanta Journal and Constitution,* 9 April 1993, 12.

26. Harry S. Truman, quoted in Bernard C. Nalty and Morris J. MacGregor, eds. *Blacks in the Military* (Wilmington, DE, Scholarly Resources, 1981), 239.

27. Defense Authorization Act, Public Law 102–190, December 5, 1991.

28. Edwin Dorn, "Race and the American Military: Past and Present." P. 115 in N. F. Dreisziger, ed., *Ethnic Armies,* (Waterloo, Ontario: Wilfrid Laurier University Press, 1990), 89–122.

29. Les Aspin, Memorandum on "Policy on the Assignment of Women in the Armed Forces" (April 28, 1993).

30. Survey cited by Don Ward, "Women Not Welcome—Yet," *Navy Times,* 4 January 1993, 30.

31. C. R. Myers, "Breaking the Military Mold," *Washington Post,* 25 May 1993, 18.

32. Jeanne Holm, *Women in the Military* (Novato, CA: Presidio Press, 1982); Stiehm, *Bring Me Men and Women.*

33. "Equality—Not Equivocation," *Los Angeles Times,* 15 April 1993, 10.

34. Bob Woodward, "The Secretary of Analysis," *Washington Post Magazine*, 21 February 1993, 9–11, 20, 22–30.

35. Jim Wooten, "Don't Make Military a Laboratory," *Atlanta Journal and Constitution* (April 11, 1993): G–5.

36. David S. Jones and Hagen W. Frank, quoted in Suzanne Fields, "When the Uniform is Not Cut to Fit," *Washington Times*, 8 April 1993, G–1.

37. Lawrence Korb, quoted in Eric Schmitt's "Calm Analysis Dominates Panel Hearing on Gay Ban," *New York Times*, 1 April 1993, 1.

38. RAND Corp., *Sexual Orientation and U.S. Military Personnel Policy: Options and Assessment* (Santa Monica, CA: RAND, 1993): xxiii, 27.

39. Paradigm shifts are major changes in world views, and occur whenever a major change causes us to view the world differently. For example, Darwinian evolution forced a paradigm shift in how we view human evolution. Likewise, major cultural change can force a paradigm shift, as shown by the American civil rights movement during the 1960s.

40. There seems to be some paradigm shift from the military's traditional combat identity. In his "Bottom-Up Review" (presented to the House Armed Services Committee on 30 March 1993), former Secretary Aspin noted that the Fiscal Year 1994 budget includes $398 million for anticipated peacekeeping, humanitarian, and disaster relief operations. In addition, Mr. Aspin cited "economic danger" as one of four post-Cold War dangers that the military must plan for in the future. The Army recently adopted new doctrinal thinking (Field Manual 100–5, "Operations") which includes peacekeeping, humanitarian assistance, and disaster relief among its military missions. All of these actions suggest a paradigm shift from the traditional combat identity to a broader view of the military that encompasses both combat and noncombat roles.

41. There appears to be some paradigm shift from the military's traditional masculine warrior identity. For example, in the wake of Tailhook '91, Admiral Frank Kelso (former Chief of Naval Operations) acknowledged that, "Tailhook brought to light the fact that we had an institutional problem in how we treated women. . . . In that regard, it was a watershed event that has brought about cultural changes." (See John Lancaster, "Tailhook Probe Implicates 140 Officers," *Washington Post*, 24 April 1993, 1). Shortly after his statement, Admiral Kelso offered to open Navy combat roles to women. Such statements and actions indicate a paradigm shift in the Navy (or at least Admiral Kelso), shifting from a masculine-warrior paradigm to a more inclusionary, egalitarian paradigm.

42. National Opinion Research Center, annual survey (February-April, 1991), cited in the American Enterprise, *Public Opinion and Demographic Report* (March/April, 1993), 82.

43. Gallup Poll for Newsweek (January 1993), cited in the American Enterprise, *Public Opinion and Demographic Report* (March/April, 1993), 83.

44. General Merrill A. McPeak, quoted in John Lancaster's "Accused of Ridiculing Clinton, General Faces Air Force Probe," *Washington Post*, 8 June 1993, 1.

45. Michael Crichton, *Jurassic Park* (New York: Ballatine Books, 1990); 314.

20

Leaders, Managers, and Command Climate

Lt. Gen. Walter F. Ulmer, Jr.

The Setting

In spite of the enormous contemporary stresses upon the institution, America's military continues to be better than it has been in at least forty years. Whether or not this same laudatory evaluation will be accurate five years from now is unclear. Dwindling budgets, awesome advances in technology, structural reconfigurations associated with "downsizing," a widening array of missions, and critical scrutiny of roles and doctrines have created extraordinary pressures on our armed forces. The decade of the 90's has seen competence and tradition in action—from the spectacular 1991 excursion in the Gulf through the confusion of Mogadishu, the peculiarities of Haiti, and the "peacekeeping" in Bosnia, not to mention the hurricane and flood relief tasks close at home. However, in spite of many indicators of robustness and tactical excellence, we are far from capitalizing on the human potential in our armed forces. In order to sustain the reliable and efficient military machine our nation needs, we must attend immediately to the revitalization of the overall organizational climate.

No institution is more serious about inculcation of leadership and managerial techniques than our armed forces. Still, we have imprecise, unstudied, and randomly supervised concepts for building and sustaining a climate that fosters innovation, aggressiveness, calculated risk-taking, and the special unit tenacity necessary for battlefield superiority. Listening to students at War College seminars or reading the professional journals, one might conclude that different officers had come from different armies.

Revised by the author from *Armed Forces Journal International* (July 1986), pp. 54–69. Reprinted by permission.

Their stories of motivational techniques, leader priorities, organizational values, training distracters (i.e., any activity required of a commander or his troops that takes away from the critical training mission), and mentoring are extraordinarily diverse. The good stories reveal the enormous power of a proper command climate. The others describe frustration amid mindless bureaucracy . . . an invitation to avoidable and ultimately debilitating mediocrity.

The Role of Climate

These described variations in the quality of our organizations do not stem from differences in geography, new equipment, or availability of training devices. Nor do they derive exclusively from leadership style differences. Rather, they evolve from diverse combinations of leadership and management competencies that produce either a supportive or a dysfunctional organizational climate. And what is the essence of a "supportive" climate that promotes esprit and gives birth to "high performing units"? It may be easier to feel or sense than to describe. Most experienced people can quickly take its measure. There is a pervasive sense of mission. There is a common agreement on the top priorities. There are clear standards. Competence is prized and appreciated. There is a willingness to share information. There is a sense of fair play. There is joy in teamwork. There are quick and convenient ways to attack problems and fix aberrations in the system. There is a sure sense of rationality and trust. Such climates are the product of strong, insightful leadership embedded in enduring values.

Recent studies confirm that within the officer corps there remain widely varying opinions about the quality of leadership and favorability of command climates. Some sources contend that the bold, creative officer cannot succeed in today's military, where only spotless and politically correct actions will ensure "survival." Naturally, some complaints may represent merely the cries of unsatisfiable idealists or the whinings of non-selectees. My personal experience and recent observations support the disturbing contention that inappropriate constraints on boldness and candor do exist. Some young officers disenchanted by their local situation are voting with their feet. However, the fact that excellent units are seen to exist side by side with those of low or erratic effectiveness confirms that pathways to high performance can be found even in today's hectic, stressful environment.

Trust and Leadership

Leadership is of course not the exclusive factor determining climate and combat effectiveness. Other non-material factors include the mental and physical abilities of the followers, the managerial skills of the leaders, the level of commitment to institutional values, and the mode of processing information through the organization. One critical component of the morale and cohesiveness mosaic, and whose absence or dilution is particularly detrimental to effectiveness over time and under stress, is *trust*. Trust plays an enormous role in large and small organizations. Trust can generate magic. Nourishing it among soldiers coming from a skeptical, periodically traumatized free society is ever more often a challenge. The development of trust represents the consummation of a thousand small acts, while its undermining may be precipitated by a single isolated event. It works or fails upward, downward, and sideways. Our future performance is significantly affected by the trust (or lack of it) our boss places in us. A World War I story has Brig. Gen. Douglas MacArthur in the trenches with an Infantry unit just before dawn. He takes the Distinguished Service Cross ribbon from his own tunic and pins it to the chest of a young major about to lead the battalion in an attack, explaining that he knows the major will do heroic deeds that day. One general officer serving in a troop command in the 1990's observed the opposite end of the spectrum: "We . . . occasionally practice what we preach, but all in all we're gripped by our collective distrust of our people." Distrust inhibits soldiers from sharing responsibility and taking initiative and is, therefore, of more than clinical interest in a military unit.

American bureaucracies have a penchant for solving problems, whether caused by individual ethical flaws or systemic discontinuities, by grafting another set of regulations or another gang of overseers onto the existing superstructure. NASA's quest for safety guarantees via checklists, the Defense Department's use of oppressive regulations to ensure integrity in the procurement process, the Environmental Protection Agency's flood of minute environmental guidelines, and some bizarre revelations of Vice President Gore' s examination of nonsense in the Federal bureaucracy highlight our tendency to rely on detailed proscriptions rather than on ethical common sense. Distrust is the lubricant for oversupervision and centralization.

A few years ago, the U.S. Army implemented a policy (that, I hope, is now forgotten) whereby a company commander could not be relieved of command without prior approval of a general officer (except in tactical or life-threatening emergencies). This directive sent two messages. The message policymakers intended to send was that relief was a serious move and that company commanders should be protected from arbitrary and capricious actions by battalion and brigade commanders; the second, unintended message was that the system did not trust the judgment of battalion and brigade commanders. The second message was stronger. The directive was severely misguided, and its author to this day probably remains unaware of his damage.

Some military scholars and defense establishment thinkers have developed recently the concept of a contemporary *Revolution in Military Affairs (RMA)*. The initials *RMA* are starting to appear in military journals and Department of Defense memoranda here and there. The basic postulate of the *RMA* is that the microprocessor and other technological innovations will enable a smaller force propelled by creative doctrine to substitute for the larger, slower formations of the Cold War. In the current discussion of structural and doctrinal change that happens to fit comfortably into the era of reduced defense spending, there are few references to the challenges to leadership and leader development that will attend any such an *RMA*. At the top levels of the Department of Defense in particular, fascination with technology, finances, and geopolitics continue to relegate human issues—except for a few pet social projects—to the back bench. In fact, any *RMA* will sooner than later come to depend more on the sustainment of fighting spirit than on the utilization of cyberspace.

The tools for building routinely supportive organizational climates are available. Development and implementation of a systematic approach to climate-building are the specific avenues to dramatically improved combat readiness. And the prescription is not expensive. The question is not one of leadership versus management, it is one of good leadership versus bad leadership, good management versus bad management, and integrating enlightened leadership and sensible management to create the proper climate. It is absurd to imply that skilled managers cannot be skilled leaders. On the contrary, leadership and management must be complimentary to create the climates from which high-performing units emerge.

Measuring and Developing Leaders

If we are serious about identifying and developing leaders, we must provide a model for measuring leadership. In this context we define "leadership" as essentially an influence process whereby one gains the trust and respect of subordinates and moves them toward goals *without reliance upon positional authority*. (Exercise of positional authority is of course legitimate and often necessary, but *reliance* on formal authority alone does not constitute "leadership" as we are using that term.) Given that our standard mode of performance appraisal is exclusively superiors assessing subordinates, it is remarkable that we do as well as we do in selection and development. We would do much better by having subordinates augment the system with periodic input about their superiors. When, as occasionally happens, a general makes a spectacle of himself through arrogant or capricious behavior, his boss is often surprised and disappointed. The troops might be disappointed also. But they are never surprised.

An Army War College study in the early 1970's examined leader behavior from three perspectives—self/peer, superior, and subordinate—and eventually incorporated input from more than thirty thousand questionnaires. The data confirmed what we intuitively knew: Self-delusion about leadership effectiveness is commonplace. Peers, superiors, and subordinates often see an officer quite differently from how the officer views himself. These data are similar to that collected in the corporate sector fifteen years later by researchers at the Center for Creative Leadership. Leadership, no matter which definition you use, does not speak of something that happens to, or occurs within, the leader; it speaks of something that happens to, or occurs within, a group of followers. Only followers reliably know how well the leader has led. This is particularly true in evaluating such leader behaviors as candor, commitment, and caring. In any formal organization, but within the long shadow of military tradition in particular, accepting the fact that our subordinates are the ultimate judges of even one facet of our performance is difficult And such acceptance becomes even more threatening and counterintuitive as we become "successful" and more chronologically gifted!

Why does any leader ever promote somebody who everybody but the leader knows is the wrong person for the job? The answer is rarely cronyism or disregard for leader behaviors. The leader is simply ignorant of the leadership reputation of his candidate. Seniors' evaluations of colonels or brigadier generals are especially difficult to make because they are often based on infrequent or intermittent personal contact and tend to be skewed by single, highly visible incidents. Rarely do we provide useful developmental feedback to colonels and generals—or admirals either. The crucial model of successful adult learning with performance feedback as the essential ingredient is absent from our leadership texts and from our service school curricula. (As of this 1995 writing, there are embryonic efforts to confront these realities. The fact that such issues are being seriously discussed is encouraging; the history of sustained implementation of leader development at senior levels in either military or commercial organizations is not.)

Because superiors cannot alone measure leadership capability reliably, we must conclude that peer and subordinate input into the evaluation system are essential if the organization wants to identify, reward, and develop leadership. There is simply no alternative, particularly remembering that leadership strengths and weaknesses and ethical imperfections often reveal themselves last to even an experienced boss.

Peer and subordinate ratings raise emotional issues of competitiveness among peers and perceived challenges to authority, often creating theoretical confusion between popularity and competency. Such ratings have been used at our service academies, in other officer training programs, in Ranger school, and in special situations. However, although it is essential for decision makers to have access to the viewpoints of subordinates and peers when assessing leader effectiveness, any such input is not intended to substitute for the commander's decision. There may be justifiable occasions when the boss says, "I know he is not a great leader, but I need him in that job anyway." And finally, input from subordinates and peers can be packaged and administered in relatively unemotional and supportive formats and provided as constructive feedback even within the constraints of an hierarchical organization.

A second powerful, underutilized mechanism for providing insight regarding leader strengths and weaknesses is the behavioral assessment. Our senior service colleges have been using a limited battery of psychological tests to provide some awareness of individual tendencies of personality. A longer, more comprehensive session of assessment earlier in an officer's career is warranted. Assessment should be integrated into the normal sequence of promotion, schooling, and assignment and made a formal part of our programs. The results should be used for screening prior to commissioning and for self-development in the middle years, and should be made available to selection boards for key staff and command positions in grades of colonel.

Further, we should give serious consideration to an outrageous concept proposed by Army Col. Mike Malone. He suggests that an officer make application for the position of brigade commander or equivalent, and that the application process would include anonymous evaluations of the candidate's leadership from designated peers and subordinates in his prior command assignments.

To further complicate the process of evaluating leadership outcomes is the unseemly reality that we are not capable of assessing accurately the short-term changes in unit combat effectiveness. Not only are important attributes such as morale, pride, and mental toughness difficult to appraise, but also even the more tangible components of readiness, such as materiel status or tactical proficiency, defy precise peacetime evaluation. The inherent difficulty of evaluating unit effectiveness is exacerbated by the omission of that subject within the military education system.

Climate and Quality

Examinations of climate and culture are anything but new. Systematic but aborted organizational effectiveness initiatives in the military and similar efforts in industry have spotlighted the interaction between environment and productivity. Industrial giants such as Goodyear, Procter and Gamble, General Electric, and Ford continue to invest big money in reshaping the motivational context of work. "Self directing," or "self-managing," teams (SMT's) have moved past the conceptual stage. Total Quality Management

(TQM) has entered the lexicon. Both SMT's and TQM have erratic records of success in the corporate world. They will fare no better in the governmental sector. These attempts toward greater employee autonomy coupled with a dispersed sense of responsibility for quality output were not conceived from altruistic motives. These efforts stem from a bottom-line necessity to remain competitive in the international marketplace. However, we have found that such efforts ultimately succeed or fail within the context of a supportive organizational climate. When top leaders know how to lead and manage, SMT's and TQM can produce wonders. When leadership and knowledge of organizational climates and culture are lacking, SMT's and TQM become passing fads or chaos builders. Still, decentralization, trust, clarity of organizational vision, and empowerment appear to be the direct route to unlocking American initiative and producing better tires, paper towels, and switchboards. But it takes leadership of greater energy and confidence to decentralize and empower than to exercise rigid, centralized control! "Freedom to do one's work" (meaning latitude in getting the job done) within the realm of clear goals and priorities is *the* key stimulant to productivity. Environmental factors in the workplace are even more powerful than personal qualities of the workforce—including exceptional cognitive abilities—in producing innovative solutions. A stifling, overpressured climate with poorly articulated goals and priorities and a dearth of trust is also the primary stimulant for ethical misbehavior as employees or soldiers attempt to meet impossible goals with marginal resources. Arthur D. Little, Inc., concludes in its report, Management Perspectives on Innovation, that "creating a favorable climate is the most important single factor in encouraging innovations. " And "innovation" translates quickly into the mind-set of intelligent risk taking and creative problem-solving needed by every fighting element in our armed forces, with or without the *RMA*. We must get serious about unleashing and focusing our enormous, uniquely American reservoir of human initiative. Too much of it remains pinned beneath the weight of a relentless bureaucracy.

Enhancing Organizational Climate

How can we change the organizational climate? Effective climate-building steps will mean altering the managerial and leadership habits of many of our colonels and generals. Therefore, it must be supported and over-watched by the top team. Crucial to leadership at the flag officer level is an understanding of the following: how to communicate a clear vision of an idealized future, how to build supportive, coordinated, internal operating systems, how to modernize methods for evaluating people and units, and how to reinforce traditional values through personal behavior.

As we move to create an environment that builds high-performing units, the criticality of competence in management must be recognized. While the MacNamara era did emphasize "management" to the detriment of "leadership," any diminution of managerial competence and practice is as threatening to organizational effectiveness as is incompetent leadership. Poor managerial practices soak up so much energy that leaders become too tired and frustrated to lead. Current systems for evaluating unit readiness, for tracking fund expenditure, and for ensuring rationality in local procurement of supplies, for example, create an administrative morass that can cripple any efforts to create a positive climate. Again, our service schools have not taught us about the essentiality of a supportive climate, or how to create, sustain, and measure it. Our systems for measuring progress in units—systems that often highlight short-term results, compromise morale, distort priorities, and worship statistics—represent another area of managerial challenge. They sit alongside the challenges of articulating a vision, decentralizing while maintaining high standards, developing loyal disagreement, generating trust, and scrubbing the nonsense out of the systems.

In relative terms, the American military as an institution may be as good as there is on earth. That special aura of selfless commitment and wonderful camaraderie unique to the brotherhood of arms still permeates most of our units. But we must be better if we are to survive the perilous times ahead. That can only be done by attracting, developing, and retaining individuals of strong character and quick intellect throughout the forces, and in the first instance by constructing organizational climates that will nurture and excite the enormous human potential at our disposal. Good people are increasingly intolerant of organizational stupidity and vacillating leadership. Poor organizational climates will slowly and quite silently demotivate the brightest and the best. We need to analyze and learn from specific successes and failures of senior officers as they energize or demoralize their commands. Supportive climates will sustain hope and build the emotional muscle necessary for battlefield success. Their teachable creation can be commonplace even in an era of budget austerity. They are in fact the most cost effective force multiplier imaginable. And the responsibility for moving from routine good intentions to routine best practice clearly falls on those of us who have been, are, or will be the senior leaders of our armed forces.

PART FIVE

The New Realities

Make the most of yourself, for that is all there is to you.
—Emerson

We continue to set impossible expectations for our leaders. Position descriptions for the top jobs in business, government, and the military define requirements that few people can meet. Leaders are supposed to take charge, create a vision, set impossible goals, be innovative in their ideas, perform magic with inadequate budgets, maintain harmony with every conceivable constituency, adhere to all laws and policies, and keep everyone challenged and satisfied. They must anticipate change in internal and external environments while presenting acceptable responses to those changes. Some focus on the short-run effectiveness of unit efficiency, and others expect a commitment to the long view for mission accomplishment; the leader must give full attention to both. Past and present actions of the leader are given close scrutiny by friend and foe. Performance expectations are high, and we do not respond well to those who fall short.

Military leadership is global in scope. Even though there is a relative peace within, international peacekeeping missions throughout the world are challenging our defense resources. The variety of multicultural and cross-cultural issues must be addressed. This diversity adds new dimensions to leadership, and we are still learning how to cope with them. Military leaders are faced with an environment that is ambiguous and complex. Alternatives are constantly changing the form and substance of leadership style.

At the same time, information technologies can be both resources and constraints. Power is based upon our ability to access, analyze, and disseminate information. Telecommunications technologies give us instant access to the world and what it knows. We are able to (and do) collect more data than ever before; yet leaders and commanders face a critical problem: They are overloaded with data and starved for information. The result is that leaders are often tempted to wait until they have more information before making a decision.

Effective leaders understand that intuition is the best guide. Intuition is truly our education and experience as we have recorded it. Synthesizing what we know sometimes confounds logic; the data say one thing but we really "know" something else. Effective leaders will go with their intuition because, in many respects, it is based upon information, not data. Military legend is replete with examples of how true leadership occurred when the leader acted on "gut" or intuition.

Leadership and Management

At the same time, there continue to be debates about the similarities between leadership and management. Our position is that they are two distinct but complementary systems of action.

Many people define management as a set of functions—planning, organizing, and controlling—that can be taught and learned. The resources managers work with are people, money, materiel, information, and time. All are applied to accomplish the unit or organizational objective. Thus, the skillful manager employs many tools and techniques acquired through a combination of education and experience.

Leadership is an influence process. The end result is evaluation in terms of the unit or organizational objective. However, leaders work through people, and effective leaders are skilled in relating to others. Specific methods are not well defined because influence is a product of individual personalities and human interactions. There are still questions as to whether people can be educated or trained to be leaders. Our belief is that through self-knowledge will come self-confidence—a true understanding of one's strengths and shortcomings that allows the individual to realize just how he or she can be effective as a leader.

Managers do not necessarily lead, and leaders are not necessarily good managers. However, we find that successful leadership and good management go hand in hand. The best leaders have also distinguished themselves as superb managers.

Style and Substance

What leaders do is important; how they do it is critical. Substance relates directly to getting the job done. Style reflects the process by which the leader interacts with others in accomplishing the task. Achieving a goal is success, but how we feel about what is accomplished also has significant meaning.

Much of the leadership research is focused on style and behaviors. The two most common references are to the autocratic and democratic types, the latter representing a more collaborative approach between leader and followers. Shared leadership is a more open concept because it creates positive, long-term effects on the people in an organization. It seems to provide participants (leader and followers) with a sense of ownership of the actions taken, creating greater personal ownership, satisfaction, and commitment to the organization.

Style is more than a question of one type versus another. There is no one best style for all situations. Complex or ambiguous tasks may require a greater variety of inputs than relatively simple, routine tasks that can be directed by a leader acting alone.

Timing is also an important consideration. Participative styles are time consuming. Shared leadership includes consultation with followers. The path to consensus decisions is often long and tedious. In situations where quick decisions are necessary for survival, the leader must review available information and take immediate action. To some extent, style depends upon the time demands placed on the leader and followers.

The Quest for Leadership

Many speakers and writers try to create formulas for leadership success. They describe deeds and opinions of successful leaders, creating lists of behaviors necessary for effective leadership. Students struggle with trying to learn and execute these behaviors, thinking of them as specific leadership skills. The fact is that these are not *skills*. There is no pattern of activities, no single path to leadership. Over a period of time, an organization can be led successfully by individuals with very different personalities and styles. A leader can succeed in one organization and fail in another even though his or her style remains relatively constant.

Effective leaders seem to behave in ways that fit their personalities, the situation, and the needs of the group that they are leading. They act normally, exhibiting empathy for their followers while displaying self-knowledge and confidence. There is no set of acquired behaviors. One cannot fake a dynamic, enthusiastic commitment to leadership.

Some leaders take firm charge. Others nurture the group so that everyone accepts responsibility. We know leaders who are great orators. There are also those who are quiet and uninspiring with words but lead by example. Leaders come in all statures and from all cultures. Some act decisively; others act with slow deliberation. Effective leaders set the stage with personality and expectations, presenting a consistent image.

We evaluate leaders by the success of the organization *and* by their personal effectiveness. Apart from the organization's measurement systems, leaders have subjective feelings about their performance. Their egos are involved. Leaders are continually engaged in self-evaluation because making a difference is important to them.

The role a leader chooses to play (or is expected to play) also relates to effectiveness. In the headship role, the leader is a communicator who represents the goals and values of the organization to the outside world. A leader can also choose to focus internally, functioning as a buffer between the followers and external environments while concentrating his or her efforts on actions within the organizational boundaries. A leader may elect to be a storyteller, working primarily to inspire members to work toward a common objective. Many people simply lead by example, working the hardest and making the sacrifices that create an energizing environment in which everyone wants to contribute.

Thus, we again come to the issue of personality. *Who* the leader is in large part determines the nature of the role. What an organization *needs* is critical. We cannot expect leaders to respond equally well to every shift in organizational emphasis. Some people can adapt well as leaders. Effective leaders know their strengths and weaknesses and act accordingly.

There are two basic leadership strategies: transactional and transformational. Transactional leaders recognize what participants want to get from their work and exchange rewards (and punishments) for performance and effort. The leader clarifies the role the follower must play to attain the desired outcomes, giving participants the direction necessary to achieve organizational goals. Properly implemented, transactional leadership is effective and desirable in many situations.

Transformational leadership involves strong personal identification between followers and the leader. They join in a shared vision, placing group goals above self-interest. The transformational leader motivates participants to perform beyond their expectations by creating opportunities to build self-esteem and self-actualization. Transformational leadership is visionary leadership. A visionary leader helps followers develop a mental picture of the goal and transforms purpose into action.

There are three major aspects to visionary leadership. The first consists of constructing a vision, creating an ideal image of the organization and its culture. The second is defining an organizational philosophy that succinctly states the vision and then developing programs and policies that put the philosophy into practice. The third aspect centers on the leaders' own practices, the specific actions in which leaders engage on a one-to-one basis in order to create and share ownership in the vision.

Understanding the New Realities

Ambiguity and uncertainty abound as a result of a rapidly changing world. To paraphrase Shelley, successful military leaders must see the present in the past and the future in the present. Thus, in this section, we provide some views of the challenges and opportunities presented to the military leader of today and tomorrow. There are many issues searching for answers. Our intent is to provide you with some insights. How you understand yourself as a leader will determine the way in which you deal with these issues.

In "New Ideas from the Army (Really)" (Chapter 21), Lee Smith describes the downsized military as adaptive, flexible, and a learning enterprise—the same attributes of successful business organizations in a rapidly changing global environment. Smith is especially complimentary of the Army's After Action Reports, where commanders and troops actively engage in critiques of exercises. Everyone has a chance to provide feedback, and there is learning at all levels. This affirms that the best information is not always at the top. The author presents a number of anecdotes about military commanders looking to the future in terms of where and how battles might be fought. The military understands the importance of information and how to use it. Through careful planning that involves everyone, some degree of certainty can be provided in the actual combat situation. Yet, Smith notes, effective leadership is the preparation for a violent, uncertain, complex, and ambiguous world. Other organizations have a lot to learn from the military.

In a counterperspective, Colonel Herbert Harback makes important linkages in his "Leadership Lessons from Downsized Corporate America" (Chapter 22). He uses research from 64 civilian corporations representing over 400 companies for ideas that can be employed in the modern military. Among the emerging lessons learned are mentorship (where an individual is guided through a development plan) and culture change (where restructuring must be led and the failure to respond to change is high). Harback further suggests that empowerment means loosening centralized control, necessary to effectiveness in a smaller workforce, and encouraging cross-functional teamwork. In downsized organizations, great concern must be given to the "survivors," who must work harder and are fearful of additional reductions in force, and to retention of the organization's core values. The demands on leadership are heavy. For the military, the lessons relate to cultural change, core value recognition, survivor care and involvement, empowerment, and situational task force orientation.

Richard Kohn presents a perspective on current issues with "Women in Combat, Homosexuals in Uniform: The Challenge of Military Leadership" (Chapter 23). He suggests that leaders who oppose the social changes need to think carefully. With regard to gender, history has demonstrated that women have fought successfully with men in other times. Fairness, practicality, and cohesion must be approached differently as military leaders cope with change. The services must redefine acceptable behavior, and Kohn is confident that military leaders will adjust, just as they have throughout history. The strength of the military depends ultimately upon the bonds of the people, their values and ideals, because it is the people who are served by the military.

Finally, we present an interesting perspective of leadership in the information age in Thomas Ricks's "Battle Plans: In Wake of Cold War, An Intellectual Leads Army in New Missions" (Chapter 24), which cites the accomplishments of a contemporary army officer who is a soldier and scholar and who has been a theorist and commander. Col. James McDonough wrote a book on his experiences in the Vietnam War that was a best seller and made into a movie. McDonough wrote a textbook about mechanized warfare and, more recently, a novel. At the same time, this officer has extensive practical experience with the global challenges of a modern military where his insights are tested by the realities of downsizing, all-volunteer troops, and new threats requiring a redefinition of military structure and mission. Interestingly, Ricks quotes some who believe that McDonough's intellectual pursuits will prevent him from being promoted to general officer. McDonough himself appears to be less concerned with that issue than in doing his best.

I have three precious things which I hold fast and prize. The first is gentleness; the second is frugality; and the third is humility, which keeps me from putting myself before others. Be gentle and you can be bold; be frugal and you can be liberal; avoid putting yourself before others and you can become a leader.

—Lao-Tzu

21

New Ideas from the Army (Really)

Lee Smith

Picture the U.S. Army three years ago, just after it had demolished Saddam Hussein's fearsome regiments in one of the fastest and most one-sided battles in history. The Army emerged as the world's premier land force. To draw commercial parallels, it was as supreme as IBM ruling over the dominion of mainframes. It was as commanding as General Motors when it owned more than half the American market. In short, the Army seemed rumbling merrily toward a breathtaking fall. What organization, after all, would be more likely to be suckered by success and blind-sided by the future than the Army: rigid, hierarchical, the archetypal command-and-control organization in which a smug and remote Pentagon hands down orders to the field. As the old saying goes, the Army was an organization designed by geniuses to be run by idiots.

Remarkably, the Army isn't like that anymore. It's no secret that the service had improved enormously since its near-death experience in Vietnam. But what's surprising is that it has continued to force itself through reexamination and self-renewal since the triumph of Desert Storm, a time when the temptation might have been to repose on its laurels. Dee Hock, founder of the Visa credit card company, toured some bases at the Pentagon's invitation recently. "I came away mildly astonished," he says. "Officers on every level were discussing change, in many ways ahead of business."

The Army is striving to become everything the modern organization is supposed to be—adaptive, flexible, a learning enterprise, even getting closer to, um, the needs of the customer. Army Chief of Staff General Gordon Sul-

Reprinted by permission from *Fortune*, 130:6 (September 19, 1994), pp. 203–212. Copyright © 1994 by Time, Inc. All rights reserved.

livan—in effect the CEO—finds it useful at times to think of possible adversaries as customers. The exercise helps clarify what services they will require for their control or, perhaps, elimination.

To civilians, the Gulf war looked like an effortless Nintendo engagement that put the Americans megagenerations ahead of any adversary. But to Sullivan and other generals it revealed weakness: terrible inventory control, a slipping lead in crucial technologies, and a communication system that was still stuck in World War II.

Forcing this bureaucratic body to change are many of the same forces that obsess business. The Army's annual appropriation has dropped from $90 billion in 1989 to $60 billion this year (about the revenue of IBM or GE). Downsizing has reduced the number of troops in uniform from 780,000 to 565,000 within a year or so. Like business, the Army is looking out on a world that is volatile and often inscrutable. Says Sullivan: "We are trying to change this organization to do things we can't even predict."

Sullivan, 57, saw combat in Vietnam, but his look and manner are less those of a hell-fire commander than of an archbishop shepherding a flock confused about the expectations of the modern church. Now that the Soviet satan is dead, what does it mean to be a soldier? Since the Gulf war, troops have been dispatched on dozens of unconnected missions, at least one of them botched. Soldiers went off to feed children in Somalia, and because of multiple misunderstandings 29 of them died. Recently troops have purified water for Rwandan refugees, fought forest fires in the Pacific Northwest, and taught their Russian counterparts how to rescue hostages, and Colombians how to chase drug lords.

What's next? Police duty in Haiti, maybe? Sullivan doesn't protest the diversity of the demand. Without those needs Americans might forget they have an Army that has to be paid and provisioned. But how does he keep the organization ready and adaptive? That, of course, is a major challenge for business as well.

Maybe even Alexander the Great worried about how to keep his generals from re-fighting the last campaign. Top management certainly puzzles over how to get executives in mid-career to change the way they solve problems. "You get a chance to indoctrinate people in your culture and your way of thinking in their early years," says Richard Pascale, a former Stanford business school professor who counsels companies on adapting to new circumstances. "But it's very hard to retrain them when your culture has to change because the world is different."

Pascale greatly admires the Army's solution: Put everyone from PFCs to brigadier generals through maneuvers that stress them to the breaking point. Then subject them to the After Action Review, a performance appraisal—in public.

In the most elaborate form of the critique, an Army brigade of 3,000 or so travels to the National Training Center in California, where it has to go muzzle to muzzle with crack units based at the center. These elite units constantly develop new combat techniques so that the visitors never get the same fight twice. The exercise is videotaped in detail while observer-controllers swarm all over the battlefield taking notes and at times redirecting the action.

The After Action Review is unemotional—and devastating. Colonels see where the lieutenants sinned, and vice versa. "There was a lot of resistance," says Sullivan, "but we do it because in high-performance organizations, the parts are supposed to talk to one another." A junior officer is informed that enemy "crunchies" (tanker slang for foot solders) slipped past his platoon and disabled the fuel trucks. With M1 tanks guzzling two gallons a mile, the loss of fuel trucks rendered them useless. And an observer-controller asks the colonel respectfully but pointedly, "What were you thinking, sir, when you ordered the column to move right instead of left?"

No other army is so egalitarian. "Delegations who come to study our ways are dumbfounded when they see an AAR," says a Pentagon colonel. "There is no way they would subject their senior officers to embarrassment." Nor are there many corporations in which senior executives sit down with those who will eventually succeed them and explain how under pressure they overlooked some vital information that blew the deal.

"There is more interest in learning in the military than in most organizations I've seen," says Margaret Wheatley, an organizational consultant who has advised dozens of FORTUNE 500 companies. "Generals take time to think." Sullivan, one of the most intellectual chiefs in recent Army history, reads and studies broadly, even into such arcana as chaos theory.

Business folk can point out that in the relative security of the post–Cold War era the brass has the luxury of being able to ruminate abstractly about the Next Big One. Those in commerce, on the other hand, are actually in combat, struggling daily with ferocious competitors.

Corporate chief executives often promise to step aside from their company's latest battles and look ahead. Worthy sentiment, but hard to live by. "Too many CEOs have so structured their jobs that they will always be involved in the day-to-day," maintains Wheatley. "They assume their companies can't get along without them." For whatever reason, absent a wall topped with barbed wire, it's tough to keep the boss out of today's crisis.

Congress, in effect, constructed such a handy barrier for the Army and the other services in the Goldwater-Nichols Act of 1986. The chain of command for combat now runs directly from the President and Defense Secretary to the regional commander in the field. For example, General Sullivan is not directly involved in the strategy for repelling a possible onslaught by the North Koreans. That's the worry of General Gary Luck, who leads all U.S. forces in Korea.

Sullivan is free therefore to put his head just where he wants it—in the year 2010. That's distant but not so far away that today's soldiers will think of it as remote. The two-star generals who will command divisions in that year are majors today. Sullivan, now in the final year of a four-year tour, has to hope that his successors share his vision and that Congress funds it.

His aim is to create the world's first Information Age army. "If you know just where you are and just where the enemy is, you have a tremendous advantage," says Sullivan. Sounds banal, but for most of history, commanders have not known those fundamentals. That's part of the fog of war. Knowledge is especially critical for the U.S. Army, which must compensate for its relatively puny size. With roughly half a million men and women in uniform, it is only the world's eighth-largest land force (outnumbered by those of China, Russia, India, North Korea, Vietnam, South Korea, and Pakistan).

For all of history up until the 1860s, armies were what Sullivan refers to as Agrarian Age forces, fighting battle by battle, mostly with cottage-made weapons. "When Grant left Culpepper, Virginia, in pursuit of Lee in 1864 he ushered in the Industrial Age war," says Sullivan. Grant's objective was not so much to beat Lee in the field as to destroy the South's industrial base, which he did.

Industrial Age strategy prevailed until Desert Storm, the first Information Age war. The U.S. won quickly because it deprived the Iraqis of information by vaporizing radar and telecommunications systems, and used its own information to point cruise missiles and other smart weapons precisely on target.

The war went smoothly—except to Sullivan and others who looked closely enough to see the cracks: Some 40,000 U.S. containers of the size that tractor-trailers haul arrived in Saudi Arabia—unmarked. Many had to be opened and their contents of spare tires, generators, and such sorted out. There was far more than the Army could ever use, partly because supply sergeants traditionally order everything three times in the expectation that two requisitions will go astray in unmarked containers. Huge overshipments are not only expensive; they also put a strain on transportation, a serious weakness in the U.S. ability to fight far away. As a result of that experience, containers are now bar-coded to list their contents, and sensors signal their whereabouts to anxious sergeants via satellite.

American soldiers had an enormous advantage in the Gulf because they had infrared equipment such as goggles and gun sights that enabled them to fight at night, when the Iraqis were effectively blind. Since the end of the war, however, the French have produced night-vision equipment about as good, and cheaper and available to anyone who wants to buy it. Other technological advantages slip away fast. U.S. troops had to leave Somalia by ship because commanders feared that warlords might have Stinger missiles that could bring down 747s.

A lot of useful intelligence about enemy troop placements, weather, and such never got down to battlefront troops in Iraq because the communications system was primitive. "I stood looking out of my turret, and jotted down observations in my spiral notebook and spoke to the troops by radio," says Colonel Pat Ritter, who commanded a battalion of 58 tanks in the Gulf. "There wasn't much going on that George Patton wouldn't have recognized."

What Sullivan wants to create, among other things, is an Army of 2010 that is joined by electronic mail, plus digitally transmitted data and video pictures. The effect on command and control will be staggering. In corporations E-mail tends to erode hierarchies and break down the barriers between functions as, for example, marketing communicates directly with production.

In the same way the Army's communications will tend to fuse the service's branches. The Army hopes to buy a new helicopter now in prototype, the Comanche, to hover over the battlefield, spot enemy positions, and transmit them digitally to tanks, infantry, and artillery. But Sullivan's civilian superiors in the Pentagon and Congress may decide to save $2 billion or so by killing the Comanche, so the adaptable Army will have to retrofit today's helicopters for the job. Either way, the ground detachments will simultaneously exchange data, select and assign targets, and fire.

The troops of 2010 are already in basic training; that is, they are in kindergarten, tapping joyously on computer keyboards. More difficult is finding the managers, the officers, to prepare the workplace for them. Without question the officer corps is the best educated the U.S. has ever had. Two-thirds of the Army's 55,000 officers have advanced degrees, including 2,000 with MBAs.

Nonetheless, Sullivan estimates that about 5% of active duty officers still have their heads locked in the Cold War; about 65% have caught up to the Gulf War; and only 30% are with Sullivan, standing 15 years in the future and figuring out how to get there from here.

One of Sullivan's fellow visionaries is Brigadier General Bert Maggart, 50, who oversees the Army's battle lab for mounted operations at Fort Knox, Kentucky. Technicians and troops tinker endlessly with dozens of tank simulators, fitting them with new instruments and preparing them for novel fighting tactics. The electronics are so elaborate that soon simulators at Knox will be plugged into maneuvers with actual tanks in Texas or Germany, and affect the outcomes of those mock battles. Drivers and gunners in the real machines will see the simulators as friendly or menacing icons on their displays.

Maggart—smart, intense, and demanding—has created a brain trust of a dozen captains (and one sergeant first class with a Ph.D. in history) whom he challenges to solve the problems of future combat. He bangs a forefinger on a baffling grid map that displays tanks scattered over rugged terrain. "I want to teach lieutenants to see everything that a colonel can see here," he says, pointing out a troubling paradox that will face the Information Age army. The colonel in command of 50 tanks will know in massive detail and second by second where they are, how much fuel and ammunition they have, and so on, but the battle will unfold so rapidly he will have knowledge without control.

Thus, the lieutenant in charge of four of those tanks will be on his own. So Maggart's captains devise simulated battles that will age lieutenants in a hurry, such as scenarios in which the colonel is killed and they have to take over the battalion.

Preparing to fight the lightning-quick wars of the next century could be the easy part. The real leadership challenge for Sullivan and his successors will be developing soldiers, officers in particular, who not only can adapt month to month to different climates and cultures but also can continually adjust and readjust their reflexes.

Soldiers understand what's expected of them when they have to get ready for an all-out fight. Getting ready for conditions other than war is a much fuzzier assignment. How does a soldier, or anyone else, understand the fine distinctions and rules of engagement (when it's okay to shoot) during peacekeeping, peacemaking, humanitarian rescue, nation building, whatever?

By and large the Army doesn't attract those who thrive on soft information and carrying out instructions that are vague or mutate from day to day. Nor are soldiers comfortable in the midst of unfamiliar values and alien behavior. That's one of the reasons given by the military for insisting that gays keep their sexual preferences quiet.

Wander among the Army elite, the 15,000 members of the 82nd Airborne Division at Fort Bragg, North Carolina. They are great soldiers— motivated and single-minded in their determination to win. There's not a Type B in the outfit. "People even mow their lawns at a faster pace," a recently arrived officer's wife wrote in the local newspaper.

That's just the temperament required for jumping out of planes and seizing enemy airfields, the mission the 82nd rehearses again and again. But once the target is taken, is it reasonable to expect them or soldiers like them to walk police beats in Haiti, say? It may not be clear who the enemy is or how strongly he should be dealt with. Tom Surles, a retired colonel who commanded a battalion in Korea, considers such missions a serious mismatch. "We train to fire our weapons and hit things with them," says

Surles. "To send the military in and say 'Don't shoot'—well, you've got the wrong people to do that."

Sullivan strongly disagrees with that view. He notes that his troops are now carrying out noncombative missions in 105 countries, without incident. Moreover, restraint is incorporated in training programs. At Fort Polk, Louisiana, troops practice fighting while nuns and journalists wander among them. "Killing" civilians costs a soldier points.

Sullivan urges his officers to model themselves on jazz musicians Dave Brubeck and Wynton Marsalis, who although trained in the classics have the gift of being able to improvise in action. The 19th-century strategies of Karl von Clausewitz and the other standards will not suffice in a confusing and turbulent era.

Fast-track colonels at the Army War College in Carlisle, Pennsylvania, are told time and again that they are preparing for leadership roles in a world that is violent, uncertain, complex, and ambiguous. They hear it so often they have taken to calling the place, with tongue-in-cheek sarcasm, VUCA U. The world of commerce is teaching the same lesson to millions of business people every day. Most could benefit from studying it with the Army's discipline and zeal.

22

Leadership Lessons from Downsized Corporate America

Herbert F. Harback

With incentive regulation accomplished, we could concentrate on the business growth strategies. But none of our strategies could be achieved with the company culture in place after the breakup. So I had to focus on the culture first. The operating companies had an implementation mentality. They did not understand the initiative, innovation, risks and accountability necessary to meet our business goals. Managers were held accountable for implementation of a process or practice exactly as it was written, not for the end result. Managers simply could not imagine rewriting a process even if they knew a better one. In a large business, the most important determinant of success is the effectiveness of millions of day-to-day interactions between human beings. If those contacts are contentious, turf-oriented, and parochial, the company will flounder, bureaucracies will grow, and internal competition will be rampant.
—Raymond Smith, Chief Executive Officer of Bell Atlantic

We are at a major crossroads in the development of our future military leaders. It is called "downsizing," and we need to be concerned with the impact it will have on our Army. This article discusses some of the preliminary findings of a current study on corporate change and its potential implications for the Army.

I have had the unique opportunity to work with American corporations that recently underwent significant change. They found themselves having to restructure because of outside influences. For most, that restructuring has been in cutting costs and firing people—corporate downsizing. For all of them, it has been painful. Some have not survived, many are still strug-

Reprinted by permission from *Military Review,* 73:8 (August 1993), pp. 24–31.

gling and some are far better now than before—but all carry scars of costly decisions and emotional dilemmas.

Many corporate downsizing lessons are of direct value to the Army as it takes on a reduction in force. To date, 64 civilian corporations representing over 400 companies have been studied through in-depth, executive-level interviews. The initial results are significant, time sensitive and applicable to us. Examined in terms of leadership development requirements for our downsized Army, these lessons quickly focus on the organizational issues of mentorship and culture change and the employee issues of empowerment and survivor care.

Emerging Lessons Learned

Mentorship.   Mentorship is a process in which an individual is guided through a developmental plan designed to rapidly move him to the executive, decision-making level. Gaining key experience at different critical corporate ladder nodes is the objective. It is more than the recognition of excellent work or simple job succession and replacement identification. Mentorship is the earmarking and nurturing of future corporate captains. The challenge is that the more a company downsizes, the greater the need to protect its leader development program from the natural tendency to cut low near-term benefit programs. A company's focus may be myopic; immediate cost cutting overrides future investments as one is confronted with the need to downsize.

The initial research's viewpoint was that a system of mentoring would be assumed within any modern corporation. That is no longer a strong belief. Each company did have its own program of identifying potential, but the degree to which the programs are endorsed and actually carried out varies greatly.

In downsizing, it becomes critical that the organization recognizes how its executives need to be developed. The greater the number of companies and the more homogeneous the final product or service within the industry, the lesser the need for formal mentorship.

The more unique the service offered and the smaller the industry, the greater the need for a mentorship program. The more unique the company, the less likely there will be executive lateral movement into the company, and the more likely it will consider executive talent as a "we grow our own." Given the fact that the Army is within this description, it should have a highly formalized mentorship program. The challenge is that the past ways of developing leaders through more structured methods may not be available because of staff and funding cuts. New approaches are in order.

The most successfully downsized corporations offer a solution called "Task Force Analysis." A task force is seen as a temporary grouping, at corporate level, of key individuals tasked to solve a problem or develop new market opportunities. These individuals are brought in from subordinate operating units, presented a mission and a time limit and quickly go to work. The leader of the group is not necessarily the most senior or the most technically qualified. The leader is selected because of his "leadership" abilities in moving the task force to completion.

The significance of such an approach is that it provides answers to many downsizing issues. It increases a networking and team-building environment, shortcuts bureaucratic demands, drastically cuts decision making and implementation times and minimizes the inherently expensive large standing staff. Additionally, and of key note within the topic of mentorship, it provides a very effective approach to selective leader training. The task force experience in a downsized corporation becomes the training classroom for the "fast track" leader. For the Army, it is a proven method that can be employed to help educate our future leaders in successfully functioning within a downsized force.

Cultural Changes.   In the movie "Other People's Money," Gregory Peck as Jorgey, the chief executive officer of a small New England business, gives an emotional speech in an attempt to save his company. He talks about its history as a family business, the need to hang together, the ugliness of people trying to change the company and his commitment to ensuring lifelong jobs for his employees. Great speech, but then Danny DeVito, as Larry "the Liquidator" Garfield, has the floor. His comment is "Amen. Where I come from we are taught to say 'Amen' after a prayer, and that's what you just heard—a prayer for a miracle." Jorgenson, a super individual, had failed to keep his company competitive within the current environment. The company had failed to change its culture with the changing times.

What Garfield was saying is that change is a part of the business world. As such, an organization needs to change in order to keep pace with its market. When a company fails to change, it will find itself quickly distanced from its market goals. If a company, or the Army, views "change" as alien and something that must be fought, then economic and emotional conflicts are inevitable. Standing still is simply that. The Army needs to recognize that change is a part of our world.

"Row harder," a term used by one of the corporations interviewed, provides a great mental picture. It is a classic situation where employees are fired in a cost-cutting move, but the structure remains. Row harder places us aboard a great war ship. We look around to see some empty seats as the captain tells us the sad news about the newly dismissed shipmates. He tells us we need to show more teamwork and that we just have to row harder. Why? Because we have the same large boat and the same logistics aboard. What happens? We go slower, get more winded and frustrated, and the ship takes on water and goes down. Unless action is taken to educate and rededicate, the past ways of doing business will still be tried. Frustration, fatigue and failure come from a row harder mentality. We must question the value added from each process and restructure ourselves and our organization to do better. Leaders of our downsized Army must understand this concept. They must be in the forefront of the restructuring of the "ship" and the re-training of the "crews."

Wess Roberts, in his book *Leadership Secrets of Attila the Hun,* gives us a clear orientation for leaders in a downsized Army: "Huns should be taught to focus on opportunities rather than problems." As long as change is seen as an obstacle, all that flows from it will also be obstacles. As such, we will stop to lament and consider and wish we were back in the "good old days." Those days were not that good and are gone. What is needed is a view that change is natural and provides us opportunities for positive growth and better days.

Two related lessons from the research are clear. First, downsizing must be leader led. Care is required not to delegate downsizing implementation to a functional (finance, personnel, and so on) staff. The result will be a false focus on increased internal efficiencies. Increased performance, a leader type of concern, will be secondary. The focus must go beyond functional expertise in order to successfully implement change. Managerial traits focus on the efficiencies of the operation. They seldom support the total movement and commitment of the organization. A successfully downsized effort is leader driven. It goes beyond internal cost efficiencies to an orienta-tion on market and long-term performance. Leadership, not management, is the critical element of a downsized army.

The second related cultural change issue is that the failure to respond to change, moreover, to be a part of it, is high. Simply put, treading water never wins the race. Doing nothing does cost us in time, money and oppor-tunities. The result is that later, far more is expended to correct the problem as the problem grows in size and severity. Downsized military leadership needs to be one of decisiveness and speed.

Emerging Human Resources Lessons Learned

Empowerment. At the start of the research, the term "empowerment" was used to describe one of the anticipated positive fallouts of downsizing. At first, it was glossed over as just another word for the Army's "powering down" to subordinate leaders. It provides a clear authority to leadership positions already tagged with certain responsibilities.

As the Army refined this concept, "accountability" was added to respon-sibility and authority, making these three terms equal parts of any leader position. Further, the extent of powering down was linked with mission success—powering down to the lowest leader level capable of fulfilling the mission. It focuses on a recognized leader position, and it provides the tools needed to successfully accomplish the job. Empowerment, an important part of successful downsizing, is significantly different and is essential in successful downsized leadership. It is the organizational expansion of leadership. Its focus is on redefining staff and managerial positions. Empowerment adds a new facet to the current responsibilities of a position; it is the expansion of decision making within the structure.

This difference has many significant aspects. First, empowerment means the loosening of centralized control. The challenge is that this relationship of empowerment and increased decentralization is not always in sync. The existence of pockets of "resistance" to the release of authority and the inherent power of that resistance are frequent observations made by the downsizing organization. Although solutions vary, they do have one thing in common. Empowerment is a top-driven action requiring executive commitment and guidance.

It cannot be assumed that the action of conferring authority, responsibility and authority to a position will automatically lead to enlightened decision making and increased organizational performance. The key lesson is that constructive empowerment requires training the new decision makers and redefining responsibilities, relationships and work flows. That is a key lesson. This implies that there are additional expenses in money, time and effort in order to properly prepare the organization for increased employee empowerment as a part of downsizing.

Second, empowerment supports the success of long-term staff reductions. If a staff reduction is initiated without decentralization and increased empowerment, there will be a tendency to continue to act within old ways. This will lead to a rebuilding of the staff to past levels in order to respond to past demands. What is needed is a breaking of the old staff structure paradigms. Staff reductions are best executed through layer deletions. Empowerment ensures this by redefining the decision-making sequence and providing to more people the ability to act with authority and without dependency on old staff layers. Is this practical for the Army? Yes, but it will take strong and up-to-date leadership to do it.

In a traditional hierarchical organization, empowerment is reluctantly given, at times too little and too late, as a part of a decentralized move. One cannot assume that the delegation of decision making will automatically be in the direction of empowerment. It may very well follow an easier flow—that of upward delegation. This is common when new training and job redefining have not been properly done and staff reductions have been on a piecemeal basis. The lesson is that empowerment is an essential part of downsizing but requires a well-thought-out plan of action.

Finally, empowerment encourages cross-functional teamwork essential in quality management improvement. With reduced staff layers and increased decentralization, individuals now empowered in decision making will seek information across functional boundaries. With the absence of old staff layers, the empowered person finds himself having to cross over and coordinate with others as a part of decision making. This movement enhances teamwork, efficiency and overall performance.

Empowerment does not make a leader, but it does provide for the opportunity for better leadership. It moves a job position from being one of a managerial control of resources to that of decision making. The corporate lessons on empowerment stress that it is the source of quality management, product excellence and long-term performance; it is also an impossible move to make without significant cultural change to the corporation.

Survivor Care.   The bottom line of downsizing is that there are fewer employees. It is clearly recognized that recently fired employees—the nonsurvivors—are faced with numerous problems, and the company can provide timely transition assistance. What is not as quickly recognized, but is being surfaced as the most important downsizing issue, is that the company must place focus on the caring of the remaining employees—the survivors. Four survivor lessons arise from the research interviews.

First, are employee communications and commitment. It is key that the employees, before any corporate change, understand how the corporation is affected by economic conditions. Too often the corporation is viewed as the pivotal center of all economic woes that batter upon the employees' lives. This cultural belief, at times encouraged by the corporations themselves, is a situation in which the fate of the employee and his family are solely linked to, and are assumed to be the total responsibility of the corporation. This must be changed. The employees must learn the realities of their economy and how global market conditions, as well as other outside influences, impact upon the company, forcing it, in turn, to constantly adjust itself in order to survive. This is a long-term proposition and very difficult to execute once downsizing begins. Nevertheless, it is an essential cultural change. "Evolutionary, not revolutionary" is the phrase aptly stated by one corporation when looking at this lesson learned.

What we are finding out is that employees can very well understand the realities of life and are dealing with economic challenges in their everyday decisions outside of the workplace. Many corporations, though, have viewed the employee as not interested in or not capable of dealing with the harsh turmoil of the outside economic world. Although that may have been the case some time ago, the clear lesson cited by the corporations is the opposite. The more informed the employees are on economic conditions and issues, the more they understand the need for corporate flexibility and change. The focus must be on employee education and participation; for example, leaders need to better understand and communicate to the soldiers the impact that national security decisions have upon the Army.

The second survivor issue is that of performance appraisal. It is easier to implement change if the change is based on a "level field" concept of equity and performance evaluation. One-time special appraisals and order of merit lists for termination selection are sure methods to employee mistrust and corporate problems. If a system is in place, then as the need to downsize comes, there will have already been an initial sorting out of options by all employees. "Footlocker" counseling, written performance appraisals and evaluation support forms increase in a downsized army.

The third survivor care issue is the corporation's core values. These must be appropriate, clearly defined, recognized and followed. These values, such as loyalty, sense of worth, recognition for contribution, just pay, dignity and trust, are seen as properties that cannot be treaded upon without consequence. When the downsizing process crosses over any of these, there is a high risk of employees seeing such actions as a breach of faith by the corporation. The solution is to recognize what the core values are and to shape those values over time to be in consonance with the market actions of the corporation. Corporate actions and corporate values need to be in sync. Translated—our actions need to follow from our past communications. Actions, not words, will judge the leader's commitment to the Army's values and overall culture.

The fourth survivor issue is the recognition that downsizing causes a complete break of trust between the employees and the organization. This is generally recognized between the company and those to be fired, but the research shows that it is a major point to employees who survive the reduction in force. It is a vital lesson learned in survivor care. Too often, the company assumes that the traumas of being fired are limited to only those that are actually fired—not true. The company must not assume that the bond between the company and the surviving employees is still intact; it is not. The firm needs to develop a program that enforces the core value bonds during periods of change, while the employees must understand that change is a part of market survival.

Survivors exist during voluntary severance actions, as well as during involuntary changes. There is a tendency to look only at termination events as times that may cause the need to care for survivors. Whether voluntary or not, change impacts on those that remain within the organization, as well as those that do not. The corporation needs to understand that survivor care is an issue during any type of organizational change. The key is that people do not hold steady in thought and view while the company is changing. Additional time and effort are required in addressing survivor concerns.

Three research findings in the area of nonsurvivors deserve discussion. First, the actual firing needs to be fast and deep. A key comment throughout the research was to avoid drawing out the downsizing. Disaster is almost certain when an organization opts for a phased process or one which represents a "Chinese dripping water" torture method. Employees want both shoes to drop so that it can end. Likewise, any employee reduction error must be on the side of cutting too deep rather than too little. The organization will better function with a large cut than a shallow slice. Additionally, the focus needs to be on reducing employee numbers, not employee benefits. Survivors should be able to focus on a new workplace with greater challenges, speed, excitement and rewards. "Lightening the load" for this new adventure is understood far more than the cutting out of benefits to those who remain, especially when enhanced severance packets are used to help cull out employees. The lesson is simple—protect the benefits while decisively moving in on employee reductions. The follow-on lesson is that the new organization needs to actually be better off in focus and reward than before, not worse.

The second issue is that nonsurvivor care must be placed into the hands of a third party. The use of an independent outplacement agency is essential. Those fired go through an emotional sequence that is better done outside the workplace. The focus must be on an honest self-appraisal followed by a full-time personal commitment to find new employment. In-house services slow this process down and negatively impact upon those still in the organization. Outplacement services need to be outside the organization and conducted by a neutral agency. Survivors expect the organization to be fair with those fired; "fairness" means being evenhanded, treating people with dignity and providing a transition team as part of a more-than-minimum severance package. It does not mean that the organization must guarantee jobs to those fired at the expense of the welfare of those selected to be part of the "new winning team."

False hope is one of the most damaging aspects of this part of downsizing. It is inadvertently done by management in an attempt to reduce the pain and shock of termination. Two approaches are common. The first is the offering of part-time reemployment to fired employees. Whether promises are made about bringing the person back full time, the action of maintaining some sort of connection with the company implies a hope that it could happen. The second approach is through an outright promise of bringing a person back or through continuing conversations over time with the fired employee. Both the company, with its survivors, and the nonsurvivor himself, need to move on. Actions that do not cleanly sever the tie do not help either party.

The key is to ensure the dignity and independence of the person. Do not paint employees into a corner; they need to be, and feel as though they were, a part of the decision-making process. Employees must understand to what degree they are at risk and what plausible options remain for them. For those at risk, the best options are found in "sweetened" severance offers. The corporate consensus on dealing with nonsurvivors is to focus on the risk recognition, option development and swift movement from the company. Speed is added to the process by placing time limits on options and having the value of the options reduced over time, ending with involuntary severance with the lowest benefits.

A Call for Leadership. Every successfully downsized corporation found itself having to clearly define its purpose for existence. Essentially, it was to satisfy a need of a group of people—to provide a service or product in response to a customer's need. When one drifts away from satisfying a need of the customer, the organization starts to lose purpose.

The corporate research is ongoing, but the emerging lessons are clear and applicable to us. I did not translate each corporate issue into an Army lesson to be learned. I think it is best to let the reader do this. Army cultural change and core value recognition, survivor care and involvement, empowerment and situational task force orientation, and customer awareness and market focus, all provide thoughtful issues for consideration. This research is important in that it underscores the need for the Army to reexamine its culture and to focus on a strategy which has clearly defined its values, integrated change within its process and is geared to being a viable organization. The research is providing us the ability to learn from others and to better prepare ourselves.

It is not so much that the Army is going through a major restructuring that is important; rather, it is the recognition that change, in and of itself, is a part of organizational well being. However, change, by nature, is disruptive. Our new call for leadership is one in which we seek those who are able to integrate change into their sphere of influence. Proper leadership allows one to understand and work with it so that it is internalized within the organization.

23

Women in Combat,
Homosexuals in Uniform:
The Challenge of
Military Leadership

Richard H. Kohn

Bill Clinton's promise to end the ban on homosexuals serving openly in the military, and the continuing furor over women in combat, threaten an on-going civil-military battle that could damage military professionalism, alienate an otherwise friendly incoming Administration, and, ultimately, ruin the military effectiveness of the American armed forces for the foresee-able future. Military leaders who oppose these changes ought to consider some facts and principles that might change their minds.

First, history. Women have fought successfully, sometimes integrated with men, as in the World War II Allied underground, where they proved just as adept at slitting throats, leading men in battle, suffering torture, and dying, as men; sometimes segregated, as in Soviet air force units, which produced many female aces fighting the Germans. Homosexuals have for centuries served honorably and effectively, in the United States and abroad. Arguments against open service assume that proper policies and effective leadership will fail, even though the services succeeded in integrating African-Americans and women, switching to a draft military in 1940 and then back to an all-volunteer force after 1973, and adjusting to other very divisive social changes over the last half century.

Reprinted from *Parameters: Journal of the U.S. Army War College* (Washington, D.C.: Government Printing Office), 23:2 (Spring 1993), pp. 2–4. Copyright © 1993 by Richard H. Kohn. Reprinted by permission of the author.

Second, there is fairness. In times of emergency, service is a fundamental obligation no citizen should escape unless disqualified physically or excused on religious or moral grounds, or because their skills need to be used in some other capacity. But also, participation in combat—dying for one's country—has historically enabled minorities to claim the full privileges of equal participation in society, something basic to our form of government. That is why African-Americans for generations "fought for the right to fight" and why combat and military service are so important to women and homosexuals. Combat and service promote equal protection of the laws and undermine prejudice and discrimination.

Third, the very real practical problems can be overcome. Without question, change will be complicated and costly and take time, and military efficiency will suffer in the short term. Unless carefully explained to the American people, these changes could harm recruiting, precisely in those areas and among those groups which have been traditionally supportive of military service. To accommodate women on combat ships and in flying units (few advocate women in ground combat units), facilities and perhaps weapon systems will need modification. There will be ticklish, perhaps intractable, problems of privacy and personal discomfort (there already *are* in the military). The services will be distracted from their primary peacetime duties of readiness, preparation, and modernization. Leadership at all levels will be challenged to maintain morale and effectiveness in circumstances where, historically, macho behavior and explicit sexual banter helped forge the personal bonds that enabled units to train and fight effectively.

Cohesion, the key to military success, will be more difficult without traditional methods of male bonding. The strict authority, harsh discipline, and instant obedience required for victory in battle have always been subject to abuse, and adding more women and ending discrimination against gay men and lesbians will increase the problem. To deal with it, military leaders will have to redouble their efforts to define appropriate conduct and to punish or expel those in the ranks who cannot or will not control their language and their behavior. The problem, as Tailhook so clearly reveals, already exists; the fundamental issue in the short run will not be attitude, but behavior, and the military can be extremely effective in controlling behavior. The services will have to review policies on acceptable conduct, on and off duty. Research on maintaining cohesion without scapegoating homosexuals and treating women as sex objects will have to be undertaken. The challenge to our military leadership, at all levels, will be enormous, and it will last as long as sexism and homophobia afflict significant portions of our population.

And yet, our military can adjust—once again. It is natural to resist because change poses a diversion from the primary purposes of preparing for and deterring war, and engaging in combat. That is why as outstanding a public servant as General George C. Marshall during World War II opposed racial integration, believing it divisive and concerned that the Army could not afford to act as a "social laboratory" during a national emergency. But civilian control means that our military will be organized and will operate according to the nation's needs and desires. Historically our national security and our social, legal, and constitutional practices have had to be balanced. The services know that military efficiency and combat effectiveness do not always determine our military policies, and less so in times of peace and lessened threat.

If President Clinton follows through on the promise to let gay men and lesbians serve openly, and if, for reasons of fairness and justice, he permits women to fight in combat units at sea and in the air, then the American military must comply, and without resistance. To resist would only make the adjustment more time-consuming and disruptive, and would itself undermine military effectiveness.

In the long run, the services should find that their effectiveness, as in the experience of racial and gender integration, will be enhanced rather than diminished. The strength of our military depends ultimately upon its bonds to the people; the armed forces will be stronger the more they reflect the values and ideals of the society they serve.

24

Battle Plans: In Wake of Cold War, An Intellectual Leads Army in New Missions

---

Thomas E. Ricks

Col. James McDonough, the officer most likely to lead American troops into Bosnia, jumps from his Blackhawk helicopter and jogs into the noisy chaos of Landing Zone Bravo.

The U.S. Army's big rehearsal for going into Bosnia is in full swing. Two twin-rotored CH-47 Chinook helicopters thump into the grassy landing zone. An Apache attack helicopter, its 16 Hellfire missiles bristling, hovers just behind them. Overhead, two F-16 jets peel down the Bavarian valley looking for a mortar emplacement. Dozens of flak-jacketed troops, their faces painted in green and black camouflage, run to the Chinooks. Radios crackle with military chatter.

The short, balding colonel surveys the tumult. "Believe it or not," he says with a grin, "this all makes sense."

It better—for his sake and America's. What is happening here is a major step toward creation of the post-Cold War U.S. Army. Col. McDonough is right in the middle of it, first as a theorist who directed the Army's School of Advanced Military Studies and now as the commander of one of its most unusual units. Under his command, the Italy-based, 1,700-man airborne force has evolved in 18 months into one of the Army's hottest units, the one most likely to see action in the near future.

Like his unit, Col. McDonough is unusual: a military analyst who helped reshape the Army's thinking over the past five years and a noteworthy author. His first book was *Platoon Leader*, a Vietnam memoir that sold more than 250,000 copies and became a movie. Then came *The Defense of Hill 781*, a textbook on modern mechanized warfare praised by *Infantry* magazine as "essential reading for professionals." His latest is a novel about the battle of Waterloo that meditates on *The Limits of Glory*, its title. In it, he has the Duke of Wellington somberly conclude that war is "a form of . . . mass murder." Now he is contemplating a novel about Rwanda, where he led the U.S. task force last year in Kigali, the capital.

'Other Than War'

Most significantly for the action swirling around him on LZ Bravo, Col. McDonough played a key role in producing the 1990s edition of a crucial Army manual, "FM 100-5: Operations"—the basic document describing how the Army conducts business. Army insiders say he waged a long campaign to insert in this service bible for the first time a prescient chapter on "operations other than war." Since then, the U.S. military has been dispatched on just such "contingency operations" to Somalia, Haiti and Rwanda.

Previous editions of "Operations" focused on tanks slugging it out with the Red Army on the plains of Central Europe. Col. McDonough's version envisions a light, helicopter-oriented force ready to travel long distances to fight small wars, monitor peace accords or feed refugees.

Bosnia may provide the first major test of all that theorizing. Whatever the U.S. does there, Col. McDonough's brigade will probably be in the forefront. Pentagon officials expect U.S. troops to extract United Nations peacekeepers or monitor a peace agreement or perhaps both. And they expect that in either case, some rogue armed bands of Serbs and Muslims will violently challenge the American troops.

SWAT Team

For months, Col. McDonough's brigade has been preparing for a mission code-named "Daring Lion," the job of lifting peacekeepers from remote enclaves. In a larger peacekeeping effort involving perhaps 15,000 U.S. troops, his unit—which, among other things, has the Army's only paratrooper battalion with its own artillery—might well be the rapid-deployment force rushed by helicopter to hot spots.

The scenario his brigade rehearses here in Bavaria's forested hills assumes that a peace agreement has been reached but not yet implemented. It preserves the enclave of Gorazde as a Muslim area—but a rogue Bosnian Serb commander is moving armored vehicles toward the town. The colonel's orders are to evacuate U.N. personnel and American citizens.

It is a crucial assignment, but, ironically, it may not do much for his career.

James McDonough began Army life stereotyped as a boxer from Brooklyn. In Vietnam, he recalls, he was always introduced as "the West Point boxing champion"—which he was in 1968 and 1969.

While in Vietnam, he learned how to command troops. When a disgruntled soldier fired a 40mm grenade past his ear, this quiet man cocked an M-16 rifle under the soldier's chin, lifted him to tiptoe and warned him to be more accurate next time—or else. He also fully expected to someday step on a booby trap. On patrol, he wrote in *Platoon Leader*, "I tried hard to feel my legs so I would remember them after they were blown off."

His books, and a degree in political science from Massachusetts Institute of Technology, changed his image from boxer to intellectual—not necessarily a step up in the eyes of his peers. Despite his influence, few expect him to make general. To put it bluntly, he is deemed too much of a thinker to be invited into the club. "The Army has a hard time with that sort of person," says Raoul Alcala, a retired colonel. "Generals tend to select people in their own image—heroic, good leaders, but not particularly cerebral."

Retired Gen. John Galvin, a former West Point English professor who became the top U.S. commander in Europe, calls Col. McDonough "one of the best thinkers" in the service. It seemed only natural when the colonel became director of Fort Leavenworth's School of Advanced Military Studies, where the best and brightest think about how to conduct future campaigns.

Sent to Italy

Two years ago, Col. McDonough's success in revamping Army thinking was rewarded with what seemed a booby prize: command of an airborne unit at an Italian post known as a waiting room for retirement because, during the Cold War, paratroopers had no real role in Europe. Even worse, he was put on the sleepy side of the Alps, far from Central Europe. For decades, U.S. troops in Italy simply guarded nuclear weapons—which were removed in 1992. "Until recently, it was sort of the lost brigade—everybody knew they were there but nobody knew why," says Ben Covington, a retired Army colonel.

"Now," he adds, "they are being looked on as the tip of the spear."

That change occurred over the past year, but not easily. Col. McDonough's assignment was to expand a battalion into a full-scale brigade capable of supporting itself as it carried out contingency operations. He relished the job, which he saw as a chance to put his ideas into practice.

But on arriving in January 1994, he recalls, "I didn't see a corresponding smile on the U.S. Army in Europe." He was told no office space was available, so he set up temporary headquarters in his bedroom. The new brigade had no flag, so his sergeant major made a plaque—only to get orders forbidding that it be posted.

Col. McDonough began building his unit from bones of the old Army in Europe, scrounging antiaircraft missiles, trucks and communications gear from units leaving for the States. To staff his headquarters, he even invited old friends in the National Guard to resume active duty for a few months. He also reached out to other U.S. military units. Navy SEALs parachuted in exercises with his unit and set up an "assault command post," which put him in touch with the flight deck of the Saratoga, a U.S. carrier then in the Adriatic, nine minutes after he jumped. (Now 49 years old, he still parachutes with his troops about once a month.)

Into Africa

The preparation paid off in July 1994, when his brigade was abruptly ordered to Rwanda. In 72 hours, he had troops on the ground. The relief mission vindicated his work on the Army's new doctrine, he says: "It was a force-projection operation, moving a great distance to conduct an operation other than war that required creative leadership and unorthodox solutions."

Moreover, Rwanda was a radical departure from the 1980s Caspar Weinberger/Colin Powell doctrine of hitting the ground with overwhelming force. In the colonel's view, the weight of all that power can mire some operations. He kept most of his combat force in nearby Uganda.

In some ways, Rwanda was an out-of-town rehearsal for Bosnia. Knowing when and how to use force is the biggest challenge Col. McDonough and his troops face in getting ready for the main event, and it is the core of their weeklong sojourn here in Bavaria. It calls for a far different set of skills than those that paratroopers traditionally need—the old ability to jump into an area, seize an objective and kill anybody trying to stop them.

The exercise concentrates just about every recent Balkan nightmare into just four hours: Mortar shells begin hitting refugees in an enclave. Shoulder-fired missiles are launched against incoming U.S. helicopters. A U.N. vehicle turns its machine gun on U.N. troops.

The infantrymen of the brigade's Alpha Company are purposely whip-sawed between two wildly different "rules of engagement"—the orders governing the use of force. First, the company is deposited in a deadly firefight at a landing zone. Creeping through woods to rescue some besieged "British peacekeepers," they unleash their M-60 machine guns and quickly "kill" the six members of the "Danubian National Army" threatening them.

An hour later, the company finds itself under far more restrictive rules as it protects the perimeter of another landing zone from curious "civilians" and gun-toting "militiamen" who may or may not be friendly. As the civilians approach—they and the militiamen really are role-playing soldiers—the troops yell the Serbo-Croatian phrase each has on a yellow "rules of engagement" card: *Stani ili pucam*— "stop or I'll shoot." In the mouths of the young soldiers, still pumped with adrenaline from the firefight, this becomes "stolly olly poochie" and then a simple: "Get the f___ down."

When one civilian persists, a soldier "shoots" him in the leg. Another squad watches and critiques the action. "That wasn't hostile enough" for him to be shot, one disgusted soldier says.

Essentially, the soldiers are practicing making national policy at the squad level. "There's a sense that any encounter, at the lowest level, could be on the front pages of tomorrow's newspaper," Capt. Bill Burleson, Alpha's 29-year-old commander, says later. "Shooting things and blowing things up is what they learn from the day they come in the Army. This is a gray area between combat and peace, and it really requires mental gymnastics." When Lt. Jason Joose, who leads Alpha's 1st platoon, concludes the lesson of today's exercise is that you should shoot anybody who threatens you, the captain quietly warns him away from sudden escalation. If any shooting is required, he says later, it probably will be done by an American sniper looking over the company's shoulder.

While the nuclear warhead was the characteristic weapon of the Cold War, the sniper's rifle may best define the new era. "Recent years, all the conflicts we've been in, the lesson learned is that snipers are worth their weight in gold," says Lt. Col. Mike Scaparrotti, the colonel's battalion commander. If sent into Bosnia, he plans to use them liberally to protect his men.

Fire When Really Ready

Even big artillery pieces are fired in a careful way. At one point, the exercise has U.S. troops shelled by a mortar hidden in the "oldest castle in the Balkans," an important cultural monument. The brigade's fire-support officer asks Capt. Edward Hayes, the staff lawyer, whether they can hit back. He clears the use of five shells. But after most land on target, he says next time he would recommend only two—"the minimum force necessary."

Hearing a little too much talk about "minimal force," Col. McDonough uses a commander's briefing to hammer home the formulation he prefers: "the judicious use of force." He tells the brigade staff: "Fires, though judiciously applied, will be devastating. Scare the s___ out of them—and then kill them."

The next day, the colonel shows his men what he means. During the full-scale exercise, a company of "Bosnian Serb" armored vehicles threatens the landing zone. Col. McDonough orders six Apache helicopters to blast them—and they end the threat. The evacuation goes smoothly.

It is a tricky environment the Army couldn't have handled 20 years ago, says the brigade's top sergeant, Sgt. Maj. Gerald Parks. "I come from an Army that was full of drugs," the 24-year veteran says. "I wouldn't have trusted a lot of those soldiers to do this job. These soldiers have got to be trained and disciplined enough to deal with high-intensity conflict and then go use the minimum force necessary to take control of another situation."

Col. McDonough, soldier and scholar, is well-suited to train and lead troops in ambiguous, post-Cold War situations, says Andrew Krepinevich, a former Army strategist who now directs the Defense Budget Project, a Washington think tank. Mr. Krepinevich has heard the Pentagon gossip that Col. McDonough won't make general, and he worries about the signal that sends. "The Army may require a very different kind of officer in the future than it has in the past," he says, "as we move into these fuzzy situations that put a premium on commanders with a cultural sensitivity and an ability to adapt rapidly."

Col. McDonough also has heard the gossip. Good soldier that he is, he stoically says he doesn't expect to become a general: "I don't believe I am among the very best that the Army will pick from."

About the Book and Editors

In the twelve years since the first edition of this book, countless books and articles have been written on the subject of leadership. In many respects, the topic has been popularized with "how to" publications, seminars, and workshops. As the intensity of interest increased, more experts appeared to provide the definitive message. Yet interest in leadership remains strong. Perhaps we are best off by devoting ourselves to the *study* of leadership rather than looking for a single, best answer.

The authors review scores of indexes and electronic databases each year in an attempt to keep current with ideas and revelations about leaders and leadership. Convinced that leadership is both an art and a science, they find that much of what we know is continually rewritten in a variety of formats. Both have extensive experience in the military and private sector as followers and leaders, and in command. Through their teaching and scholarship, the editors consistently provide innovative overviews of leadership with the best writings available.

Over 200 articles were reviewed for this third edition, most written in the past six years. The reader will find many new pieces and some of the classic readings from previous editions. Writers in the fields of history, business, religion, politics, and education continue their attempts to explain the phenomenon of leadership. Unique to the third edition is the section on the realities of the peacetime military in a rapidly changing social environment. Each chapter will stimulate the reader to think about his or her own understanding of leadership. The editors focus on the understanding of challenges and opportunities for effective leadership in today's military. A variety of perspectives reflects the richness of ideas that characterize the self-knowledge and self-confidence necessary for effective leadership in the military of today.

This edition again combines some of the best contributions from within and outside the military to provoke meaningful discussions on themes important to the study of leadership. Although military leadership continues to have a unique heritage, both civilian and military readers will find similarities in the ideas and concepts of those pursuing leader effectiveness.

Robert L. Taylor (Lt. Col., USAF, ret.) is dean, College of Business and Public Administration, at the University of Louisville. He previously served as a missile launch control officer, a combat defense operations officer, and professor and head of the Department of Management at the USAF Academy.

William E. Rosenbach (Col., USAF, ret.) is the Evans Professor of Eisenhower Leadership Studies and professor of management at Gettysburg College. He has served as an aviator, staff officer, professor, and acting head of the Department of Behavioral Sciences and Leadership at the USAF Academy.